W9-CTA-016

HELP YOUR KIDS WITH

m√a/th

HELP YOUR KIDS WITH

ma√th

A UNIQUE STEP-BY-STEP VISUAL GUIDE

LONDON, NEW YORK, MELBOURNE,
MUNICH, AND DELHI

Project Art Editor
Mark Lloyd

Project Editor
Nathan Joyce

Designers
Nicola Erdpresser, Riccie Janus,
Maxine Pedliham, Silke Spingies,
Rebecca Tennant

Editors
Nicola Deschamps, Martha Evatt,
Lizzie Munsey, Martyn Page, Laura Palosuo,
Peter Preston, Miezan van Zyl

Design Assistants
Thomas Howey, Fiona Macdonald

US Editor
Jill Hamilton

Production Editor
Luca Frassinetti

US Consultant
Alison Tribley

Production
Erika Pepe

Indexer
Jane Parker

Jacket Designer
Duncan Turner

Managing Editor
Sarah Larter

Managing Art Editor
Michelle Baxter

Publishing Manager
Liz Wheeler

Art Director
Phil Ormerod

Reference Publisher
Jonathan Metcalf

First American Edition, 2010
This Edition, 2014

Published in the United States by
DK Publishing
345 Hudson Street
New York, New York 10014

10 11 12 13 14 10 9 8 7 6 5 4 3 2 1
006–263995 – July/14

Copyright © 2010, 2014 Dorling Kindersley Limited

All rights reserved. Without limiting the rights under copyright reserved above, no part of this
publication may be reproduced, stored in a retrieval system, or transmitted in any form or by any
means (electronic, mechanical, photocopying, recording, or otherwise) without prior written
permission of the copyright owner and the above publisher of this book.
Published in Great Britain by Dorling Kindersley Limited.

A catalog record for this book is available from the
Library of Congress.

ISBN 978-1-4654-3400-5

DK books are available at special discounts when purchased in bulk for sales promotions,
premiums, fund-raising, or educational use. For details contact: DK Publishing Special Markets,
345 Hudson Street, New York, New York 10014 or SpecialSales@dk.com.

Printed and bound by South China Printing Company, China

Discover more at
www.dk.com

CAROL VORDERMAN M.A.(Cantab), MBE is one of Britain's best-loved TV personalities and is renowned for her excellent math skills. She has hosted numerous shows, from light entertainment with **Carol Vorderman's Better Homes** and **The Pride of Britain Awards**, to scientific programs such as **Tomorrow's World**, on the BBC, ITV, and Channel 4. Whether co-hosting Channel 4's **Countdown** for 26 years, becoming the second-best-selling female nonfiction author of the 2000s in the UK, or advising Parliament on the future of math education in the UK, Carol has a passion for and devotion to explaining math in an exciting and easily understandable way.

BARRY LEWIS (Consultant Editor, Numbers, Geometry, Trigonometry, Algebra) studied math in college and graduated with honors. He spent many years in publishing, as an author and as an editor, where he developed a passion for mathematical books that presented this often difficult subject in accessible, appealing, and visual ways. He is the author of **Diversions in Modern Mathematics**, which subsequently appeared in Spanish as **Matemáticas modernas. Aspectos recreativos**.

He was invited by the British government to run the major initiative **Maths Year 2000,** a celebration of mathematical achievement with the aim of making the subject more popular and less feared. In 2001 Barry became the president of the UK's Mathematical Association, and was elected as a fellow of the Institute of Mathematics and its Applications, for his achievements in popularizing mathematics. He is currently the Chair of Council of the Mathematical Association and regularly publishes articles and books dealing with both research topics and ways of engaging people in this critical subject.

ANDREW JEFFREY (Author, Probability) is a math consultant, well known for his passion and enthusiasm for the teaching and learning of math. A teacher for over 20 years, Andrew now spends his time training, coaching, and supporting teachers and delivering lectures for various organizations throughout Europe. He has written many books on the subject of math and is better known to many schools as the "Mathemagician."

MARCUS WEEKS (Author, Statistics) is the author of many books and has contributed to several reference books, including DK's **Science: The Definitive Visual Guide** and **Children's Illustrated Encyclopedia**.

SEAN MCARDLE (Consultant) was head of math in two primary schools and has a Master of Philosophy degree in Educational Assessment. He has written or co-written more than 100 mathematical textbooks for children and assessment books for teachers.

Contents

Foreword

Hello

Welcome to the wonderful world of math. Research has shown just how important it is for parents to be able to help children with their education. Being able to work through homework together and enjoy a subject, particularly math, is a vital part of a child's progress.

However, math homework can be the cause of upset in many households. The introduction of new methods of arithmetic hasn't helped, as many parents are now simply unable to assist.

We wanted this book to guide parents through some of the methods in early arithmetic and then for them to go on to enjoy some deeper mathematics.

As a parent, I know just how important it is to be aware of it when your child is struggling and equally, when they are shining. By having a greater understanding of math, we can appreciate this even more.

Over nearly 30 years, and for nearly every single day, I have had the privilege of hearing people's very personal views about math and arithmetic. Many weren't taught math particularly well or in an interesting way. If you were one of those people, then we hope that this book can go some way to changing your situation and that math, once understood, can begin to excite you as much as it does me.

CAROL VORDERMAN

π=**3.14**1592653589793238462643383 2795028841971693993751058209749 4459230781640628620899862803485 3421170679821480865132823066470 9384460955058223172535940812848 1117450284102701938521105559644 6229489549303819644288109756659 3344612847564823378678316527120 1909145648566923460348610454326 6482133936072602491412737245870 0660631558817488152092096282925 4091715364367892590360011330530 5488204665213841469519451160943 3057270365759591953092186117381 9326117931051185480744623799627 49567351885752724891227938183011 9491

Introduction

This book concentrates on the math tackled in schools between the ages of 9 and 16. But it does so in a gripping, engaging, and visual way. Its purpose is to teach math by stealth. It presents mathematical ideas, techniques, and procedures so that they are immediately absorbed and understood. Every spread in the book is written and presented so that the reader will exclaim, "Ah ha—now I understand!" Students can use it on their own; equally, it helps parents understand and remember the subject and thus help their children. If parents too gain something in the process, then so much the better.

At the start of the new millennium I had the privilege of being the director of the United Kingdom's **Maths Year 2000**, a celebration of math and an international effort to highlight and boost awareness of the subject. It was supported by the British government and Carol Vorderman was also involved. Carol championed math across the British media, and is well known for her astonishingly agile ways of manipulating and working with numbers—almost as if they were her personal friends. My working, domestic, and sleeping hours are devoted to math—finding out how various subtle patterns based on counting items in sophisticated structures work and how they hang together. What united us was a shared passion for math and the contribution it makes to all our lives—economic, cultural, and practical.

How is it that in a world ever more dominated by numbers, math—the subtle art that teases out the patterns, the harmonies, and the textures that make up the relationships between the numbers—is in danger? I sometimes think that we are drowning in numbers.

As employees, our contribution is measured by targets, statistics, workforce percentages, and adherence to budget. As consumers, we are counted and aggregated according to every act of consumption. And in a nice subtlety, most of the products that we do consume come complete with their own personal statistics—the energy in a can of beans and its "low" salt content; the story in a newspaper and its swath of statistics controlling and interpreting the world, developing each truth, simplifying each problem. Each minute of every hour, each hour of every day, we record and publish ever more readings from our collective life-support machine. That is how we seek to understand the world, but the problem is, the more figures we get, the more truth seems to slip through our fingers.

The danger is, despite all the numbers and our increasingly numerate world, math gets left behind. I'm sure that many think the ability to do the numbers is enough. Not so. Neither as individuals, nor collectively. Numbers are pinpricks in the fabric of math, blazing within. Without them we would be condemned to total darkness. With them we gain glimpses of the sparkling treasures otherwise hidden.

This book sets out to address and solve this problem. Everyone can do math.

BARRY LEWIS

Former President, **The Mathematical Association**; Director **Maths Year 2000.**

Numbers

2 Introducing numbers

COUNTING AND NUMBERS FORM THE FOUNDATION OF MATHEMATICS.

Numbers are symbols that developed as a way to record amounts or quantities, but over centuries mathematicians have discovered ways to use and interpret numbers in order to work out new information.

What are numbers?

Numbers are basically a set of standard symbols that represent quantities—the familiar 0 to 9. In addition to these whole numbers (also called integers) there are also fractions (see pp.48–55) and decimals (see pp.44–45). Numbers can also be negative, or less than zero (see pp.34–35).

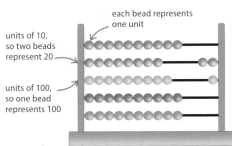

each bead represents one unit

units of 10, so two beads represent 20

units of 100, so one bead represents 100

◁ **Abacus**
The abacus is a traditional calculating and counting device with beads that represent numbers. The number shown here is 120.

whole number   negative number   fraction   decimal

$$1 \quad -2 \quad \frac{1}{3} \quad 0.4$$

△ **Types of numbers**
Here 1 is a positive whole number and -2 is a negative number. The symbol $\frac{1}{3}$ represents a fraction, which is one part of a whole that has been divided into three parts. A decimal is another way to express a fraction.

▽ **First number**
One is not a prime number. It is called the "multiplicative identity," because any number multiplied by 1 gives that number as the answer.

▽ **Even prime number**
The number 2 is the only even-numbered prime number—a number that is only divisible by itself and 1 (see pp.26–27).

LOOKING CLOSER

Zero

The use of the symbol for zero is considered an important advance in the way numbers are written. Before the symbol for zero was adopted, a blank space was used in calculations. This could lead to ambiguity and made numbers easier to confuse. For example, it was difficult to distinguish between 400, 40, and 4, since they were all represented by only the number 4. The symbol zero developed from a dot first used by Indian mathematicians to act a placeholder.

zero is important for 24-hour timekeeping

◁ **Easy to read**
The zero acts as a placeholder for the "tens," which makes it easy to distinguish the single minutes.

△ **Perfect number**
This is the smallest perfect number, which is a number that is the sum of its positive divisors (except itself). So, $1 + 2 + 3 = 6$.

△ **Not the sum of squares**
The number 7 is the lowest number that cannot be represented as the sum of the squares of three whole numbers (integers).

REAL WORLD

Number symbols

Many civilizations developed their own symbols for numbers, some of which are shown below, together with our modern Hindu–Arabic number system. One of the main advantages of our modern number system is that arithmetical operations, such as multiplication and division, are much easier to do than with the more complicated older number systems.

Modern Hindu–Arabic	1	2	3	4	5	6	7	8	9	10
Mayan	•	••	•••	••••	—	⊙	⊙⊙	⊙⊙⊙	⊙⊙⊙⊙	═
Ancient Chinese	一	二	三	四	五	六	七	八	九	十
Ancient Roman	I	II	III	IV	V	VI	VII	VIII	IX	X
Ancient Egyptian	I	II	III	IIII	IIIII	IIIIII	IIIIIII	IIIIIIII	IIIIIIIII	∩
Babylonian	𒁹	𒐖	𒐗	𒐘	𒐙	𒐚	𒐛	𒐜	𒐝	𒌋

▽ **Triangular number**
This is the smallest triangular number, which is a positive whole number that is the sum of consecutive whole numbers. So, 1 + 2 = 3.

▽ **Composite number**
The number 4 is the smallest composite number —a number that is the product of other numbers. The factors of 4 are two 2s.

▽ **Prime number**
This is the only prime number to end with a 5. A 5-sided polygon is the only shape for which the number of sides and diagonals are equal.

△ **Fibonacci number**
The number 8 is a cube number ($2^3 = 8$) and it is the only positive Fibonacci number (see p.171), other than 1, that is a cube.

△ **Highest decimal**
The number 9 is the highest single-digit whole number and the highest single-digit number in the decimal system.

△ **Base number**
The Western number system is based on the number 10. It is speculated that this is because humans used their fingers and toes for counting.

+ Addition

NUMBERS ARE ADDED TOGETHER TO FIND THEIR TOTAL.
THIS RESULT IS CALLED THE SUM.

SEE ALSO

Subtraction	17 ❯
Positive and negative numbers	34–35 ❯

Adding up

An easy way to work out the sum of two numbers is a number line. It is a group of numbers arranged in a straight line that makes it possible to count up or down. In this number line, 3 is added to 1.

move three steps along

+1 +1 +1

start at 1　　total

0　1　2　3　4　5

◁ **Use a number line**
To add 3 to 1, start at 1 and move along the line three times—first to 2, then to 3, then to 4, which is the answer.

▷ **What it means**
The result of adding 3 to the start number of 1 is 4. This means that the sum of 1 and 3 is 4.

sign for addition

equals sign leads to answer

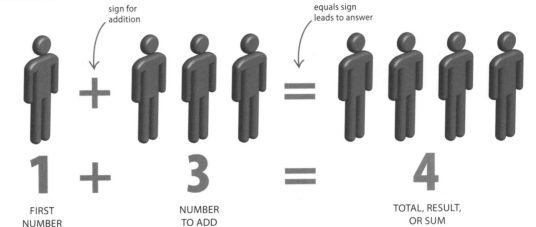

1　+　3　=　4

FIRST NUMBER　　NUMBER TO ADD　　TOTAL, RESULT, OR SUM

Adding large numbers

Numbers that have two or more digits are added in vertical columns. First, add the ones, then the tens, the hundreds, and so on. The sum of each column is written beneath it. If the sum has two digits, the first is carried to the next column.

hundreds
tens
ones

928
+ 191

space at foot of column for sum

working from right, first add ones

928
+ 191
9

carry 1
add tens

1
928
+ 191
19

the first 1 of 11 goes in the thousands column, while the second goes in the hundreds column

9 + 1 + the carried 1 = 11

1
928
+ 191
1,119

the answer is 1,119

First, the numbers are written with their ones, tens, and hundreds directly above each other.

Next, add the ones 1 and 8 and write their sum of 9 in the space underneath the ones column.

The sum of the tens has two digits, so write the second underneath and carry the first to the next column.

Then add the hundreds and the carried digit. This sum has two digits, so the first goes in the thousands column.

− Subtraction

A NUMBER IS SUBTRACTED FROM ANOTHER NUMBER TO FIND WHAT IS LEFT. THIS IS KNOWN AS THE DIFFERENCE.

SEE ALSO
‹ 16 Addition
Positive and negative numbers 34–35›

Taking away

A number line can also be used to show how to subtract numbers. From the first number, move back along the line the number of places shown by the second number. Here 3 is taken from 4.

start at 4, then move three places to left

◁ **Use a number line**
To subtract 3 from 4, start at 4 and move three places along the number line, first to 3, then 2, and then to 1.

sign for subtraction

equals sign leads to answer

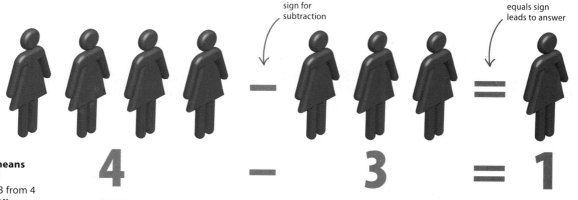

▷ **What it means**
The result of subtracting 3 from 4 is 1, so the difference between 3 and 4 is 1.

4 FIRST NUMBER   **−**   **3** NUMBER TO SUBTRACT   **= 1** RESULT OR DIFFERENCE

Subtracting large numbers

Subtracting numbers of two or more digits is done in vertical columns. First subtract the ones, then the tens, the hundreds, and so on. Sometimes a digit is borrowed from the next column along.

hundreds / tens / ones — number to be subtracted from
928
− 191 — number to subtract

First, the numbers are written with their ones, tens, and hundreds directly above each other.

subtract ones
928
− 191
  7

Next, subtract the unit 1 from 8, and write their difference of 7 in the space underneath them.

first, borrow 1 from hundreds / then, carry 1 to tens
8 1
9̷28
− 191
 37

In the tens, 9 cannot be subtracted from 2, so 1 is borrowed from the hundreds, turning 9 into 8 and 2 into 12.

subtract 1 from 8
8 1
9̷28
− 191
737 — the answer is 737

In the hundreds column, 1 is subtracted from the new, now lower number of 8.

Multiplication

MULTIPLICATION INVOLVES ADDING A NUMBER TO ITSELF A NUMBER OF
TIMES. THE RESULT OF MULTIPLYING NUMBERS IS CALLED THE PRODUCT.

SEE ALSO

❮ 16–17 Addition and Subtraction

| Division | 22–25 ❯ |
| Decimals | 44–45 ❯ |

What is multiplication?

The second number in a multiplication sum is the
number to be added to itself and the first is the
number of times to add it. Here the number of rows
of people is added together a number of times
determined by the number of people in each row.
This multiplication sum gives the total number of
people in the group.

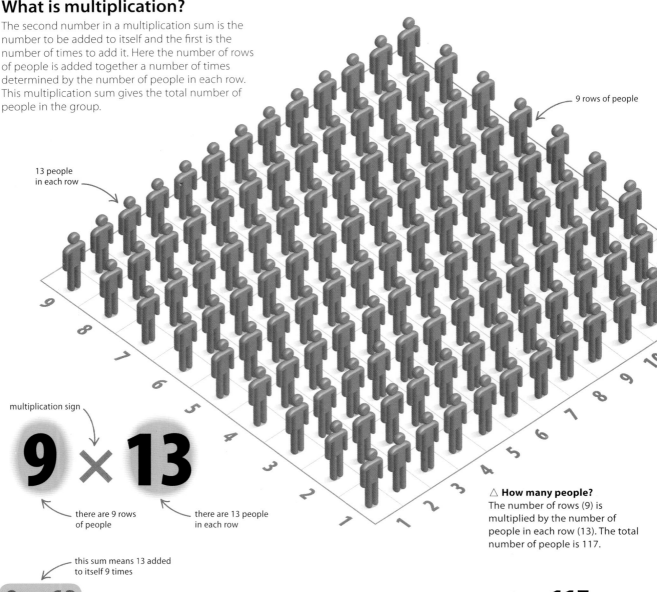

9 rows of people

13 people
in each row

multiplication sign

9 × 13

there are 9 rows
of people

there are 13 people
in each row

△ **How many people?**
The number of rows (9) is
multiplied by the number of
people in each row (13). The total
number of people is 117.

this sum means 13 added
to itself 9 times

9 × 13 = 13 + 13 + 13 + 13 + 13 + 13 + 13 + 13 + 13 = **117**

product of 9
and 13 is 117

Works both ways

It does not matter which order numbers appear in a multiplication sum because the answer will be the same either way. Two methods of the same multiplication are shown here.

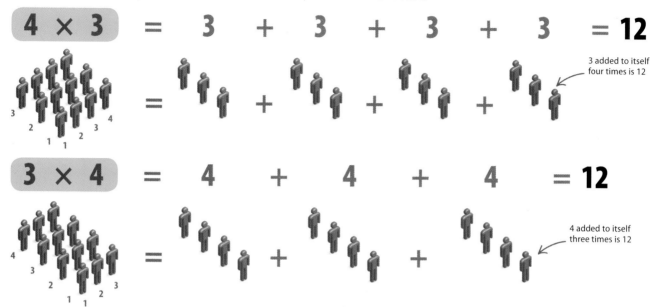

4×3 = 3 + 3 + 3 + 3 = **12**

3 added to itself four times is 12

3×4 = 4 + 4 + 4 = **12**

4 added to itself three times is 12

Multiplying by 10, 100, 1,000

Multiplying whole numbers by 10, 100, 1,000, and so on involves adding one zero (0), two zeroes (00), three zeroes (000), and so on to the right of the number being multiplied.

add 0 to end of number

$$34 \times 10 = \mathbf{340}$$

add 00 to end of number

$$72 \times 100 = \mathbf{7,200}$$

add 000 to end of number

$$18 \times 1,000 = \mathbf{18,000}$$

Patterns of multiplication

There are quick ways to multiply two numbers, and these patterns of multiplication are easy to remember. The table shows patterns involved in multiplying numbers by 2, 5, 6, 9, 12, and 20.

PATTERNS OF MULTIPLICATION		
To multiply	**How to do it**	**Example to multiply**
2	add the number to itself	$2 \times 11 = 11 + 11 = \mathbf{22}$
5	the last digit of the number follows the pattern 5, 0, 5, 0	5, 10, 15, 20
6	multiplying 6 by any even number gives an answer that ends in the same last digit as the even number	$6 \times 12 = 72$ $6 \times 8 = 48$
9	multiply the number by 10, then subtract the number	$9 \times 7 = 10 \times 7 - 7 = \mathbf{63}$
12	multiply the original number first by 10, then multiply the original number by 2, and then add the two answers	$12 \times 10 = 120$ $12 \times 2 = 24$ $120 + 24 = \mathbf{144}$
20	multiply the number by 10 then multiply the answer by 2	$14 \times 20 =$ $14 \times 10 = 140$ $140 \times 2 = \mathbf{280}$

MULTIPLES

When a number is multiplied by any whole number the result (product) is called a multiple. For example, the first six multiples of the number 2 are 2, 4, 6, 8, 10, and 12. This is because $2 \times 1 = 2$, $2 \times 2 = 4$, $2 \times 3 = 6$, $2 \times 4 = 8$, $2 \times 5 = 10$, and $2 \times 6 = 12$.

MULTIPLES OF 3

$3 \times 1 = 3$
$3 \times 2 = 6$
$3 \times 3 = 9$
$3 \times 4 = 12$
$3 \times 5 = 15$

first five multiples of 3

MULTIPLES OF 8

$8 \times 1 = 8$
$8 \times 2 = 16$
$8 \times 3 = 24$
$8 \times 4 = 32$
$8 \times 5 = 40$

first five multiples of 8

MULTIPLES OF 12

$12 \times 1 = 12$
$12 \times 2 = 24$
$12 \times 3 = 36$
$12 \times 4 = 48$
$12 \times 5 = 60$

first five multiples of 12

Common multiples

Two or more numbers can have multiples in common. Drawing a grid, such as the one on the right, can help find the common multiples of different numbers. The smallest of these common numbers is called the lowest common multiple.

24

Lowest common multiple
The lowest common multiple of 3 and 8 is 24 because it is the smallest number that both multiply into.

multiples of 3

multiples of 8

multiples of 3 and 8

▷ **Finding common multiples**
Multiples of 3 and multiples of 8 are highlighted on this grid. Some multiples are common to both numbers.

1	2	3	4	5	6	7	8	9	10
11	12	13	14	15	16	17	18	19	20
21	22	23	24	25	26	27	28	29	30
31	32	33	34	35	36	37	38	39	40
41	42	43	44	45	46	47	48	49	50
51	52	53	54	55	56	57	58	59	60
61	62	63	64	65	66	67	68	69	70
71	72	73	74	75	76	77	78	79	80
81	82	83	84	85	86	87	88	89	90
91	92	93	94	95	96	97	98	99	100

Short multiplication

Multiplying a large number by a single-digit number is called short multiplication. The larger number is placed above the smaller one in columns arranged according to their value.

4 carried to tens column → 4
196
× 7
— 2
6 written in ones column
2 written in ones column

6 carried to hundreds column → 6 4
196
× 7
— 72
7 written in tens column

1 written in hundreds column → 6 4
196
× 7
— 1,372
3 written in hundreds column; 1 written in thousands column
1,372 is final answer

To multiply 196 and 7, first multiply the ones 7 and 6. The product is 42, the 4 of which is carried.

Next, multiply 7 and 9, the product of which is 63. The carried 4 is added to 63 to get 67.

Finally, multiply 7 and 1. Add its product (7) to the carried 6 to get 13, giving a final product of 1,372.

Long multiplication

Multiplying two numbers that both contain at least two digits is called long multiplication. The numbers are placed one above the other, in columns arranged according to their value (ones, tens, hundreds, and so on).

428 multiplied by 1
428
× 111
— 428

428 multiplied by 10
428
× 111
— 428
4,280
add 0 when multiplying by 10

428 multiplied by 100
428
× 111
— 428
4,280
42,800
add 00 when multiplying by 100

428
× 111
— 428
4,280
+ 42,800
= 47,508

First, multiply 428 by 1 in the ones column. Work digit by digit from right to left so 8 × 1, 2 × 1, and then 4 × 1.

Multiply 428 digit by digit by 1 in the tens column. Remember to add 0 when multiplying by a number in the tens place.

Multiply 428 digit by digit by 1 in the hundreds column. Add 00 when multiplying by a digit in the hundreds place.

Add together the products of the three multiplications. The answer is 47,508.

LOOKING CLOSER

Box method of multiplication

The long multiplication of 428 and 111 can be broken down further into simple multiplications with the help of a table or box. Each number is reduced to its hundreds, tens, and ones, and multiplied by the other.

▷ **The final step**
Add together the nine multiplications to find the final answer.

		428 WRITTEN IN 100S, 10S, AND ONES		
		400	**20**	**8**
111 WRITTEN IN 100S, 10S, AND ONES	**100**	400 × 100 = 40,000	20 × 100 = 2,000	8 × 100 = 800
	10	400 × 10 = 4,000	20 × 10 = 200	8 × 10 = 80
	1	400 × 1 = 400	20 × 1 = 20	8 × 1 = 8

40,000
2,000
800
4,000
200
80
400
20
+ 8
= 47,508
this is the final answer

Division

DIVISION INVOLVES FINDING OUT HOW MANY TIMES ONE NUMBER GOES INTO ANOTHER NUMBER.

SEE ALSO

⟨ 16–17 Addition and subtraction

⟨ 18–21 Multiplication

Ratio and proportion   **56–59 ⟩**

There are two ways to think about division. The first is sharing a number out equally (10 coins to 2 people is 5 each). The other is dividing a number into equal groups (10 coins into piles containing 2 coins each is 5 piles).

How division works

Dividing one number by another finds out how many times the second number (the divisor) fits into the first (the dividend). For example, dividing 10 by 2 finds out how many times 2 fits into 10. The result of the division is known as the quotient.

◁ **Division symbols**
There are three main symbols for division that all mean the same thing. For example, "6 divided by 3" can be expressed as $6 \div 3$, $6/3$, or $\frac{6}{3}$.

▽ **Division as sharing**
Sharing equally is one type of division. Dividing 4 candies equally between 2 people means that each person gets the same number of candies: 2 each.

4 CANDIES **÷ 2** PEOPLE **= 2** CANDIES PER PERSON

DIVIDEND
The number that is being divided or shared by another number

DIVISOR
The number that is being used to divide the dividend

LOOKING CLOSER

How division is linked to multiplication

Division is the direct opposite or "inverse" of multiplication, and the two are always connected. If you know the answer to a particular division, you can form a multiplication from it and vice versa.

◁ **Back to the beginning**
If 10 (the dividend) is divided by 2 (the divisor), the answer (the quotient) is 5. Multiplying the quotient (5) by the divisor of the original division problem (2) results in the original dividend (10).

$$10 \div 2 = 5 \qquad 5 \times 2 = 10$$

Another approach to division

Division can also be viewed as finding out how many groups of the second number (divisor) are contained in the first number (dividend). The operation remains the same in both cases.

This example shows 30 soccer balls, which are to be divided into groups of 3:

group of three

There are exactly 10 groups of 3 soccer balls, with no remainder, so 30 ÷ 3 = **10**.

10 CANDIES

▽ **Introducing remainders**
In this example, 10 candies are being divided among 3 girls. However, 3 does not divide exactly into 10—it fits 3 times with 1 left over. The amount left over from a division sum is called the remainder.

10

DIVISION

3 GIRLS

3 CANDIES EACH

3   3
3
3   1 REMAINING CANDIES

3
1

= **3**

QUOTIENT
The result of the division

3 remainder 1

REMAINDER
The amount left over when one number cannot divide exactly into another

DIVISION TIPS		
A number is divisible by	**If...**	**Examples**
2	the last digit is an even number	12, 134, 5,000
3	the sum of all digits when added together is divisible by 3	18 1+8 = 9
4	the number formed by the last two digits is divisible by 4	732 32÷4 = 8
5	the last digit is 5 or 0	25, 90, 835
6	the last digit is even and the sum of its digits when added together is divisible by 3	3,426 3+4+2+6 = 15
7	no simple divisibility test	
8	the number formed by the last three digits is divisible by 8	7,536 536 ÷ 8 = 67
9	the sum of all of its digits is divisible by 9	6,831 6+8+3+1 = 18
10	the number ends in 0	30, 150, 4,270

Short division

Short division is used to divide one number (the dividend) by another whole number (the divisor) that is less than 10.

start on the left with the first 3 (divisor)

dividing line

result is 132

1
3|396

396 is the dividend

13
3|396

132
3|396

Divide the first 3 into 3. It fits once exactly, so put a 1 above the dividing line, directly above the 3 of the dividend.

Move to the next column and divide 3 into 9. It fits three times exactly, so put a 3 directly above the 9 of the dividend.

Divide 3 into 6, the last digit of the dividend. It goes twice exactly, so put a 2 directly above the 6 of the dividend.

Carrying numbers

When the result of a division gives a whole number and a remainder, the remainder can be carried over to the next digit of the dividend.

start on the left

divisor

5|2,765

2,765 is the dividend

divide 5 into first 2 digits of dividend

carry remainder 2 to next digit of dividend

5
5|2,²7²65

Start with number 5. It does not divide into 2 because it is larger than 2. Instead, 5 will need to be divided into the first two digits of the dividend.

Divide 5 into 27. The result is 5 with a remainder of 2. Put 5 directly above the 7 and carry the remainder.

carry remainder 1 to next digit of dividend

the result is 553

55
5|2,²7²6¹5

553
5|2,²7²6¹5

Divide 5 into 26. The result is 5 with a remainder of 1. Put 5 directly above the 6 and carry the remainder 1 to the next digit of the dividend.

Divide 5 into 15. It fits three times exactly, so put 3 above the dividing line, directly above the final 5 of the dividend.

LOOKING CLOSER

Converting remainders

When one number will not divide exactly into another, the answer has a remainder. Remainders can be converted into decimals, as shown below.

remainder

22 r 2
4|90

22.
4|9¹0.0

Remove the remainder, 2 in this case, leaving 22. Add a decimal point above and below the dividing line. Next, add a zero to the dividend after the decimal point.

22.
4|9¹0.²0

Carry the remainder (2) from above the dividing line to below the line and put it in front of the new zero.

22.5
4|9¹0.²0

Divide 4 into 20. It goes 5 times exactly, so put a 5 directly above the zero of the dividend and after the decimal point.

LOOKING CLOSER

Making division simpler

To make a division easier, sometimes the divisor can be split into factors. This means that a number of simpler divisions can be done.

816÷6

divisor is 6, which is 2 × 3. Splitting 6 into 2 and 3 simplifies the sum

result is 136

816÷2 = 408 ➡ **408÷3 = 136**

divide by first factor of divisor

divide by second factor of divisor

This method of splitting the divisor into factors can also be used for more difficult divisions.

405÷15

splitting 15 into 5 and 3, which multiply to make 15, simplifies the problem

result is 27

405÷5 = 81 ➡ **81÷3 = 27**

divide by first factor of divisor

divide result by second factor of divisor

Long division

Long division is usually used when the divisor is at least two digits long and the dividend is at least 3 digits long. Unlike short division, all the workings out are written out in full below the dividing line. Multiplication is used for finding remainders. A long division sum is presented in the example on the right.

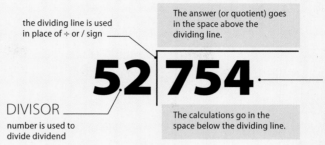

the dividing line is used in place of ÷ or / sign

The answer (or quotient) goes in the space above the dividing line.

DIVISOR
number is used to divide dividend

The calculations go in the space below the dividing line.

DIVIDEND
number that is divided by another number

put result of second division above last digit being divided into

result is 1

1

52 754

divide divisor into first two digits of dividend

multiply 1 (the number of times 52 goes into 75) by 52 to get 52

1

52 754
−52
23

subtract 52 from 75

amount left over from first division

divide divisor into 234

14

52 754
−52
234

bring down last digit of dividend and join it to remainder

Begin by dividing the divisor into the first two digits of the dividend. 52 fits into 75 once, so put a 1 above the dividing line, aligning it with the last digit of the number being divided.

Work out the first remainder. The divisor 52 does not divide into 75 exactly. To work out the amount left over (the remainder), subtract 52 from 75. The result is 23.

Now, bring down the last digit of the dividend and place it next to the remainder to form 234. Next, divide 234 by 52. It goes four times, so put a 4 next to the 1.

14

52 754
−52
234
−**208**
26

multiply 4 (the number of times 52 goes into 234) by 52 to get 208

amount left over from second division

add a decimal point then a zero

14

52 754.0
−52
234
−208
260

bring down zero and join it to remainder

add decimal point above other one

14.5

52 754.0
−52
234
−208
260

put result of last sum after decimal point

Work out the second remainder. The divisor, 52, does not divide into 234 exactly. To find the remainder, multiply 4 by 52 to make 208. Subtract 208 from 234, leaving 26.

There are no more whole numbers to bring down, so add a decimal point after the dividend and a zero after it. Bring down the zero and join it to the remainder 26 to form 260.

Put a decimal point after the 14. Next, divide 260 by 52, which goes five times exactly. Put a 5 above the dividing line, aligned with the new zero in the dividend.

11 Prime numbers

ANY WHOLE NUMBER LARGER THAN 1 THAT CANNOT BE DIVIDED
BY ANY OTHER NUMBER EXCEPT FOR ITSELF AND 1.

SEE ALSO
❰ 18–21 Multiplication
❰ 22–25 Division

Introducing prime numbers

Over 2,000 years ago, the Ancient Greek mathematician Euclid noted that
some numbers are only divisible by 1 or the number itself. These numbers
are known as prime numbers. A number that is not a prime is called a
composite—it can be arrived at, or composed, by multiplying together
smaller prime numbers, which are known as its prime factors.

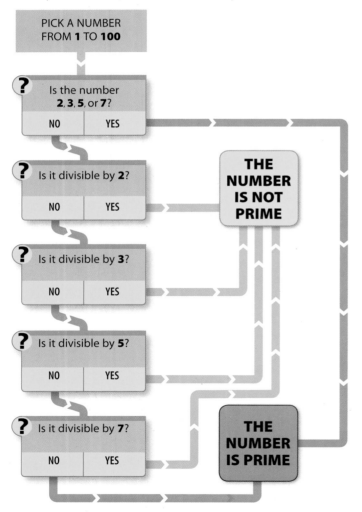

△ **Is a number prime?**
This flowchart can be used to determine whether a
number between 1 and 100 is prime by checking if it
is divisible by any of the primes 2, 3, 5, and 7.

1 is not a prime number or a
composite number

2 is the only even prime number.
No other even number is prime
because they are all divisible by 2

▷ **First 100 numbers**
This table shows the prime
numbers among the first
100 whole numbers.

KEY

17

Prime number
A blue box indicates that the number is prime. It has no factors other than 1 and itself.

42
2 3 7

Composite number
A yellow box denotes a composite number, which means that it is divisible by more than 1 and itself.

smaller numbers show whether the number is divisible by 2, 3, 5, or 7, or a combination of them

6	7	8	9	10
2 3		2	3	2 5
16	17	18	19	20
2		2 3		2 5
26	27	28	29	30
2	3	2 7		2 3 5
36	37	38	39	40
2 3		2	3	2 5
46	47	48	49	50
2		2 3	7	2 5
56	57	58	59	60
2 7	3	2		2 3 5
66	67	68	69	70
2 3		2	3	2 5 7
76	77	78	79	80
2	7	2 3		2 5
86	87	88	89	90
2	3	2		2 3 5
96	97	98	99	100
2 3		2 7	3	2 5

Prime factors

Every number is either a prime or the result of multiplying together prime numbers. Prime factorization is the process of breaking down a composite number into the prime numbers that it is made up of. These are known as its prime factors.

prime factor ⟶   ⟵ remaining factor

30 = **5** × **6**

To find the prime factors of 30, find the largest prime number that divides into 30, which is 5. The remaining factor is 6 (5 × 6 = 30), which needs to be broken down into prime numbers.

largest prime factor ⟶

6 = **3** × **2**

Next, take the remaining factor and find the largest prime number that divides into it, and any smaller prime numbers. In this case, the prime numbers that divide into 6 are 3 and 2.

list prime factors in descending order ⟶

30 = **5** × **3** × **2**

It is now possible to see that 30 is the product of multiplying together the prime numbers 5, 3, and 2. Therefore, the prime factors of 30 are 5, 3, and, 2.

REAL WORLD

Encryption

Many transactions in banks and stores rely on the Internet and other communications systems. To protect the information, it is coded using a number that is the product of just two huge primes. The security relies on the fact that no "eavesdropper" can factorize the number because its factors are so large.

▷ **Data protection**
To provide constant security, mathematicians relentlessly hunt for ever bigger primes.

Units of measurement

UNITS OF MEASUREMENT ARE STANDARD SIZES USED TO MEASURE TIME, MASS, AND LENGTH.

Basic units

A unit is any agreed or standardized measurement of size. This allows quantities to be accurately measured. There are three basic units: time, weight (including mass), and length.

LOOKING CLOSER

Distance

Distance is the amount of space between two points. It expresses length, but is also used to describe a journey, which is not always the most direct route between two points .

plane flies set distance between two cities

distance between cities A and B

A

B

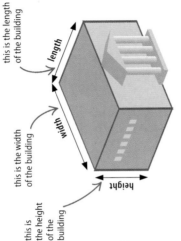

this is the length of the building

length

this is the width of the building

width

this is the height of the building

height

△ Time

Time is measured in milliseconds, seconds, minutes, hours, days, weeks, months, and years. Different countries and cultures may have calendars that start a new year at a different time.

these two units are lighter

these three units are heavier

△ Weight and mass

Weight is how heavy something is in relation to the force of gravity acting upon it. Mass is the amount of matter that makes up the object. Both are measured in the same units, such as grams and kilograms, or ounces and pounds.

△ Length

Length is how long something is. It is measured in centimeters, meters, and kilometers in the metric system, or in inches, feet, yards, and miles in the imperial system (see pp.242–245).

Compound measures

A compound unit is made up of more than one of the basic units, including using the same unit repeatedly. Examples include area, volume, speed, and density.

▽ Volume

Volume is measured in cubed units. The volume of a cuboid is the product of its height, width, and length; if they were all measured in meters (m), its area would be m × m × m, or m³.

length

width

height

$$\text{volume} = \text{length} \times \text{width} \times \text{height}$$

volume is a compound of three of the same units, because width and height are technically lengths

▽ Area

Area is measured in squared units. The area of a rectangle is the product of its length and width; if they were both measured in meters (m) its area would be m × m, which is written as m².

width

length

$$\text{area} = \text{length} \times \text{width}$$

area is made up of two of the same units, because width is also a length

Speed

Speed measures the distance (length) traveled in a given time. This means that the formula for measuring speed is length ÷ time. If this is measured in kilometers and hours, the unit for speed will be km/h.

$$\textbf{Speed} = \frac{\textbf{distance}}{\textbf{time}}$$

△ Speed formula triangle
The relationships between speed, distance, and time can be shown in a triangle. The position of each unit in the triangle indicates how to use the other two measurements to calculate that unit.

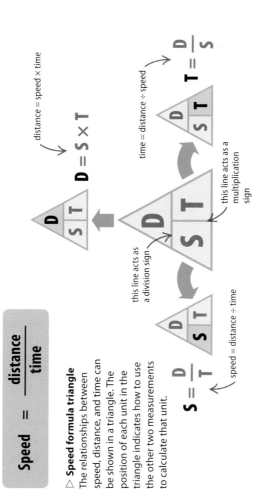

this line acts as a division sign

this line acts as a multiplication sign

$$S = \frac{D}{T}$$

speed = distance ÷ time

$$D = S \times T$$

distance = speed × time

$$T = \frac{D}{S}$$

time = distance ÷ speed

▷ Finding speed
A van travels 20 km in 20 minutes. From this information its speed in km/h can be found.

20 km

divide 20 by 60 to find its value in hours

$$20 \text{ minutes} = \frac{20}{60} = \frac{1}{3} \textbf{ hour}$$

First, convert the minutes into hours. To convert minutes into hours, divide them by 60, then cancel the fraction—divide the top and bottom numbers by 20. This gives an answer of ¹/₃ hour.

distance is 20 km

$$S = \frac{D}{T} = 60 \text{ km/h}$$

time is ¹/₃ hour

Then, substitute the values for distance and time into the formula for speed. Divide the distance (20 km) by the time (¹/₃ hour) to find the speed, in this case 60 km/h.

Density

Density measures how much matter is packed into a given volume of a substance. It involves two units—mass and volume. The formula for measuring density is mass ÷ volume. If this is measured in grams and centimeters, the unit for density will be g/cm³.

$$\textbf{Density} = \frac{\textbf{mass}}{\textbf{volume}}$$

△ Density formula triangle
The relationships between density, mass, and volume can be shown in a triangle. The position of each unit of measurement in the triangle shows how to calculate that unit using the other two measurements.

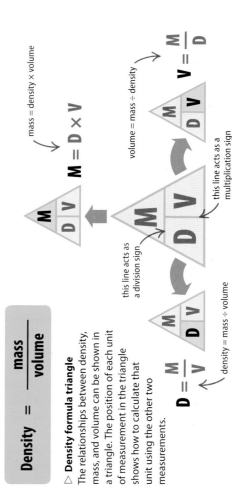

this line acts as a division sign

this line acts as a multiplication sign

$$D = \frac{M}{V}$$

density = mass ÷ volume

$$M = D \times V$$

mass = density × volume

$$V = \frac{M}{D}$$

volume = mass ÷ density

▷ Finding volume
Lead has a density of 0.0113 kg/cm³. With this measurement, the volume of a lead weight that has a mass of 0.5 kg can be found.

0.5 kg

density of lead is constant, regardless of mass

mass is 0.5 kg

$$V = \frac{M}{D} = 44.25 \text{ cm}^3$$

density is 0.0113 kg/cm³

△ Using the formula
Substitute the values for mass and density into the formula for volume. Divide the mass (0.5 kg) by the density (0.0113 kg/cm³) to find the volume, in this case 44.25 cm³.

Telling the time

TIME IS MEASURED IN THE SAME WAY AROUND THE WORLD.
THE MAIN UNITS ARE SECONDS, MINUTES, AND HOURS.

SEE ALSO
‹ 14–15 Introducing numbers
‹ 28–29 Units of measurement

Telling the time is an important skill and one that is
used in many ways: What time is breakfast? How long
until my birthday? Which is the quickest route?

Measuring time

Units of time measure how long events take and the gaps
between the events. Sometimes it is important to measure time
exactly, in a science experiment for example. At other times,
accuracy of measurement is not so important, such as when we
go to a friend's house to play. For thousands of years time was
measured simply by observing the movement of the sun, moon,
or stars, but now our watches and clocks are extremely accurate.

Bigger units of time

This is a list of the most commonly used
bigger units of time. Other units include
the Olympiad, which is a period of 4 years
and starts on January 1st of a year in which
the summer Olympics take place.

7 days is 1 week

▼

**Fortnight is short for
14 nights and is the
same as 2 weeks**

▼

**Between 28 and 31 days
is 1 month**

▼

**365 days is 1 year
(366 in a leap year)**

▼

10 years is a decade

▼

100 years is a century

▼

1000 years is a millennium

1 second	2	3	4	5	6	7	8	9	10
11	12	13	14	15	16	17	18	19	20
21	22	23	24	25	26	27	28	29	30
31	32	33	34	35	36	37	38	39	40
41	42	43	44	45	46	47	48	49	50
51	52	53	54	55	56	57	58	59	60

1 minute

◁ **Units of time**
The units we use around
the world are based on
1 second as measured
by International Atomic
Time. There are 86,400
seconds in one day.

There are
60 seconds in
each minute.

There are
60 minutes
in each hour.

1 minute	2	3	4	5	6	7	8	9	10
11	12	13	14	15	16	17	18	19	20
21	22	23	24	25	26	27	28	29	30
31	32	33	34	35	36	37	38	39	40
41	42	43	44	45	46	47	48	49	50
51	52	53	54	55	56	57	58	59	60

1 hour

1 hour	2	3	4	5	6
7	8	9	10	11	12
13	14	15	16	17	18
19	20	21	22	23	24

1 day

There are 24 hours in each day.

Reading the time

The time can be told by looking carefully at where the hands point on a clock or watch. The hour hand is shorter and moves around slowly. The minute hand is longer than the hour hand and points at minutes "past" the hour or "to" the next one. Most clock faces show the minutes in groups of five and the in-between minutes are shown by a short line or mark. The second hand is usually long and thin, and sweeps quickly around the face every minute, marking 60 seconds.

The short hand indicates what hour it is. This hour hand shows 11.

Between each number is 5 minutes.

The second hand shows 40 seconds on this clock face.

The hands move in this direction. This is called the clockwise direction.

The number of small marks are the number of minutes or seconds.

The long hand shows the minutes. On this clock face 20 minutes have passed.

△ A clock face
A clock face is a visual way to show the time easily and clearly. There are many types of clock and watch faces.

When the minute hand points to 12, the time is "on the hour" as shown by the hour hand.

5 to

5 past

10 to

10 past

If the minute hand is pointing to 9, the time is "quarter to" the hour.

quarter to

to the hour

past the hour

quarter past

When the minute hand points to 3, the time is "quarter past" the hour.

20 to

20 past

If the minute hand points to 6, the time is "half past" the hour.

25 to

25 past

half past

◁ Quarters and halves
A clock can show the time as a "quarter past" or a "quarter to." The quarter refers to a quarter of an hour, which is 15 minutes. Although we say "quarter" and "half," we do not normally say "three-quarters" in the same way. We might say something took "three-quarters of an hour," though, meaning 45 minutes.

10 o'clock

Quarter past 1

Half past 3

Quarter to 7

Analogue time

Most clocks and watches only go up to 12 hours, but there are 24 hours in one day. To show the difference between morning and night, we use AM or PM. The middle of the day (12 o'clock) is called midday or noon.

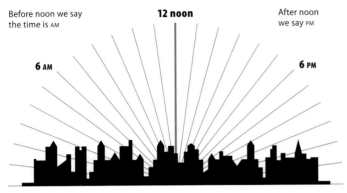

Before noon we say the time is AM

12 noon

After noon we say PM

6 AM

6 PM

△ **AM or PM**
The initials AM and PM stand for the Latin words **a**nte **m**eridiem (meaning "before noon") and **p**ost **m**eridiem (meaning "after noon"). The first 12 hours of the day are called AM and the second 12 hours of the day are called PM.

Digital time

Traditional clock faces show time in an analogue format but digital formats are also common, especially on electrical devices such as computers, televisions, and mobile phones. Some digital displays show time in the 24-hour system; others use the analogue system and also show AM or PM.

△ **Hours and minutes**
On a digital clock, the hours are shown first followed by a colon and the minutes. Some displays may also show seconds.

△ **24-hour digital display**
If the hours or minutes are single digit numbers, a zero (called a leading zero) is placed to the left of the digit.

△ **Midnight**
When it is midnight, the clock resets to 00:00. Midnight is an abbreviated form of "middle of the night."

△ **12-hour digital display**
This type of display will have AM and PM with the relevant part of the day highlighted.

24-hour clock

The 24-hour system was devised to stop confusion between morning and afternoon times, and runs continuously from midnight to midnight. It is often used in computers, by the military, and on timetables. To convert from the 12-hour system to the 24-hour system, you add 12 to the hour for times after noon. For example, 11 PM becomes 23:00 (11 + 12) and 8:45 PM becomes 20:45 (8:45 + 12).

12-hour clock	24-hour clock
12:00 midnight	00:00
1:00 AM	01:00
2:00 AM	02:00
3:00 AM	03:00
4:00 AM	04:00
5:00 AM	05:00
6:00 AM	06:00
7:00 AM	07:00
8:00 AM	08:00
9:00 AM	09:00
10:00 AM	10:00
11:00 AM	11:00
12:00 noon	12:00
1:00 PM	13:00
2:00 PM	14:00
3:00 PM	15:00
4:00 PM	16:00
5:00 PM	17:00
6:00 PM	18:00
7:00 PM	19:00
8:00 PM	20:00
9:00 PM	21:00
10:00 PM	22:00
11:00 PM	23:00

Roman numerals

DEVELOPED BY THE ANCIENT ROMANS, THIS SYSTEM USES
LETTERS FROM THE LATIN ALPHABET TO REPRESENT NUMBERS.

SEE ALSO

❰ 14–15 Introducing numbers

Understanding Roman numerals

The Roman numeral system does not use zero. To make a number,
seven letters are combined. These are the letters and their values:

| 1 | 5 | 10 | 50 | 100 | 500 | 1000 |

Forming numbers

Some key principles were observed by the ancient Romans to
"create" numbers from the seven letters.

First principle When a smaller number appears after a larger number,
the smaller number is added to the larger number to find the total value.

$$XI = X + I = 11 \qquad XVII = X + V + I + I = 17$$

Second principle When a smaller number appears before a larger number,
the smaller number is subtracted from the larger number to find the total value.

$$IX = X - I = 9 \qquad CM = M - C = 900$$

Third principle Each letter can be repeated up to three times.

$$XX = X + X = 20 \qquad XXX = X + X + X = 30$$

Using Roman numerals

Although Roman numerals are not widely used today, they still appear on some
clock faces, with the names of monarchs and popes, and for important dates.

Time

Names

Henry VIII
Henry the eighth

Dates

MMXIV
2014

Number	Roman numeral
1	I
2	II
3	III
4	IV
5	V
6	VI
7	VII
8	VIII
9	IX
10	X
11	XI
12	XII
13	XIII
14	XIV
15	XV
16	XVI
17	XVII
18	XVIII
19	XIX
20	XX
30	XXX
40	XL
50	L
60	LX
70	LXX
80	LXXX
90	XC
100	C
500	D
1000	M

Positive and negative numbers

A POSITIVE NUMBER IS A NUMBER THAT IS MORE THAN ZERO,
WHILE A NEGATIVE NUMBER IS LESS THAN ZERO.

A positive number is shown by a plus sign (+), or has no sign in front of it.
If a number is negative, it has a minus sign (−) in front of it.

SEE ALSO

❰ **14–15** Introducing numbers
❰ **16–17** Addition and subtraction

Why use positives and negatives?

Positive numbers are used when an amount is counted up from zero, and negative numbers when it is counted down from zero. For example, if a bank account has money in it, it is a positive amount of money, but if the account is overdrawn, the amount of money in the account is negative.

negative numbers

number line continues forever

−5 −4 −3 −2

Adding and subtracting positives and negatives

Use a number line to add and subtract positive and negative numbers. Find the first number on the line and then move the number of steps shown by the second number. Move right for addition and left for subtraction.

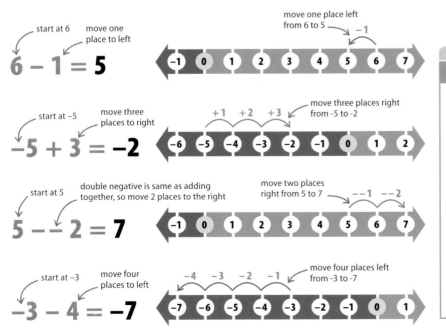

start at 6 move one place to left

move one place left from 6 to 5 −1

$6 − 1 = 5$

−1 0 1 2 3 4 5 6 7

start at −5 move three places to right

+1 +2 +3 move three places right from -5 to -2

$−5 + 3 = −2$

−6 −5 −4 −3 −2 −1 0 1 2

start at 5 double negative is same as adding together, so move 2 places to the right

move two places right from 5 to 7 −−1 −−2

$5 − −2 = 7$

−1 0 1 2 3 4 5 6 7

start at −3 move four places to left

−4 −3 −2 −1 move four places left from -3 to -7

$−3 − 4 = −7$

−7 −6 −5 −4 −3 −2 −1 0 1

LOOKING CLOSER

Double negatives

If a negative or minus number is subtracted from a positive number, it creates a double negative. The first negative is cancelled out by the second negative, so the result is always a positive, for example 5 minus −2 is the same as adding 2 to 5.

— — = +

△ **Like signs equal a positive**
If any two like signs appear together, the result is always positive. The result is negative with two unlike signs together.

▽ Number line
A number line is a good way to get to grips with positive and negative numbers. Draw the positive numbers to the right of 0, and the negative numbers to the left of 0. Adding color makes them easier to tell apart.

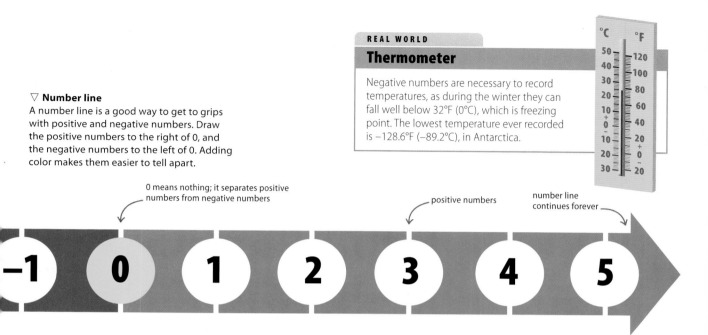

REAL WORLD

Thermometer
Negative numbers are necessary to record temperatures, as during the winter they can fall well below 32°F (0°C), which is freezing point. The lowest temperature ever recorded is −128.6°F (−89.2°C), in Antarctica.

0 means nothing; it separates positive numbers from negative numbers

positive numbers

number line continues forever

−1   0   1   2   3   4   5

Multiplying and dividing
To multiply or divide any two numbers, first ignore whether they are positive or negative, then work out if the answer is positive or negative using the diagram on the right.

$2 \times 4 = 8$

8 is positive because
$+ \times + = +$

$-1 \times 6 = -6$

−6 is negative because
$- \times + = -$

$-4 \div 2 = -2$

−2 is negative because
$- \div + = -$

$-2 \times 4 = -8$

−8 is negative because
$- \times + = -$

$-2 \times -4 = 8$

8 is positive because
$- \times - = +$

$-10 \div -2 = 5$

5 is positive because
$- \div - = +$

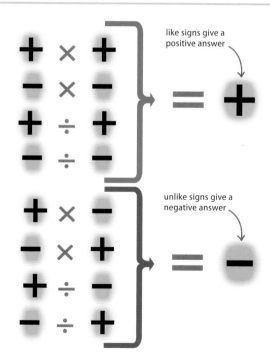

like signs give a positive answer

$+ \times +$
$- \times -$
$+ \div +$
$- \div -$
$= +$

unlike signs give a negative answer

$+ \times -$
$- \times +$
$+ \div -$
$- \div +$
$= -$

△ Positive or negative answer
The sign in the answer depends on whether the signs of the values are alike or not.

Powers and roots

A POWER IS THE NUMBER OF TIMES A NUMBER IS MULTIPLIED BY
ITSELF. THE ROOT OF A NUMBER IS A NUMBER THAT, MULTIPLIED
BY ITSELF, EQUALS THE ORIGINAL NUMBER.

Introducing powers

A power is the number of times a number is multiplied by itself. This
is indicated as a smaller number positioned to the right above the
number. Multiplying a number by itself once is described as "squaring"
the number; multiplying a number by itself twice is described as
"cubing" the number.

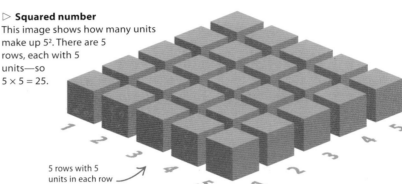

5^4

this is the power, which shows how
many times to multiply the number
(5^4 means $5 \times 5 \times 5 \times 5$)

this is the number that
the power relates to

$$5 \times 5 = 5^2$$
$$= 25$$

this is the power;
5^2 is called "5 squared"

▷ **Squared number**
This image shows how many units
make up 5^2. There are 5
rows, each with 5
units—so
$5 \times 5 = 25$.

5 rows with 5
units in each row

△ **The square of a number**
Multiplying a number by itself gives the
square of the number. The power for a
square number is ^{2}, for example 5^2 means
that 2 number 5's are being multiplied.

$$5 \times 5 \times 5 = 5^3$$
$$= 125$$

this is the power;
5^3 is called "5 cubed"

△ **The cube of a number**
Multiplying a number by itself twice
gives its cube. The power for a cube
number is ^{3}, for example 5^3, which
means there are 3 number 5's being
multiplied: $5 \times 5 \times 5$.

5 vertical rows

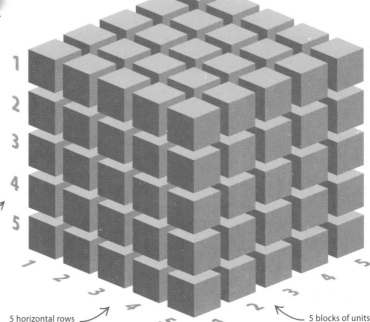

▷ **Cubed number**
This image shows how many units make
up 5^3. There are 5 horizontal rows and
5 vertical rows, each with 5 units in each
one, so $5 \times 5 \times 5 = 125$.

5 horizontal rows

5 blocks of units

Square roots and cube roots

A square root is a number that, multiplied by itself once, equals a given number. For example, one square root of 4 is 2, because $2 \times 2 = 4$. Another square root is -2, as $(-2) \times (-2) = 4$; the square roots of numbers can be either positive or negative. A cube root is a number that, multiplied by itself twice, equals a given number. For example, the cube root of 27 is 3, because $3 \times 3 \times 3 = 27$.

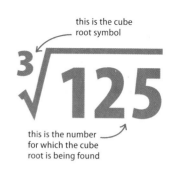

this is the square root symbol

this is the cube root symbol

$$\sqrt{25}$$

$$\sqrt[3]{125}$$

this is the number for which the square root is being found

this is the number for which the cube root is being found

square root symbol

this is the square root of 25

$$\sqrt{25} = 5 \text{ because } 5 \times 5 = 25$$

25 is 5^2

△ **The square root of a number**
The square root of a number is the number which, when squared (multiplied by itself), equals the number under the square root sign.

cube root symbol

this is the cube root of 125

125 is 5^3

$$\sqrt[3]{125} = 5 \text{ because } 5 \times 5 \times 5 = 125$$

△ **The cube root of a number**
The cube root of a number is the number that, when cubed (multiplied by itself twice), equals the number under the cube root sign.

COMMON SQUARE ROOTS

Square root	Answer	Why?
1	1	Because $1 \times 1 = 1$
4	2	Because $2 \times 2 = 4$
9	3	Because $3 \times 3 = 9$
16	4	Because $4 \times 4 = 16$
25	5	Because $5 \times 5 = 25$
36	6	Because $6 \times 6 = 36$
49	7	Because $7 \times 7 = 49$
64	8	Because $8 \times 8 = 64$
81	9	Because $9 \times 9 = 81$
100	10	Because $10 \times 10 = 100$
121	11	Because $11 \times 11 = 121$
144	12	Because $12 \times 12 = 144$
169	13	Because $13 \times 13 = 169$

LOOKING CLOSER

Using a calculator

Calculators can be used to find powers and square roots. Most calculators have buttons to square and cube numbers, buttons to find square roots and cube roots, and an exponent button, which allows them to raise numbers to any power.

△ **Exponent**
This button allows any number to be raised to any power.

$$3^5 = \boxed{3} \ \boxed{X^y} \ \boxed{5}$$
$$= 243$$

◁ **Using exponents**
First enter the number to be raised to a power, then press the exponent button, then enter the power required.

△ **Square root**
This button allows the square root of any number to be found.

$$25 = \boxed{\sqrt{}} \ \boxed{25}$$
$$= 5$$

◁ **Using square roots**
On most calculators, find the square root of a number by pressing the square root button first and then entering the number.

Multiplying powers of the same number

To multiply powers that have the same base number, simply add the powers. The power of the answer is the sum of the powers that are being multiplied.

add the powers

the first power

the second power

$$6^2 \times 6^3 = 6^5$$

the power of the answer is: $2 + 3 = 5$

because

▷ **Writing it out**
Writing out what each of these powers represents shows why powers are added together to multiply them.

$$(6 \times 6) \times (6 \times 6 \times 6) = 6 \times 6 \times 6 \times 6 \times 6$$

6^2 is 6×6 6^3 is $6 \times 6 \times 6$ $6 \times 6 \times 6 \times 6 \times 6$ is 6^5

Dividing powers of the same number

To divide powers of the same base number, subtract the second power from the first. The power of the answer is the difference between the first and second powers.

subtract the second power from the first

the first power

the second power

$$4^4 \div 4^2 = 4^2$$

the power of the answer is: $4 - 2 = 2$

because

▷ **Writing it out**
Writing out the division of the powers as a fraction and then canceling the fraction shows why powers to be divided can simply be subtracted.

4^4 is $4 \times 4 \times 4 \times 4$

$$\frac{4 \times 4 \times 4 \times 4}{4 \times 4} \Rightarrow \frac{\cancel{4} \times \cancel{4} \times 4 \times 4}{\cancel{4} \times \cancel{4}} = 4 \times 4$$

4^2 is 4×4 cancel the fraction to its simplest terms 4×4 is 4^2

LOOKING CLOSER

Zero power

Any number raised to the power 0 is equal to 1. Dividing two equal powers of the same base number gives a power of 0, and therefore the answer 1. These rules only apply when dealing with powers of the same base number.

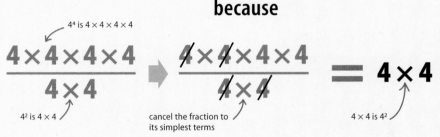

the first power

the second power

the power of the answer is: $3 - 3 = 0$

$$8^3 \div 8^3 = 8^0 = 1$$

any number to the power $0 = 1$

because

▷ **Writing it out**
Writing out the division of two equal powers makes it clear why any number to the power 0 is always equal to 1.

8^3 is $8 \times 8 \times 8$

$$\frac{8 \times 8 \times 8}{8 \times 8 \times 8} = \frac{512}{512} = 1$$

any number divided by itself $= 1$

Finding a square root by estimation

It is possible to find a square root through estimation, by choosing a number to multiply by itself, working out the answer, and then altering the number depending on whether the answer needs to be higher or lower.

$$\sqrt{32} = ?$$

$\sqrt{25} = 5$ and $\sqrt{36} = 6$, so the answer must be somewhere between 5 and 6. Start with the midpoint between the two, 5.5:

$5.5 \times 5.5 = 30.25$ ▼ Too low

$5.75 \times 5.75 = 33.0625$ ▲ Too high

$5.65 \times 5.65 = 31.9225$ ▼ Too low

$5.66 \times 5.66 = \textbf{32.0356}$

↖ the square root of 32 is approximately 5.66   ↖ this would round down to 32

$$\sqrt{1{,}000} = ?$$

$\sqrt{1{,}600} = 40$ and $\sqrt{900} = 30$, so the answer must be between 40 and 30. 1,000 is closer to 900 than 1,600, so start with a number closer to 30, such as 32:

$32 \times 32 = 1{,}024$ ▲ Too high

$31 \times 31 = 961$ ▼ Too low

$31.5 \times 31.5 = 992.25$ ▼ Too low

$31.6 \times 31.6 = 998.56$ ▼ Too low

$31.65 \times 31.65 = 1{,}001.72$ ▲ Too high

$31.62 \times 31.62 = \textbf{999.8244}$

the square root of 1,000 is approximately 31.62 ↗

↖ this would round up to 1,000 as the nearest whole number

Finding a cube root by estimation

Cube roots of numbers can also be estimated without a calculator. Use round numbers to start with, then use these answers to get closer to the final answer.

$$\sqrt[3]{32} = ?$$

$3 \times 3 \times 3 = 27$ and $4 \times 4 \times 4 = 64$, so the answer is somewhere between 3 and 4. Start with the midpoint between the two, 3.5:

$3.5 \times 3.5 \times 3.5 = 42.875$ ▲ Too high

$3.3 \times 3.3 \times 3.3 = 35.937$ ▲ Too high

$3.1 \times 3.1 \times 3.1 = 29.791$ ▼ Too low

$3.2 \times 3.2 \times 3.2 = 32.768$ ▲ Too high

$3.18 \times 3.18 \times 3.18 = \textbf{32.157432}$

↖ the cube root of 32 is approximately 3.18

↖ this would be 32.2 rounded to the tenths place, which would round to 32

$$\sqrt[3]{800} = ?$$

$9 \times 9 \times 9 = 729$ and $10 \times 10 \times 10 = 1{,}000$, so the answer is somewhere between 9 and 10. 800 is closer to 729 than 1000, so start with a number closer to 9, such as 9.1:

$9.1 \times 9.1 \times 9.1 = 753.571$ ▼ Too low

$9.3 \times 9.3 \times 9.3 = 804.357$ ▲ Too high

$9.27 \times 9.27 \times 9.27 = 796.5979$ ▼ Too low

$9.28 \times 9.28 \times 9.28 = 799.1787$ ▼ Very close

$9.284 \times 9.284 \times 9.284 = \textbf{800.2126}$

↖ the cube root of 800 is approximately 9.284

↖ this would round down to 800

Surds

SEE ALSO

❮ 36–39 Powers and roots

Fractions **48–55 ❯**

A SURD IS A SQUARE ROOT THAT CANNOT BE WRITTEN
AS A WHOLE NUMBER. IT HAS AN INFINITE NUMBER OF
DIGITS AFTER THE DECIMAL POINT.

Introducing surds

Some square roots are whole numbers and are easy to write. But some are irrational
numbers—numbers that go on forever after the decimal point. These numbers cannot
be written out in full, so the most accurate way to express them is as square roots.

irrational number

$$\sqrt{5} = 2.2360679774...$$

rational number

$$\sqrt{4} = 2$$

△ **Surd**
The square root of 5 is an irrational number—it goes
on forever. It cannot accurately be written out in full,
so it is most simply expressed as the surd √5.

△ **Not a surd**
The square root of 4 is not a surd.
It is the number 2, a whole, or
rational, number.

Simplifying surds

Some surds can be made simpler by taking out factors that can be
written as whole numbers. A few simple rules can help with this.

▷ **Square roots**
A square root is the number
that, when multiplied by
itself, equals the number
inside the root.

$$\sqrt{a} \times \sqrt{a} = a$$

$$\sqrt{3} \times \sqrt{3} = 3$$

multiply the surd by itself
to get the number inside
the square root

▷ **Multiplying roots**
Multiplying two numbers
together and taking the
square root of the result
equals the same answer as
taking the square roots of
the two numbers and
mutiplying them together.

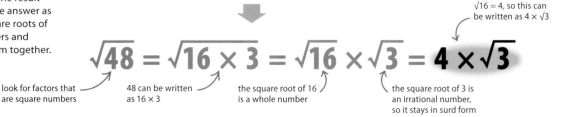

$$\sqrt{ab} = \sqrt{a} \times \sqrt{b}$$

√16 = 4, so this can
be written as 4 × √3

$$\sqrt{48} = \sqrt{16 \times 3} = \sqrt{16} \times \sqrt{3} = 4 \times \sqrt{3}$$

look for factors that
are square numbers

48 can be written
as 16 × 3

the square root of 16
is a whole number

the square root of 3 is
an irrational number,
so it stays in surd form

▷ **Dividing roots**
Dividing one number by another and taking the square root of the result is the same as dividing the square root of the first number by the square root of the second.

$$\sqrt{\frac{a}{b}} = \frac{\sqrt{a}}{\sqrt{b}}$$

$$\sqrt{\frac{7}{16}} = \frac{\sqrt{7}}{\sqrt{16}} = \frac{\sqrt{7}}{4}$$

√7 is irrational (2.6457...), so leave as a surd

16 is 4 squared

▷ **Simplifying further**
When dividing square roots, look out for ways to simplify the top as well as the bottom of the fraction.

$$\sqrt{\frac{8}{9}} = \frac{\sqrt{8}}{\sqrt{9}} = \frac{\sqrt{8}}{3} = \frac{2 \times \sqrt{2}}{3}$$

√9 = 3
(3 x 3 = 9)

final, simplified form

$$\sqrt{8} = \sqrt{4} \times \sqrt{2} = 2 \times \sqrt{2}$$

8 is 4 × 2

4 is 2 squared

Surds in fractions

When a surd appears in a fraction, it is helpful to make sure it appears in the numerator (top of the fraction) not the denominator (bottom of the fraction). This is called rationalizing, and is done by multiplying the whole fraction by the surd on the bottom.

▷ **Rationalizing**
The fraction stays the same if the top and bottom are multiplied by the same number.

$$\frac{1}{\sqrt{2}} = \frac{1 \times \sqrt{2}}{\sqrt{2} \times \sqrt{2}} = \frac{\sqrt{2}}{2}$$

the surd √2 is now on top of the fraction

multiply top and bottom by the surd √2

▷ **Simplifying further**
Sometimes rationalizing a fraction gives us another surd that can be simplified further.

12 and 15 can both be divided by 3 to simplify further

$$\frac{12}{\sqrt{15}} = \frac{12 \times \sqrt{15}}{\sqrt{15} \times \sqrt{15}} = \frac{12 \times \sqrt{15}}{15} = \frac{4 \times \sqrt{15}}{5}$$

multiply both top and bottom by √15

multiplying √15 by √15 gives 15

Standard Form

SEE ALSO

❮ **18–21** Multiplication
❮ **22–25** Division
❮ **36–39** Powers and roots

STANDARD FORM IS A CONVENIENT WAY OF WRITING VERY LARGE AND VERY SMALL NUMBERS.

Introducing standard form

Standard form makes very large or very small numbers easier to understand by showing them as a number multiplied by a power of 10. This is useful because the size of the power of 10 makes it possible to get an instant impression of how big the number really is.

this is the power of 10

$$4 \times 10^3$$

◁ **Using standard form**
This is how 4,000 is written as standard form—it shows that the decimal place for the number represented, 4,000, is 3 places to the right of 4.

How to write a number in standard form

To write a number in standard form, work out how many places the decimal point must move to form a number between 1 and 10. If the number does not have a decimal point, add one after its final digit.

▷ **Take a number**
Standard form is usually used for very large or very small numbers.

very large number

1,230,000

very small number

0.0006

▷ **Add the decimal point**
Identify the position of the decimal point if there is one. Add a decimal point at the end of the number, if it does not already have one.

add decimal point

1,230,000.

decimal point is already here

0.0006

▷ **Move the decimal point**
Move along the number and count how many places the decimal point must move to form a number between 1 and 10.

6 5 4 3 2 1

1,230,000.

the decimal point moves 6 places to the left

1 2 3 4

0.0006

the decimal point moves 4 places to the right

▷ **Write as standard form**
The number between 1 and 10 is multiplied by 10, and the small number, the "power" of 10, is found by counting how many places the decimal point moved to create the first number.

the power is 6 because the decimal point moved six places; the power is positive because the decimal point moved to the left

$$1.23 \times 10^6$$

the first number must always be between 1 and 10

the power is negative because the decimal point moved to the right

$$6 \times 10^{-4}$$

the power is 4 because the decimal point moved four places

Standard form in action

Sometimes it is difficult to compare extremely large or small numbers because of the number of digits they contain. Standard form makes this easier.

The mass of Earth is 5,974,200,000,000,000,000,000,000 kg

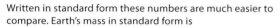

5,974,200,000,000,000,000,000,000.0 kg

The decimal point moves **24 places** to the left.

The mass of the planet Mars is

641,910,000,000,000,000,000,000.0 kg

The decimal point moves **23 places** to the left.

Written in standard form these numbers are much easier to compare. Earth's mass in standard form is

$$5.9742 \times 10^{24} \text{ kg}$$

The mass of Mars in standard form is

$$6.4191 \times 10^{23} \text{ kg}$$

▷ **Comparing planet mass**
It is immediately evident that the mass of the Earth is bigger than the mass of Mars because 10^{24} is 10 times larger than 10^{23}.

EXAMPLES OF STANDARD FORM		
Example	**Decimal form**	**Standard form**
Weight of the Moon	73,600,000,000,000,000,000,000 kg	7.36×10^{22} kg
Humans on Earth	6,800,000,000	6.8×10^{9}
Speed of light	300,000,000 m/sec	3×10^{8} m/sec
Distance of the Moon from the Earth	384,000 km	3.8×10^{5} km
Weight of the Empire State building	365,000 tons	3.65×10^{5} tons
Distance around the Equator	40,075 km	4×10^{4} km
Height of Mount Everest	8,850 m	8.850×10^{3} m
Speed of a bullet	710 m/sec	7.1×10^{2} m/sec
Speed of a snail	0.001 m/sec	1×10^{-3} m/sec
Width of a red blood cell	0.00067 cm	6.7×10^{-4} cm
Length of a virus	0.000 000 009 cm	9×10^{-9} cm
Weight of a dust particle	0.000 000 000 753 kg	7.53×10^{-10} kg

LOOKING CLOSER

Standard form and calculators

The exponent button on a calculator allows a number to be raised to any power. Calculators give very large answers in standard form.

△ **Exponent button**
This calculator button allows any number to be raised to any power.

Using the exponent button:

$$4 \times 10^{2}$$ is entered by pressing

[4] [×] [10] [X^y] [2]

On some calculators, answers appear in standard form:

1234567 × 89101112 =
1.100012925 × 10¹⁴

so the answer is approximately 110,001,292,500,000

Decimals

NUMBERS WRITTEN IN DECIMAL FORM ARE CALLED DECIMAL NUMBERS OR, MORE SIMPLY, DECIMALS.

SEE ALSO

❰ 18–21 Multiplication
❰ 22–25 Division
Using a calculator   72–73 ❱

Decimal numbers

In a decimal number, the digits to the left of the decimal point are whole numbers. The digits to the right of the decimal point are not whole numbers. The first digit to the right of the decimal point represents tenths, the second hundredths, and so on. These are called fractional parts.

whole number part is 1,234

fractional part is 56

decimal point separates the whole numbers (on the left) from the fractional numbers (on the right)

△ **Whole and fractional parts**
The whole numbers represent – moving left from the decimal point – ones, tens, hundreds, and thousands. The fractional numbers – moving right from the decimal place – are tenths then hundredths.

Multiplication

To multiply decimals, first remove the decimal point. Then perform a long multiplication of the two numbers, before adding the decimal point back in to the answer. Here 1.9 (a decimal) is multiplied by 7 (a whole number).

6 is carried to the tens column

multiply 7 by 9

$7 \times 9 = 63$, the first digit, 6, is carried to the tens column

$1 \times 7 + 6 = 13$, which is written across two columns

multiply 7 by 1

decimal point is put back in

decimal point is removed

First, remove any decimal points, so that both numbers can be treated as whole numbers.

▶ **Then multiply** the two numbers, starting in the ones column. Carry ones to the tens if necessary.

▶ **Next multiply the tens.** The product is 7, which, added to the carried 6, makes 13. Write this across two columns.

▶ **Finally, count** the decimal digits in the original numbers – there is 1. The answer will also have 1 decimal digit.

DIVISION

Dividing one number by another often gives a decimal answer. Sometimes it is easier to turn decimals into whole numbers before dividing them.

Short division with decimals

Many numbers do not divide into each other exactly. If this is the case, a decimal point is added to the number being divided, and zeros are added after the point until the division is solved. Here 6 is divided by 8.

Both numbers are whole. As 8 will not divide into 6, put in a decimal point with a 0 after it and carry the 6.

carry 6 · add a decimal point on the answer line · add a 0 after the decimal point · add a decimal point after 6

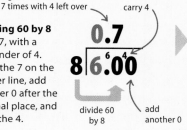

Dividing 60 by 8 gives 7, with a remainder of 4. Write the 7 on the answer line, add another 0 after the decimal place, and carry the 4.

8 goes into 60 7 times with 4 left over · carry 4 · divide 60 by 8 · add another 0

Dividing 40 by 8 gives 5 exactly, and the division ends (terminates). The answer to 6 ÷ 8 is 0.75.

answer is 0.75 · divide 40 by 8

Dividing decimals

Above, short division was used to find the decimal answer for the sum 8 ÷ 6. Long division can be used to achieve the same result.

8 fits into 6 0 times, so write 0 here · multiply 8 times 0 to get 0

First, divide 8 into 6. It goes 0 times, so put a 0 above the 6. Multiply 8 × 0, and write the result (0) under the 6.

add decimal point · bring down a 0 · divide 60 by 8

Subtract 0 from 6 to get 6, and bring down a 0. Divide 8 into 60 and put the answer, 7, after a decimal point.

multiply 8 times 7 to get 56 · first remainder is 4

Work out the first remainder by multiplying 8 by 7 and subtracting this from 60. The answer is 4.

8 goes into 40 exactly 5 times · bring down a 0 · divide 40 by 8

Bring down a zero to join the 4 and divide the number by 8. It goes exactly 5 times, so put a 5 above the line.

LOOKING CLOSER

Decimals that do not end

Sometimes the answer to a division can be a decimal number that repeats without ending. This is called a "repeating" decimal. For example, here 1 is divided by 3. Both the calculations and the answers in the division become identical after the second stage, and the answer repeats endlessly.

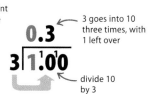

add a decimal point to the answer line · carry 1 · 3 does not divide into 1

3 does not divide into 1, so enter 0 on the answer line. Add a decimal point after 0, and carry 1.

3 goes into 10 three times, with 1 left over · divide 10 by 3

10 divided by 3 gives 3, with a remainder of 1. Write the 3 on the answer line and carry the 1 to the next 0.

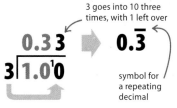

3 goes into 10 three times, with 1 left over · symbol for a repeating decimal

Dividing 10 by 3 again gives exactly the same answer as the last step. This is repeated infinitely. This type of repeating decimal is written with a line over the repeating digit.

Binary numbers

SEE ALSO
‹ 14–15 Introducing numbers
‹ 33 Roman numerals

NUMBERS ARE COMMONLY WRITTEN USING THE DECIMAL SYSTEM, BUT NUMBERS CAN BE WRITTEN IN ANY NUMBER BASE.

What is a binary number?

The decimal system uses the digits 0 through to 9, while the binary system, also known as base 2, uses only two digits—0 and 1. Binary numbers should not be thought of in the same way as decimal numbers. For example, 10 is said as "ten" in the decimal system but must be said as "one zero" in the binary system. This is because the value of each "place" is different in decimal and binary.

Decimal numbers

0 1 2 3 4 5 6 7 8 9

Binary numbers

0 1

a single binary digit is called a "bit," which is short for **b**inary dig**it**

Counting in the decimal system

When using the decimal system for column sums, numbers are written from right to left (from lowest to highest). Each column is worth ten times more than the column to the right of it. The decimal number system is also known as base 10.

	×10		×10		×10	
Thousands 1000		Hundreds 100		Tens 10		Ones 1
6		**4**		**5**		**2**

6000 + 400 + 50 + 2

= 6452

Counting in binary

Each column in the binary system is worth two times more than the column to the right of it and, as in the decimal system, 0 represents zero value. A similar system of headings may be used with binary numbers but only two symbols are used (0 and 1).

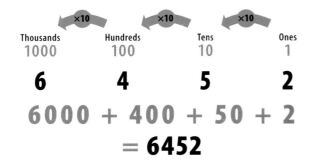

Thirty-twos 32	Sixteens 16	Eights 8	Fours 4	Twos 2	Ones 1
1	**1**	**1**	**0**	**0**	**1**

32 + 16 + 8 + 0 + 0 + 1

= 57 ← written in the decimal system

Decimal	Binary	
0	0	0
1	1	1 one
2	1 0	1 two
3	1 1	1 two + 1 one
4	1 0 0	1 four
5	1 0 1	1 four + 1 one
6	1 1 0	1 four + 1 two
7	1 1 1	1 four + 1 two + 1 one
8	1 0 0 0	1 eight
9	1 0 0 1	1 eight + 1 one
10	1 0 1 0	1 eight + 1 two
11	1 0 1 1	1 eight + 1 two + 1 one
12	1 1 0 0	1 eight + 1 four
13	1 1 0 1	1 eight + 1 four + 1 one
14	1 1 1 0	1 eight + 1 four + 1 two
15	1 1 1 1	1 eight + 1 four + 1 two + 1 one
16	1 0 0 0 0	1 sixteen
17	1 0 0 0 1	1 sixteen + 1 one
18	1 0 0 1 0	1 sixteen + 1 two
19	1 0 0 1 1	1 sixteen + 1 two + 1 one
20	1 0 1 0 0	1 sixteen + 1 four
50	1 1 0 0 1 0	1 thirty-two + 1 sixteen + 1 two
100	1 1 0 0 1 0 0	1 sixty-four + 1 thirty-two + 1 four

Adding in binary

Numbers written in binary form can be added together in a similar way to the decimal system, and column addition may be done like this:

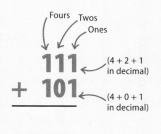

Fours
Twos
Ones

111 (4 + 2 + 1 in decimal)

+ 101 (4 + 0 + 1 in decimal)

Align the numbers under their correct place-value columns as in the decimal system. It may be helpful to write in the column headings when first learning this system.

1 + 1 = 2 (this is 10 in binary)

111
+ 101
0
1 ← carry 1

Add the ones column. The answer is 2, which is 10 in binary. The twos are shown in the next column so carry a 1 to the next column and leave 0 in the ones column.

1 + 0 + 1 = 2 (this is 10 in binary)

111
+ 101
00
1 ← carry 1

Now the digits in the twos column are added together with the 1 carried over from the ones column. The total is 2 again (10 in binary) so a 1 needs to be carried and a 0 left in the twos column.

the answer is 12 in the decimal system (8 + 4 + 0 + 0 = 12)

111
+ 101
1100
1 ← carry 1 and place in the eights column

Finally, add the 1s in the fours column, which gives us 3, (11 in binary). This is the end of the equation so the final 1 is placed in the eights column.

Subtracting in binary

Subtraction works in a similar way to the decimal system but "borrows" in different units to the decimal system—borrowing by twos instead of tens.

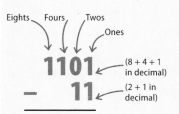

Eights
Fours
Twos
Ones

1101 (8 + 4 + 1 in decimal)

− 11 (2 + 1 in decimal)

The numbers are written in their correct place-value columns as in the decimal system.

it is helpful to add zeros   subtract the units

1101
− 0011
0

Add zeros so that there are the same number of digits in each column. Then begin by subtracting the ones column: 1 minus 1 is 0, so place a 0 in the answer space. Now move on to the twos column on the left.

we put a 2 in the twos column because the borrowed number represents 2 lots of twos

0 2
1101
− 0011
10

the answer is 10 in the decimal system (8 + 0 + 2 + 0 = 10)

The lower 1 cannot be subtracted from the 0 above it so borrow from the fours column and replace it with a 0. Then put a 2 above the twos column. Subtract the lower 1 from the upper 2. This leaves 1 as the answer.

0 2
1101
− 0011
1010

Now subtract the digits in the fours column, which gives us 0. Finally, in the eights column we have nothing to subtract from the upper 1, so 1 is written in the answer space.

Fractions

A FRACTION REPRESENTS A PART OF A WHOLE NUMBER.
THEY ARE WRITTEN AS ONE NUMBER OVER ANOTHER NUMBER.

Writing fractions

The number on the top of a fraction shows how many equal parts of the whole are being dealt with, while the number on the bottom shows the total number of equal parts that the whole has been divided into.

Numerator
The number of equal parts examined.

Dividing line
This is also written as /.

Denominator
Total number of equal parts in the whole.

$$\frac{1}{2}$$

Quarter
One fourth, or $^1/_4$ (a quarter), shows 1 part out of 4 equal parts in a whole.

$$\frac{1}{4}$$

$$\frac{1}{8}$$

Eighth
$^1/_8$ (one eighth) is 1 part out of 8 equal parts in a whole.

$$\frac{1}{16}$$

Sixteenth
$^1/_{16}$ (one sixteenth) is 1 part out of 16 equal parts in a whole.

$$\frac{1}{32}$$

$$\frac{1}{64} \quad \frac{1}{64}$$

One thirty-second
$^1/_{32}$ (one thirty-second) is 1 part out of 32 equal parts in a whole.

One sixty-fourth
$^1/_{64}$ (one sixty-fourth) is 1 part out of 64 equal parts in a whole.

▷ **Equal parts of a whole**
The circle on the right shows how parts of a whole can be divided in different ways to form different fractions.

Types of fractions

A proper fraction—where the numerator is smaller than the denominator—is just one type of fraction. When the number of parts is greater than the whole, the result is a fraction that can be written in two ways— either as an improper fraction (also known as a top-heavy fraction) or a mixed fraction.

numerator has lower value than denominator

$\frac{1}{4}$

◁ **Proper fraction**
In this fraction the number of parts examined, shown on top, is less than the whole.

numerator has higher value than denominator

$\frac{35}{4}$

◁ **Improper fraction**
The larger numerator indicates that the parts come from more than one whole.

whole number   fraction

$10\frac{1}{3}$

◁ **Mixed fraction**
A whole number is combined with a proper fraction.

Depicting fractions

Fractions can be illustrated in many ways, using any shape that can be divided into an equal number of parts.

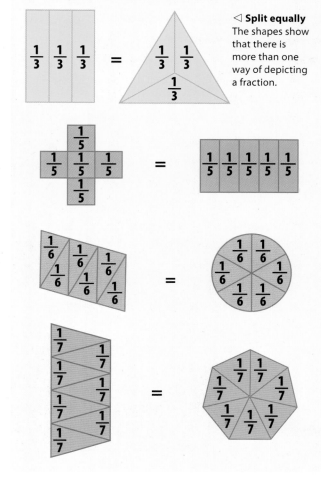

◁ **Split equally**
The shapes show that there is more than one way of depicting a fraction.

Half
$\frac{1}{2}$ (one half) is 1 part out of 2 equal parts in a whole.

Turning top-heavy fractions into mixed fractions

A top-heavy fraction can be turned into a mixed fraction by dividing the numerator by the denominator.

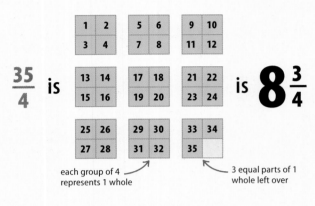

$\frac{35}{4}$ is ... is $8\frac{3}{4}$

each group of 4 represents 1 whole

3 equal parts of 1 whole left over

Draw groups of four numbers—each group represents a whole number. The fraction is eight whole numbers with ³/₄ (three quarters) left over.

numerator

whole number of 8 is produced with 3 left over

$$\frac{35}{4} = 35 \div 4 = 8\,r3 = 8\frac{3}{4}$$

denominator

Divide the numerator by the denominator, in this case, 35 by 4.

The result is the mixed fraction 8³/₄ made up of the whole number 8 and 3 parts—or ³/₄ (three quarters)—left over.

Turning mixed fractions into top-heavy fractions

A mixed fraction can be changed into a top-heavy fraction by multiplying the whole number by the denominator and adding the result to the numerator.

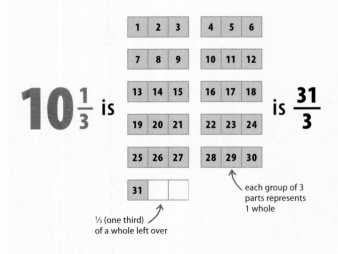

$10\frac{1}{3}$ is ... is $\frac{31}{3}$

⅓ (one third) of a whole left over

each group of 3 parts represents 1 whole

Draw the fraction as ten groups of three parts with one part left over. In this way it is possible to count 31 parts in the fraction.

whole number

multiply whole number by denominator

add to numerator

$$10\frac{1}{3} = \frac{10 \times 3 + 1}{3} = \frac{31}{3}$$

denominator

Multiply the whole number by the denominator—in this case, 10 × 3 = 30. Then add the numerator.

The result is the top-heavy fraction ³¹/₃, with a numerator (31) greater than the denominator (3).

Equivalent fractions

The same fraction can be written in different ways. These are known as equivalent (meaning "equal") fractions, even though they look different.

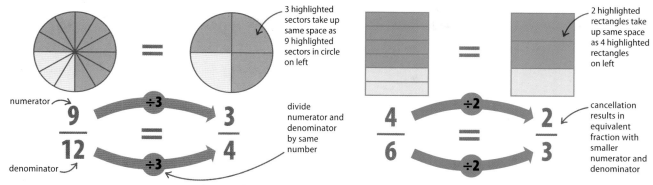

3 highlighted sectors take up same space as 9 highlighted sectors in circle on left

divide numerator and denominator by same number

2 highlighted rectangles take up same space as 4 highlighted rectangles on left

cancellation results in equivalent fraction with smaller numerator and denominator

△ **Cancellation**
Cancellation is a method used to find an equivalent fraction that is simpler than the original. To cancel a fraction divide the numerator and denominator by the same number.

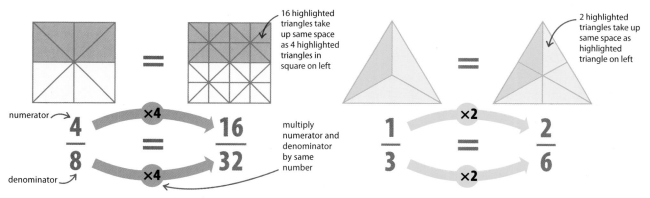

16 highlighted triangles take up same space as 4 highlighted triangles in square on left

multiply numerator and denominator by same number

2 highlighted triangles take up same space as highlighted triangle on left

△ **Reverse cancellation**
Multiplying the numerator and denominator by the same number is called reverse cancellation. This results in an equivalent fraction with a larger numerator and denominator.

Table of equivalent fractions									
$^1/_1 =$	$^2/_2$	$^3/_3$	$^4/_4$	$^5/_5$	$^6/_6$	$^7/_7$	$^8/_8$	$^9/_9$	$^{10}/_{10}$
$^1/_2 =$	$^2/_4$	$^3/_6$	$^4/_8$	$^5/_{10}$	$^6/_{12}$	$^7/_{14}$	$^8/_{16}$	$^9/_{18}$	$^{10}/_{20}$
$^1/_3 =$	$^2/_6$	$^3/_9$	$^4/_{12}$	$^5/_{15}$	$^6/_{18}$	$^7/_{21}$	$^8/_{24}$	$^9/_{27}$	$^{10}/_{30}$
$^1/_4 =$	$^2/_8$	$^3/_{12}$	$^4/_{16}$	$^5/_{20}$	$^6/_{24}$	$^7/_{28}$	$^8/_{32}$	$^9/_{36}$	$^{10}/_{40}$
$^1/_5 =$	$^2/_{10}$	$^3/_{15}$	$^4/_{20}$	$^5/_{25}$	$^6/_{30}$	$^7/_{35}$	$^8/_{40}$	$^9/_{45}$	$^{10}/_{50}$
$^1/_6 =$	$^2/_{12}$	$^3/_{18}$	$^4/_{24}$	$^5/_{30}$	$^6/_{36}$	$^7/_{42}$	$^8/_{48}$	$^9/_{54}$	$^{10}/_{60}$
$^1/_7 =$	$^2/_{14}$	$^3/_{21}$	$^4/_{28}$	$^5/_{35}$	$^6/_{42}$	$^7/_{49}$	$^8/_{56}$	$^9/_{63}$	$^{10}/_{70}$
$^1/_8 =$	$^2/_{16}$	$^3/_{24}$	$^4/_{32}$	$^5/_{40}$	$^6/_{48}$	$^7/_{56}$	$^8/_{64}$	$^9/_{72}$	$^{10}/_{80}$

Finding a common denominator

When finding the relative sizes of two or more fractions, finding a common denominator makes it much easier. A common denominator is a number that can be divided exactly by the denominators of all of the fractions. Once this has been found, comparing fractions is just a matter of comparing their numerators.

▷ **Comparing fractions**
To work out the relative sizes of fractions, it is necessary to convert them so that they all have the same denominator. To do so, first look at the denominators of all the fractions being compared.

$$\frac{2}{3} \text{ denominator} \qquad \frac{5}{8} \text{ denominator} \qquad \frac{7}{12} \text{ denominator}$$

▷ **Make a list**
List the multiples – all the whole number products of each denominator – for all of the denominators. Pick a sensible stopping point for the list, such as 100.

multiples of 3
3, 6, 9, 12, 15, 18, 21, 24, 27, 30…

multiples of 8
8, 16, 24, 32, 40, 48, 56, 64, 72…

multiples of 12
12, 24, 36, 48, 60, 72, 84, 96…

▷ **Find the lowest common denominator**
List only the multiples that are common to all three sets. These numbers are called common denominators. Identify the lowest one.

lowest common denominator of 3, 8, and 12

common denominators

24, 48, 72, 96…

▷ **Convert the fractions**
Find out how many times the original denominator goes into the common denominator. Multiply the numerator by the same number. It is now possible to compare the fractions.

largest fraction

smallest fraction

$$\frac{2}{3} \overset{\times 8}{\underset{\times 8}{=}} \frac{16}{24} \qquad \frac{5}{8} \overset{\times 3}{\underset{\times 3}{=}} \frac{15}{24} \qquad \frac{7}{12} \overset{\times 2}{\underset{\times 2}{=}} \frac{14}{24}$$

original denominator goes into common denominator 8 times, so multiply both numerator and denominator by 8

original denominator goes into common denominator 3 times, so multiply both numerator and denominator by 3

original denominator goes into common denominator 2 times, so multiply both numerator and denominator by 2

ADDING AND SUBTRACTING FRACTIONS

Just like whole numbers, it is possible to add and subtract fractions. How it is done depends on whether the denominators are the same or different.

Adding and subtracting fractions with the same denominator

To add or subtract fractions that have the same denominator, simply add or subtract their numerators to get the answer. The denominators stay the same.

$$\frac{1}{4} + \frac{2}{4} = \frac{3}{4}$$

To add fractions, add together only the numerators. The denominator in the result remains unchanged.

$$\frac{7}{8} - \frac{4}{8} = \frac{3}{8}$$

To subtract fractions, subtract the smaller numerator from the larger. The denominator in the result stays the same.

Adding fractions with different denominators

To add fractions that have different denominators, it is necessary to change one or both of the fractions so they have the same denominator. This involves finding a common denominator (see opposite).

multiply whole number by denominator then add numerator

6 is a common denominator of both 3 and 6

$5/6$ can now be added to $26/6$ as both have same denominator

remainder becomes numerator of fraction

$$4\frac{1}{3} + \frac{5}{6} \quad \frac{4\times3+1}{3} \quad \frac{13}{3} + \frac{5}{6}$$

$$\frac{13}{3} \overset{\times 2}{\underset{\times 2}{=}} \frac{26}{6} + \frac{5}{6} \quad \frac{31}{6} \Rightarrow 31 \div 6 = 5r1 = 5\frac{1}{6}$$

denominator stays same

denominator goes into common denominator 2 times, so multiply both numerator and denominator by 2

First, turn any mixed fractions that are being added into improper fractions.

The two fractions have different denominators, so a common denominator is needed.

Convert the fractions into fractions with common denominators by multiplying.

If necessary, divide the numerator by the denominator to turn the improper fraction back into a mixed fraction.

Subtracting fractions with different denominators

To subtract fractions with different denominators, a common denominator must be found.

multiply whole number by denominator then add numerator

4 is a common denominator of both 2 and 4

$3/4$ can be subtracted from $26/4$ because both have same denominator

remainder becomes numerator of fraction

$$6\frac{1}{2} - \frac{3}{4} \quad \frac{6\times2+1}{2} \quad \frac{13}{2} - \frac{3}{4}$$

$$\frac{13}{2} \overset{\times 2}{\underset{\times 2}{=}} \frac{26}{4} - \frac{3}{4} \quad \frac{23}{4} \Rightarrow 23 \div 4 = 5r1 = 5\frac{3}{4}$$

denominator stays same

denominator goes into common denominator 2 times, so multiply both numerator and denominator by 2

First, turn any mixed fractions in the equation into improper fractions by multiplying.

The two fractions have different denominators, so a common denominator is needed.

Convert the fractions into fractions with common denominators by multiplying.

If necessary, divide the numerator by the denominator to turn the improper fraction back into a mixed fraction.

MULTIPLYING FRACTIONS

Fractions can be multiplied by other fractions. To multiply fractions by mixed fractions or whole numbers, they first need to be converted into improper (top-heavy) fractions.

two equal parts

multiplying ½ by 3 is same as adding ½ to ½ to ½

$$\square \times 3 = \square + \square + \square = \square\square$$

$$\frac{1}{2} \times 3 = \frac{1}{2} + \frac{1}{2} + \frac{1}{2} = \mathbf{1\frac{1}{2}}$$

Imagine multiplying a fraction by a whole number as adding the fraction to itself that many times. Alternatively, imagine multiplying a whole number by a fraction as taking that portion of the whole number, here ½ of 3.

whole number an improper fraction with whole number as numerator and 1 as denominator

remainder becomes numerator of fraction

$$\frac{1}{2} \times \frac{3}{1} = \frac{3}{2} \implies 3 \div 2 = 1r1 = \mathbf{1\frac{1}{2}}$$

denominator stays the same

Convert the whole number to a fraction. Next, multiply both numerators together and then both denominators.

Divide the numerator of the resulting fraction by the denominator. The answer is given as a mixed fraction.

Multiplying two proper fractions

Proper fractions can be multiplied by each other. It is useful to imagine that the multiplication sign means "of"—the problem below can be expressed as "what is ½ of ¾?" and "what is ¾ of ½?".

make a fraction half as big by doubling the total number of parts—the numerator is unchanged

$$\frac{1}{2} \times \frac{3}{4} = \frac{3}{8}$$

one fraction splits another to increase number of parts in result

imagine multiplication sign means "of"

$$\frac{1}{2} \times \frac{3}{4} = \frac{3}{8}$$

increasing value of denominator decreases value of fraction

Visually, the result of multiplying two proper fractions is that the space taken by both together is reduced.

Multiply the numerators and the denominators. The resulting fraction answers both questions: "what is ½ of ¾?" and "what is ¾ of ½?".

Multiplying mixed fractions

To multiply a proper fraction by a mixed fraction, it is necessary to first convert the mixed fraction into an improper fraction.

multiply whole number by denominator

$$3\frac{2}{5} \times \frac{5}{6} \quad \frac{3 \times 5 + 2}{5}$$

add to numerator

$$\frac{17}{5} \times \frac{5}{6} =$$

remainder becomes numerator of fraction

to show in its lowest form divide both numbers by 5 to get ⁵⁄₆

$$\frac{85}{30} \implies 85 \div 30 = 2r25 = \mathbf{2\frac{25}{30}}$$

denominator stays the same

First, turn the mixed fraction into an improper fraction.

Next, multiply the numerators and denominators of both fractions to get a new fraction.

Divide the numerator of the new improper fraction by its denominator. The answer is shown as a mixed fraction.

DIVIDING FRACTIONS

Fractions can be divided by whole numbers. Turn the whole number into a fraction and find the reciprocal of this fraction by turning it upside down, then multiply it by the first fraction.

Picture dividing a fraction by a whole number as splitting it into that many parts. In this example, ¼ is split in half, resulting in twice as many equal parts.

To divide a fraction by a whole number, convert the whole number into a fraction, turn that fraction upside down, and multiply both the numerators and the denominators.

Dividing two proper fractions

Proper fractions can be divided by other proper fractions by using an inverse operation. Multiplication and division are inverse operations—they are the opposite of each other.

Dividing one fraction by another is the same as turning the second fraction upside down and then multiplying the two.

To divide two fractions use the inverse operation—turn the last fraction upside down, then multiply the numerators and the denominators.

Dividing mixed fractions

To divide mixed fractions, first convert them into improper fractions, then turn the second fraction upside down and multiply it by the first.

$$\frac{4}{3} \div \frac{9}{4} \quad \frac{4}{3} \times \frac{4}{9} = \frac{16}{27}$$

First, turn each of the mixed fractions into improper fractions by multiplying the whole number by the denominator and adding the numerator.

Divide the two fractions by turning the second fraction upside down, then multiplying the numerators and the denominators.

Ratio and proportion

RATIO COMPARES THE SIZE OF QUANTITIES. PROPORTION COMPARES THE RELATIONSHIP BETWEEN TWO SETS OF QUANTITIES.

Ratios show how much bigger one thing is than another. Two things are in proportion when a change in one causes a related change in the other.

Writing ratios

Ratios are written as two or more numbers with a colon between each. For example, a fruit bowl in which the ratio of apples to pears is 2 : 1 means that there are 2 apples for every 1 pear in the bowl.

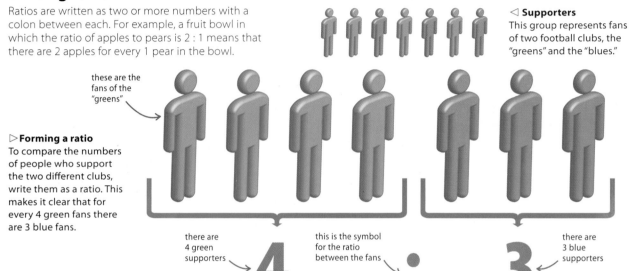

◁ **Supporters**
This group represents fans of two football clubs, the "greens" and the "blues."

these are the fans of the "greens"

▷**Forming a ratio**
To compare the numbers of people who support the two different clubs, write them as a ratio. This makes it clear that for every 4 green fans there are 3 blue fans.

there are 4 green supporters

this is the symbol for the ratio between the fans

there are 3 blue supporters

▽ **More ratios**
The same process applies to any set of data that needs to be compared. Here are more groups of fans, and the ratios they represent.

△ **1 : 2**
One fan of the greens and 2 fans of the blues can be compared as the ratio 1 : 2. This means that in this case there are twice as many fans of the blues as of the greens.

△ **1 : 3**
One fan of the greens and 3 fans of the blues can be shown as the ratio 1 : 3, which means that, in this case, there are three times more blue fans than green fans.

△ **2 : 5**
Two fans of the greens and 5 fans of the blues can be compared as the ratio 2 : 5. There are more than twice as many fans of the blues as of the greens.

Finding a ratio

Large numbers can also be written as ratios. For example, to find the ratio between 1 hour and 20 minutes, convert them into the same unit, then cancel these numbers by finding the highest number that divides into both.

ratios show information in the same way as fractions do

20 minutes is $\frac{1}{3}$ of an hour

minutes are the smaller unit

1 hour is the same as 60 minutes, so convert

this is the symbol for ratio

$60 \div 20 = 3$
$20 \div 20 = 1$

20 mins, **60** mins

20 : 60

1 : 3

Convert one of the quantities so that both have the same units. In this example use minutes.

Write as a ratio by inserting a colon between the two quantities.

Cancel the units to their lowest terms. Here both sides divide exactly by 20 to give the ratio 1 : 3.

Working with ratios

Ratios can represent real values. In a scale, the small number of the ratio is the value on the scale model, and the larger is the real value it represents.

▷ **Scaling down**
1 : 50,000 cm is used as the scale on a map. Find out what a distance of 1.5 cm represents on this map.

scale = 1 : 50,000

1.5cm

scale shows what real distance is represented by each distance on the map

▷ **Scaling up**
The plan of a microchip has the scale 40 : 1. The length of the plan is 18 cm. The scale can be used to find the length of the actual microchip.

distance on map

scale on map

actual distance represented by the map

1.5 cm × 50,000 = 75,000 cm
= 750 m

the answer is converted into a more suitable unit—there are 100 cm in a meter

length of plan

divide by scale to find actual size

actual length of microchip

18 cm ÷ 40 = 0.45 cm

Comparing ratios

Converting ratios into fractions allows their size to be compared. To compare the ratios 4 : 5 and 1 : 2, write them as fractions with the same denominator.

compare the numerators

1 : 2 = $\frac{1}{2}$
and
4 : 5 = $\frac{4}{5}$

fraction that represents ratio 1 : 2

fraction that represents ratio 4 : 5

2 × 5 is 10, the common denominator

5 × 2 is 10, the common denominator

$\frac{1}{2} = \frac{5}{10}$ ×5

$\frac{4}{5} = \frac{8}{10}$ ×2

$\frac{5}{10}$ **is smaller than** $\frac{8}{10}$

so

1:2 **is smaller than** **4:5**

First write each ratio as a fraction, placing the smaller quantity in each above the larger quantity.

Convert the fractions so that they both have the same denominator, by multiplying the first fraction by 5 and the second by 2.

Because the fractions now share a denominator, their sizes can be compared, making it clear which ratio is bigger.

PROPORTION

Two quantities are in proportion when a change in one causes a change in the other by a related number. Two examples of this are direct and indirect (also called inverse) proportion.

Direct proportion

Two quantities are in direct proportion if the ratio between them is always the same. This means, for example, that if one quantity doubles then so does the other.

▷ **Direct proportion**
This table and graph show the directly proportional relationship between the number of gardeners and the number of trees planted.

Gardeners	Trees
1	2
2	4
3	6

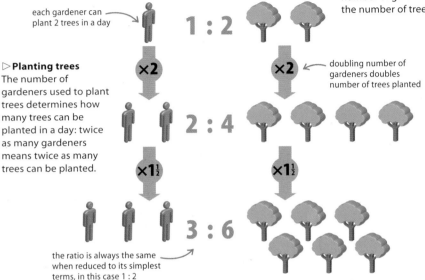

▷**Planting trees**
The number of gardeners used to plant trees determines how many trees can be planted in a day: twice as many gardeners means twice as many trees can be planted.

each gardener can plant 2 trees in a day

doubling number of gardeners doubles number of trees planted

the ratio is always the same when reduced to its simplest terms, in this case 1 : 2

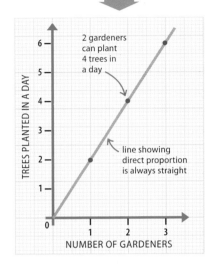

2 gardeners can plant 4 trees in a day

line showing direct proportion is always straight

TREES PLANTED IN A DAY / NUMBER OF GARDENERS

Indirect proportion

Two quantities are in indirect proportion if their product (the answer when they are multiplied by each other) is always the same. So if one quantity doubles, the other quantity halves.

▷ **Indirect proportion**
This table and graph show the indirectly proportional relationship between the vans used and the time taken to deliver the parcels.

Vans	Days
1	8
2	4
4	2

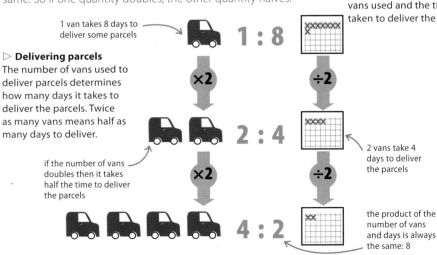

▷ **Delivering parcels**
The number of vans used to deliver parcels determines how many days it takes to deliver the parcels. Twice as many vans means half as many days to deliver.

1 van takes 8 days to deliver some parcels

if the number of vans doubles then it takes half the time to deliver the parcels

2 vans take 4 days to deliver the parcels

the product of the number of vans and days is always the same: 8

1 van takes 8 days to deliver the parcels

the line showing indirect proportion is always curved

2 vans take 4 days to deliver the parcels

TIME (DAYS) / NUMBER OF VANS

Dividing in a given ratio

A quantity can be divided into two, three, or more parts, according to a given
ratio. This example shows how to divide 20 people into the ratios 2 : 3 and 6 : 3 : 1.

**DIVIDING INTO A
TWO-PART RATIO**

2 : 3

These are the ratios to
divide the people into.

**DIVIDING INTO A
THREE-PART RATIO**

6 : 3 : 1

total number of parts in the ratio
$$2 + 3 = 5$$

Add the different
parts of the ratio to
find the total parts.

$$6 + 3 + 1 = 10$$

number of parts in the ratio

total number
of people
$$20 \div 5 = 4$$

total number
of people   total number of
parts in the ratio
$$20 \div 10 = 2$$

Divide the number of people
by the parts of the ratio.

2 in the ratio
$$2 \times 4 = 8$$

3 in the ratio
$$3 \times 4 = 12$$

6 in the
ratio
$$6 \times 2 = 12$$

12 people
represented by
6 in the ratio

3 in the
ratio
$$3 \times 2 = 6$$

6 people
represented by
3 in the ratio

Multiply each part of
the ratio by this
quantity to find the size
of the groups the ratios
represent.

1 in the
ratio
$$1 \times 2 = 2$$

2 people
represented by
1 in the ratio

12 people
represented by
3 in the ratio

8 people
represented by
2 in the ratio

Proportional quantities

Proportion can be used to solve problems involving unknown quantities. For
example, if 3 bags contain 18 apples, how many apples do 5 bags contain?

total number
of apples   bags   apples
per bag
$$18 \div 3 = 6$$

apples
per bag   number of bags
$$6 \times 5 = 30$$
total

There is a total of 18 apples in 3 bags.
Each bag contains the same number
of apples.

To find out how many apples there
are in 1 bag, divide the total number
of apples by the number of bags.

To find the number of apples
in 5 bags, multiply the number
of apples in 1 bag by 5.

Percentages

A PERCENTAGE SHOWS AN AMOUNT AS A PART OF 100.

Any number can be written as a part of 100 or a percentage. Percent means "per hundred," and it is a useful way of comparing two or more quantities. The symbol "%" is used to indicate a percentage.

SEE ALSO

❬ 44–45 Decimals
❬ 48–55 Fractions
Ratio and proportion   56–59 ❭
Rounding off   70–71 ❭

Parts of 100

The simplest way to start looking at percentages is by dealing with a block of 100 units, as shown in the main image. These 100 units represent the total number of people in a school. This total can be divided into different groups according to the proportion of the total 100 they represent.

100%

▷ **This is simply** another way of saying "everybody" or "everything." Here, all 100 figures —100%—are blue.

50%

▷ **This group** is equally divided between 50 blue and 50 purple figures. Each represents 50 out of 100 or 50% of the total. This is the same as half.

1%

▷ **In this group** there is only 1 blue figure out of 100, or 1%.

FEMALE TEACHERS
10% or
10 out of 100

MALE STUDENTS
19% or
19 out of 100

MALE TEACHERS
5% or
5 out of 100

△ **Adding up to 100**
Percentages are an effective way to show the component parts of a total. For example, male teachers (blue) account for 5% (5 out of 100) of the total.

FEMALE STUDENTS **66%** or 66 out of 100

10
9
8
7
6
5
4

▽ **Examples of percentages**
Percentages are a simple and accessible way to present information, which is why they are often used by the media.

Percentage	Facts
97%	of the world's animals are invertebrates
92.5%	of an Olympic gold medal is composed of silver
70%	of the world's surface is covered in water
66%	of the human body is water
61%	of the world's oil is in the Middle East
50%	of the world's population live in cities
21%	of the air is oxygen
6%	of the world's land surface is covered in rain forest

WORKING WITH PERCENTAGES

A percentage is simply a part of a whole, expressed as a part of 100. There are two main ways of working with percentages: the first is finding a percentage of a given amount, and the second is finding what percentage one number is of another number.

Calculating percentages

This example shows how to find the percentage of a quantity, in this case 25% of a group of 24 people.

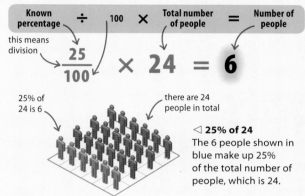

Known percentage	÷	100	×	Total number of people	=	Number of people

this means division

$$\frac{25}{100} \times 24 = 6$$

25% of 24 is 6

there are 24 people in total

◁ **25% of 24**
The 6 people shown in blue make up 25% of the total number of people, which is 24.

This example shows how to find what percentage one number is of another number, in this case 48 people out of a group of 112 people.

Number of people	÷	Total number of people	×	100	=	Percentage of total number

$$\frac{48}{112} \times 100 = 42.86$$

answer is rounded to 2 decimal places

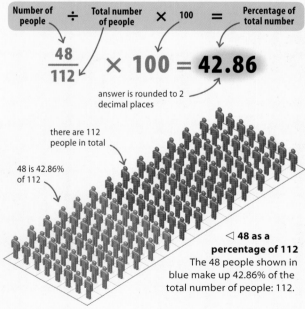

there are 112 people in total

48 is 42.86% of 112

◁ **48 as a percentage of 112**
The 48 people shown in blue make up 42.86% of the total number of people: 112.

PERCENTAGES AND QUANTITIES

Percentages are a useful way of expressing a value as a proportion of the total number. If two out of three of a percentage, value, and total number are known, it is possible to find out the missing quantity using arithmetic.

Finding an amount as a % of another amount

Out of 12 pupils in a class, 9 play a musical instrument. To find the known value (9) as a percentage of the total (12), divide the known value by the total number and multiply by 100.

| Number to turn into a % | ÷ | Total number | × | 100 | = | % of total number |

$$\frac{9}{12} \times 100 = 75\% \text{ play instruments}$$

Divide the known number by the total number (9 ÷ 12 = 0.75).

Multiply the result by 100 to get the percentage (0.75 × 100 = 75).

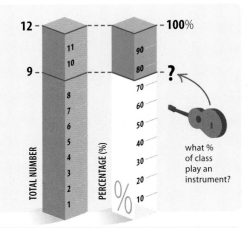

what % of class play an instrument?

Finding the total number from a %

In a class, 7 children make up 35% of the total. To find the total number of students in the class, divide the known value (7) by the known percentage (35) and multiply by 100.

| Known amount | ÷ | Known % | × | 100 | = | Total number |

$$\frac{7}{35} \times 100 = 20 \text{ students}$$

Divide the known amount by the known percentage (7 ÷ 35 = 0.2).

Multiply the result by 100 to get the total number (0.2 × 100 = 20).

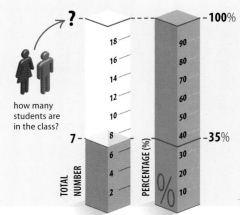

how many students are in the class?

REAL WORLD

Percentages

Percentages are all around us—in stores, in newspapers, on TV—everywhere. Many things in everyday life are measured and compared in percentages—how much an item is reduced in a sale; what the interest rate is on a mortgage or a bank loan; or how efficient a light bulb is by the percentage of electricity it converts to light. Percentages are even used to show how much of the recommended daily intake of vitamins and other nutrients is in food products.

SALE

25% OFF

PERCENTAGE CHANGE

If a value changes by a certain percentage, it is possible to calculate the new value. Conversely, when a value changes by a known amount, it is possible to work out the percent increase or decrease compared to the original.

Finding a new value from a % increase or decrease

To find how a 55% increase or decrease affects the value of 40, first work out 55% of 40. Then add to or subtract from the original to get the new value.

Known % $\div$ 100 $\times$ Original value = % of total value

$$\frac{55}{100} \times 40 = 22$$

Divide the known % by 100 (55 ÷ 100 = 0.55).

Multiply the result by the original value (0.55 × 40 = 22).

THEN Original value + or − % of total value = New value

$$40 \; \stackrel{+}{or-} \; 22 = \stackrel{62}{or \; 18}$$

Add the original value to 22 to find the % increase, or **subtract** 22 to find the % decrease.

what is 55% of 40?

?

VALUE

PERCENTAGE (%)

Finding an increase in a value as a %

The price of a donut in the school cafeteria has risen 30 cents—from 99 cents last year to $1.29 this year. To find the increase as a percent, divide the increase in value (30) by the original value (99) and multiply by 100.

Increase in value $\div$ Original value $\times$ 100 = Increase in value as %

$$\frac{30}{99} \times 100 = \textbf{30.3\%} \; \text{increase}$$

Divide the increase in value by the original value (30 ÷ 99 = 0.303).

Multiply the result by 100 to find the percentage (0.303 × 100 = 30.3), and round to 3 significant figures.

what is % increase in price of donut?

Finding a decrease in a value as a %

There was an audience of 245 at the school play last year, but this year only 209 attended—a decrease of 36. To find the decrease as a percent, divide the decrease in value (36) by the original value (245) and multiply by 100.

Decrease in value $\div$ Original value $\times$ 100 = Decrease in value as %

$$\frac{36}{245} \times 100 = \textbf{14.7\%} \; \text{decrease}$$

Divide the decrease in value by the original value (36 ÷ 245 = 0.147).

Multiply the result by 100 to find the percentage (0.147 × 100 = 14.7), and round to 3 significant figures.

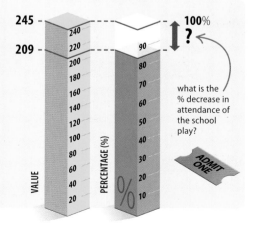

what is the % decrease in attendance of the school play?

↻ Converting fractions, decimals, and percentages

DECIMALS, FRACTIONS, AND PERCENTAGES ARE DIFFERENT WAYS OF WRITING THE SAME NUMBER.

SEE ALSO

❰ 44–45 Decimals
❰ 48–55 Fractions
❰ 60–63 Percentages

The same but different

Sometimes a number shown one way can be shown more clearly in another way. For example, if 20% is the grade required to pass an exam, this is the same as saying that 1/5 of the answers in an exam need to be answered correctly to achieve a pass mark or that the minimum score for a pass is 0.2 of the total.

75%

PERCENTAGE

A percentage shows a number as a proportion of 100.

▷ **All change**
The three ways of writing the same number are shown here: decimal (0.75), fraction (¾), and percentage (75%). They look different, but they all represent the same proportion of an amount.

Changing a **decimal** into a **percentage**

To change a decimal into a percentage, multiply by 100.

$$0.75 \rightarrow 75\%$$

$$\underset{\text{Decimal}}{0.75} \times \underset{\text{Multiply by 100}}{100} = \underset{\text{Percentage}}{75\%}$$

decimal point in 0.75 moved two places to right to make 75

Changing a **percentage** into a **decimal**

To change a percentage into a decimal, divide it by 100.

$$75\% \rightarrow 0.75$$

decimal point added two places to left of last digit

$$\underset{\text{Percentage}}{75\%} \div \underset{\text{Divide by 100}}{100} = \underset{\text{Decimal}}{0.75}$$

Changing a **percentage** into a **fraction**

To change a percentage into a fraction, write it as a fraction of 100 and then cancel it down to simplify it, if possible.

$$75\% \rightarrow \frac{3}{4}$$

divide by highest number that goes into 75 and 100

$$\underset{\text{Percentage}}{75\%} \rightarrow \underset{\substack{\text{Turn the percentage} \\ \text{into the numerator of a} \\ \text{fraction with 100 as the} \\ \text{denominator.}}}{\frac{75}{100}} \quad \overset{\div 25}{\underset{\div 25}{\rightleftarrows}} \quad \underset{\substack{\text{Fraction} \\ \text{canceled down} \\ \text{into its lowest} \\ \text{terms.}}}{\frac{3}{4}}$$

0.75
DECIMAL
A decimal is simply a number that is not whole. It always contains a decimal point.

--100% 1   1
-- 75% 0.75 $\frac{3}{4}$

PERCENTAGE   DECIMAL   FRACTION

$\frac{3}{4}$
FRACTION
A fraction shows a number as part of an equally divided whole.

Everyday numbers to remember
Many decimals, fractions, and percentages are used in everyday life—some of the more common ones are shown here.

Decimal	Fraction	%	Decimal	Fraction	%
0.1	$\frac{1}{10}$	10%	0.625	$\frac{5}{8}$	62.5%
0.125	$\frac{1}{8}$	12.5%	0.666	$\frac{2}{3}$	66.7%
0.25	$\frac{1}{4}$	25%	0.7	$\frac{7}{10}$	70%
0.333	$\frac{1}{3}$	33.3%	0.75	$\frac{3}{4}$	75%
0.4	$\frac{2}{5}$	40%	0.8	$\frac{4}{5}$	80%
0.5	$\frac{1}{2}$	50%	1	$\frac{1}{1}$	100%

Changing a **decimal** into a **fraction**
First, make the fraction's denominator (its bottom part) 10, 100, 1,000, and so on for every digit after the decimal point.

$0.75 \Rightarrow \frac{3}{4}$ — divide by highest number that goes into 75 and 100

$0.75 \Rightarrow \frac{75}{100} \xrightarrow[\div 25]{\div 25} \frac{3}{4}$

Decimal number with two digits after the decimal point.

Count the decimal places—if there is 1 digit, the denominator is 10; if there are 2, it is 100. The numerator is the number after the decimal point.

Cancel the fraction down to its lowest possible terms.

Changing a **fraction** into a **percentage**
To change a fraction into a percentage, change it to a decimal and then multiply it by 100.

$\frac{3}{4} \Rightarrow$ **75%**

divide the denominator (4) into the numerator (3)

$\frac{3}{4} \Rightarrow 3 \div 4 = 0.75 \Rightarrow 0.75 \times 100 = 75\%$

Fraction

For decimal, divide the numerator by the denominator.

Multiply by 100

Changing a **fraction** into a **decimal**
Divide the fraction's denominator (its bottom part) into the fraction's numerator (its top part).

$\frac{3}{4} \Rightarrow$ **0.75**

numerator   denominator

$\frac{3}{4} = 3 \div 4 = $ **0.75**

Fraction

Divide the numerator by the denominator.

Decimal

Mental math

EVERYDAY PROBLEMS CAN BE SIMPLIFIED SO THAT THEY
CAN BE EASILY DONE WITHOUT USING A CALCULATOR.

SEE ALSO
❮ **18–21** Multiplication
❮ **22–25** Division
Using
a calculator **72–73** ❯

MULTIPLICATION

Multiplying by some numbers can be easy. For example, to multiply by 10 either
add a 0 or move the decimal point one place to the right. To multiply by 20,
multiply by 10 and then double the answer.

▷ **Multiplying by 10**
A sports club hired 2
people last year, but
this year it needs to
hire 10 times that
number. How many
staff members will it
recruit this year?

number of staff members
recruited last year

2 staff members
recruited last year

×10

2 × 10

20 new members
of staff

zero added to give 20, which is
new number of staff members

◁ **Finding the
answer**
To multiply 2 by 10
add a 0 to the 2.
Multiplying 2
people by 10 results
in an answer of 20.

2 ×10 20

▷ **Multiplying by 20**
A shop is selling
t-shirts for the price
of $1.20 each. How
much will the price
be for 20 t-shirts?

price of a t-shirt in $

first multiply by 10, moving
decimal point one place to right

t-shirt for sale

1.2 × 10

price of 10
t-shirts in $

20 t-shirts for sale

12 × 2

price of 20 t-shirts in $

◁ **Finding the
answer**
First multiply the
price by 10, here
by moving the
decimal point one
place to the right,
and then double
that to give the
final price of $24.

1.20 ×10 12.0 ×2 24.0

▷ **Multiplying by 25**
An athlete runs 16
miles a day. If the
athlete runs the same
distance every day for
25 days, how far will
he run in total?

16 miles run in a day

athlete runs every day

16 × 100

1,600 miles run
in 100 days

athlete runs
every day for 25 days

1,600 ÷ 4

400 miles run in 25 days

◁ **Finding the
answer**
First multiply the 16
miles for one day by
100, to give 1,600
miles for 100 days,
then divide by 4 to
give the answer
over 25 days.

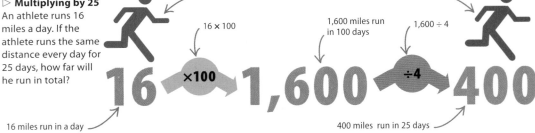

16 ×100 1,600 ÷4 400

▽ Multiplication using decimals

Decimals appear to complicate the problem, but they can be ignored until the final stage. Here the amount of carpet required to cover a floor needs to be calculated.

2.9m — width of floor to be covered
4m — length of floor to be covered
length of floor to be covered
carpet to be cut to required size

LOOKING CLOSER

Checking the answer

Because 2.9 is almost 3, multiplying 3×4 is a good way to check that the calculation to 2.9×4 is correct.

symbol for approximately equal to

$$2.9 \approx 3 \text{ and}$$

$$3 \times 4 = 12$$

close to real answer of 11.6

$$\text{so } 2.9 \times 4 \approx 12$$

width of floor
length

$$2.9 \times 4 \blacktriangleright 29 \times 4$$

width with decimal point removed

30 easier to work with than 29

length

$$\begin{aligned} 30 \times 4 \\ 1 \times 4 \end{aligned}$$

1×4 to be subtracted from 30×4

$$\begin{aligned} 120 &\leftarrow \text{sum of } 30 \times 4 \\ - \quad 4 &\leftarrow \text{sum of } 1 \times 4 \\ \hline 116 \end{aligned}$$

result of $120 - 4 \rightarrow$

decimal point moved one place to left to give answer 11.6

$$116 \blacktriangleright 11.6$$

First, take away the decimal point from the 2.9 to make the calculation 29×4.

Change 29×4 to 30×4 since it is easier to work out. Write 1×4 below (the difference between 29×4 and 30×4).

Subtract 4 (product of 1×4) from 120 (product of 30×4) to give the answer of 116 (product of 29×4).

Move the decimal point one place to the left (it was moved one place to the right in the first step).

Top tricks

The multiplication tables of several numbers reveal patterns of multiplications. Here are two good mental tricks to remember when multiplying the 9 and 11 times tables.

multipliers 1 to 10

9 TIMES TABLE									
1	2	3	4	5	6	7	8	9	10
9	18	27	36	45	54	63	72	81	90

$1 + 8 = 9$
$7 + 2 = 9$
multiples of 9

multipliers 1 to 9

11 TIMES TABLE								
1	2	3	4	5	6	7	8	9
11	22	33	44	55	66	77	88	99

$11 \times 3 = 33$, or 3 written twice
$11 \times 7 = 77$, or 7 written twice
multiples of 11

△ **Two digits are added together**
The two digits that make up the first 10 multiples of 9 each add up to 9. The first digit of the multiple (such as 1, in 18) is always 1 less than the multiplier (2).

△ **Digit is written twice**
To multiply by 11, merely repeat the two multipliers together. For example, 4×11 is two 4s or 44. It works all the way up to $9 \times 11 = 99$, which is 9 written twice.

DIVISION

Dividing by 10 or 5 is straightforward. To divide by 10, either delete a 0 or move the decimal point one place to the left. To divide by 5, again divide by 10 and then double the answer. Using these rules, work out the divisions in the following two examples.

▷ **Dividing by 10**
In this example, 160 travel vouchers are needed to rent a 10-seat mini bus. How many travel vouchers are needed for each of the 10 children to travel on the bus?

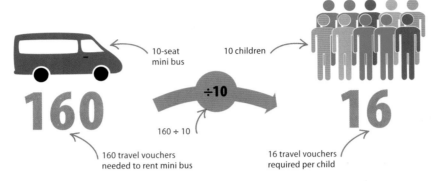

10-seat mini bus

10 children

÷10

160 ÷ 10

160 travel vouchers needed to rent mini bus

16 travel vouchers required per child

◁ **How many each?**
To find the number of travel vouchers for each child, divide the total of 160 by 10 by deleting a 0 from the 160. It gives the answer of 16 travel vouchers each.

▷ **Dividing by 5**
The cost of admission to a zoo for a group of five children is 75 tokens. How many tokens are needed for 1 of the 5 children to enter the zoo?

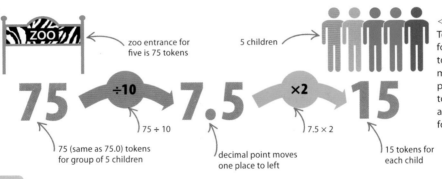

ZOO

zoo entrance for five is 75 tokens

5 children

÷10

×2

75 (same as 75.0) tokens for group of 5 children

75 ÷ 10

decimal point moves one place to left

7.5 × 2

15 tokens for each child

◁ **How many each?**
To find the admission for 1 child, divide the total of 75 by 10 (by moving a decimal point in 75 one place to the left) to give 7.5, and then double that for the answer of 15.

LOOKING CLOSER
Top tips

There are various mental tricks to help with dividing larger or more complicated numbers. In the three examples below, there are tips on how to check whether very large numbers can be divided by 3, 4, and 9.

▷ **Divisible by 3**
Add together all of the digits in the number. If the total is divisible by 3, the original number is too.

original number

digits add up to 54

$54 \div 3 = 18$, so the original number is divisible by 3

$$1665233198172 \Rightarrow 1+6+6+5+2+3+3+1+9+8+1+7+2 = 54$$

▷ **Divisible by 4**
If the last two digits are taken as one single number, and it is divisible by 4, the original number is too.

original number

5 and 6 seen as one number: 56

$56 \div 4 = 14$, so the original number is divisible by 4

$$123456123456123456 \Rightarrow 56 \div 4 = 14$$

▷ **Divisible by 9**
Add together all of the digits in the number. If the total is divisible by 9, the original number is too.

original number

add together all digits of number, their sum is 36

$36 \div 9 = 4$, so the original number is divisible by 9

$$1643951142 \Rightarrow 1+6+4+3+9+5+1+1+4+2 = 36$$

PERCENTAGES

A useful method of simplifying calculations involving percentages is to reduce one difficult percentage into smaller and easier-to-calculate parts. In the example below, the smaller percentages include 10% and 5%, which are easy to work out.

▷ **Adding 17.5 percent**
Here a shop wants to charge $480 for a new bike. However, the owner of the shop has to add a sales tax of 17.5 percent to the price. How much will it then cost?

bike for sale before sales tax

bike for sale after sales tax

+17.5%
sales tax

original price in $

final price in $

sales tax

17.5% of 480

original price of bike

2.5% of 480 is half of 5% of 480, which is half of 10% of 480

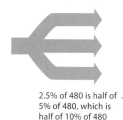

10% of 480	= 48
5% of 480	= 24
2.5% of 480	= 12

48
24
+ 12
84

results added together

84 is 17.5% of 480

First, write down the percentage price increase required and the original price of the bike.

Next, reduce 17.5% into the easier stages of 10%, 5%, and 2.5% of $480, and calculate their values.

The sum of 48, 24, and 12 is 84, so $84 is added to $480 for a price of $564.

Switching

A percentage and an amount can both be "switched," to produce the same result with each switch. For example, 50% of 10, which is 5, is exactly the same as 10% of 50, which is 5 again.

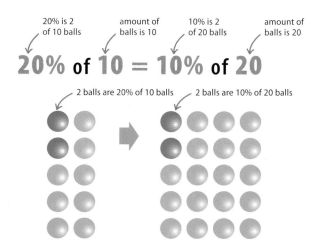

20% is 2 of 10 balls

amount of balls is 10

10% is 2 of 20 balls

amount of balls is 20

20% of 10 = 10% of 20

2 balls are 20% of 10 balls

2 balls are 10% of 20 balls

Progression

A progression involves dividing the percentage by a number and then multiplying the result by the same number. For example, 40% of 10 is 4. Dividing this 40% by 2 and multiplying 10 by 2 results in 20% of 20, which is also 4.

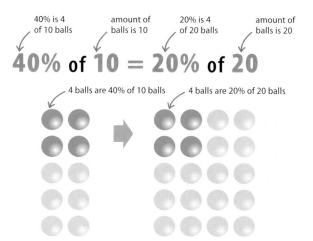

40% is 4 of 10 balls

amount of balls is 10

20% is 4 of 20 balls

amount of balls is 20

40% of 10 = 20% of 20

4 balls are 40% of 10 balls

4 balls are 20% of 20 balls

Rounding off

THE PROCESS OF ROUNDING OFF INVOLVES REPLACING ONE
NUMBER WITH ANOTHER TO MAKE IT MORE PRACTICAL TO USE.

SEE ALSO
❮ 44–45 Decimals
❮ 66–67 Mental math

Estimation and approximation

In many practical situations, an exact answer is not needed, and it is easier
to find an estimate based on rounding off (approximation). The general
principle of rounding off is that a number at or above the midpoint of
a group of numbers, such as the numbers 15–19 in the group 10–20,
rounds up, while a number below the midpoint rounds down.

▽ **Rounding to the nearest 10**
The midpoint between any two 10s is 5.
If the last digit of each number is 5 or over
it rounds up, otherwise it rounds down.

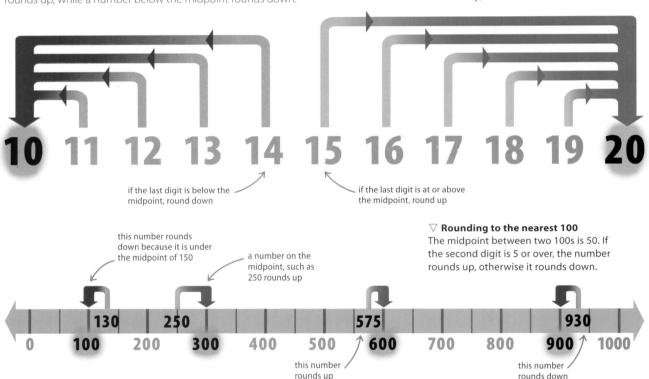

if the last digit is below the
midpoint, round down

if the last digit is at or above
the midpoint, round up

this number rounds
down because it is under
the midpoint of 150

a number on the
midpoint, such as
250 rounds up

▽ **Rounding to the nearest 100**
The midpoint between two 100s is 50. If
the second digit is 5 or over, the number
rounds up, otherwise it rounds down.

this number
rounds up

this number
rounds down

LOOKING CLOSER

Approximately equal

Many measurements are given as
approximations, and numbers are sometimes
rounded to make them easier to use. An
"approximately equals" sign is used to show when
numbers have been rounded up or down. It looks
similar to a normal equals sign (=) but with
curved instead of straight lines.

wavy lines mean
"approximately"

$$31 \approx 30 \quad \text{and} \quad 187 \approx 200$$

△ **Approximately equal to**
The "approximately equals" sign shows that the two
sides of the sign are approximately equal instead of
equal. So 31 is approximately equal to 30, and 187 is
approximately equal to 200.

Decimal places

Any number can be rounded to the appropriate number of decimal places. The choice of how many decimal places depends on what the number is used for and how exact an end result is required.

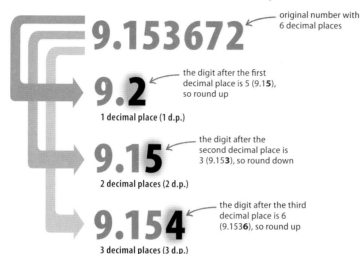

original number with 6 decimal places

9.153672

9.2
the digit after the first decimal place is 5 (9.1**5**), so round up
1 decimal place (1 d.p.)

9.15
the digit after the second decimal place is 3 (9.15**3**), so round down
2 decimal places (2 d.p.)

9.154
the digit after the third decimal place is 6 (9.153**6**), so round up
3 decimal places (3 d.p.)

LOOKING CLOSER

How many decimal places?

The more decimal places, the more accurate the number. This table shows the accuracy that is represented by different numbers of decimal places. For example, a distance in miles to 3 decimal places would be accurate to a thousandth of a mile, which is equal to 5 feet.

Decimal places	Rounded to	Example
1	$1/10$	1.1 mi
2	$1/100$	1.14 mi
3	$1/1,000$	1.135 mi

Significant figures

A significant figure in a number is a digit that counts. The digits 1 to 9 are always significant, but 0 is not. However, 0 becomes significant when it occurs between two significant figures, or if an exact answer is needed.

1 significant figure
200
Real value anywhere between 150–249

2 significant figures
200
Real value anywhere between 195–204

3 significant figures
200
Real value anywhere between 199.5–200.4

◁ **Significant zeros**
The answer 200 could be the result of rounding to 1, 2, or 3 significant figures (s.f.). Below each example is the range in which its true value lies.

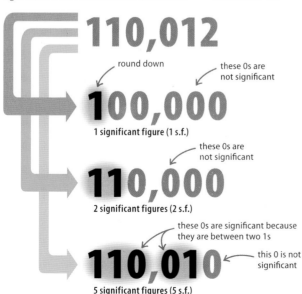

110,012

round down
these 0s are not significant
100,000
1 significant figure (1 s.f.)

these 0s are not significant
110,000
2 significant figures (2 s.f.)

these 0s are significant because they are between two 1s
110,010
this 0 is not significant
5 significant figures (5 s.f.)

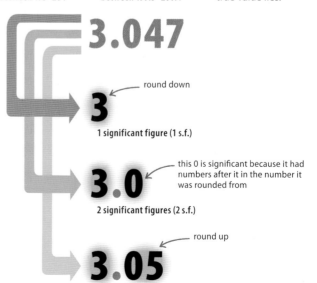

3.047

round down
3
1 significant figure (1 s.f.)

this 0 is significant because it had numbers after it in the number it was rounded from
3.0
2 significant figures (2 s.f.)

round up
3.05
3 significant figures (3 s.f.)

Using a calculator

CALCULATORS ARE MACHINES THAT WORK OUT THE ANSWERS
TO SOME MATHEMATICAL PROBLEMS.

SEE ALSO

Tools in geometry **82–83 ❭**

Collecting and
organizing data **204–205 ❭**

**Calculators are designed to make math easier, but there are
a few things to be aware of when using them.**

Introducing the calculator

A modern calculator is a handheld electronic device
that is used to find the answers to mathematical
problems. Most calculators are operated in a similar
way (as described here), but it may be necessary to
read the instructions for a particular model.

Using a calculator

Be careful that functions are entered in the correct order,
or the answers the calculator gives will be wrong.

For example, to find the answer to the calculation:

$$(7 + 2) \times 9 =$$

Enter these keys, making sure to include all parts of
the calculation, including the parentheses.

 = 81

Not

 = 25 ← calculator does
product 2 × 9 =
18, then sum
18 + 7 = 25

Estimating answers

Calculators can only give answers according to the keys that
have been pressed. It is useful to have an idea of what answer
to expect since a small mistake can give a very wrong answer.

For example

[2] [0] [0] [6] [×] [1] [9] [8]

must be close to

this would give the
answer 400,000

[2] [0] [0] [0] [×] [2] [0] [0]

So if the calculator gives the answer **40,788** it is clear that
the numbers have not been entered correctly—one "0" is
missing from what was intended:

FREQUENTLY USED KEYS

ON
This button turns the calculator on—most
calculators turn themselves off automatically if they are left
unused for a certain period of time.

Number pad
This contains the basic numbers that are needed for
math. These buttons can be used individually or in groups to
create larger numbers.

Standard arithmetic keys
These cover all the basic mathematical functions:
multiplication, division, addition, and subtraction, as well as
the essential equals sign.

Decimal point
This key works in the same way as a written decimal
point—it separates whole numbers from decimals. It is entered
in the same way as any of the number keys.

Cancel
The cancel key clears all recent entries from the
memory. This is useful when starting a new calculation because
it makes sure no unwanted values are retained.

Delete
This clears the last value that was entered into the
calculator, rather than wiping everything from the memory. It
is sometimes labeled "CE" (clear entry).

Recall button
This recalls a value from the calculator's memory—
it is useful for calculations with many parts that use numbers
or stages from earlier in the problem.

△ **Scientific calculator**
A scientific calculator has many functions—a standard calculator usually only has the number pad, standard arithmetic keys, and one or two other, simpler functions, such as percentages. The buttons shown here allow for more advanced math.

FUNCTION KEYS

Cube
This is a short cut to cubing a number, without having to key in a number multiplied by itself, and then multiplied by itself again. Key in the number to be cubed, then press this button.

ANS
Pressing this key gives the answer to the last sum that was entered. It is useful for sums with many steps.

Square root
This finds the positive square root of a positive number. Press the square root button first, then the number, and then the equals button.

Square
A short cut to squaring a number, without having to key in the number multiplied by itself. Just key in the number then this button.

Exponent
Allows a number to be raised to a power. Enter the number, then the exponent button, then the power.

Negative
Use this to make a number negative. It is usually used when the first number in a calculation is negative.

sin, cos, tan
These are mainly used in trigonometry, to find the sine, cosine, or tangent values of angles in right triangles.

Parentheses
These work the same way as enclosing part of a calculation in parentheses, to make sure the order of operations is correct.

Personal finance

KNOWING HOW MONEY WORKS IS IMPORTANT FOR
MANAGING YOUR PERSONAL FINANCES.

Personal finance includes paying tax on income,
gaining interest on savings, or paying interest on loans.

SEE ALSO

❮ **34–35** Positive and negative numbers
Business finance **76–77** ❯
Formulas **177–179** ❯

Tax

Tax is a fee charged by a government on a product,
income, or activity. Governments collect the money
they need to provide services, such as schools and
defense, by taxing individuals and companies.
Individuals are taxed on what they earn—income
tax—and also on some things they buy—sales tax.

GOVERNMENT
Part of the cost of
government spending
is collected in the form
of income tax

◁ **Income tax**
Each person is taxed on
what they earn; "take
home" is the amount
of money they have
left after paying their
income tax and other
deductions.

TAXPAYER
Everybody pays tax—through
their wages and through the
money that they spend

WAGE
This is the amount of money
that is earned by a person
who is employed

FINANCIAL TERMS	
Financial words often seem complicated, but they are easy to understand. Knowing what the important ones mean will enable you to manage your finances by helping you understand what you have to pay and the money you will receive.	
Bank account	This is the record of whatever a person borrows from or saves with the bank. Each account holder has a numeric password called a personal identification number (PIN), which should never be revealed to anyone.
Credit	Credit is money that is borrowed—for example, on a 4-year pay-back agreement or as an overdraft from the bank. It always costs to borrow money. The money paid to borrow from a bank is called interest.
Income	This is the money that comes to an individual or family. This can be provided by the wages that are paid for employment. Sometimes it comes from the government in the form of an allowance or direct payment.
Interest	This is the cost of borrowing money or the income received when saving with a bank. It costs more to borrow money from a bank than the interest a person would receive from the bank by saving the same amount.
Mortgage	A mortgage is an agreement to borrow money to buy a home. A bank lends the money for the purchase and this is paid back, usually over a long period of time, together with interest on the loan and other charges.
Savings	There are many forms of savings. Money can be saved in a bank to earn interest. Saving through a pension plan involves making regular payments to ensure an income after retirement.
Break-even	Break-even is the point where the cost, or what a company has spent, is equal to revenue, which is what the company has earned—at break-even the company makes neither a profit nor a loss.
Loss	Companies make a loss if they spend more than they earn—if it costs them more to produce their product than they earn by selling it.
Profit	Profit is the part of a company's income that is left once their costs have been paid—it is the money "made" by a company.

INTEREST

Banks pay interest on the money that savers invest with them (capital), and charge interest on money that is borrowed from them. Interest is given as a percentage, and there are two types, simple and compound.

Simple interest

This is interest paid only on the sum of money that is first saved with the bank. If $10,000 is put in a bank account with an interest rate of 0.03, the amount will increase by the same figure each year.

△ **Simple interest formula**
To find the simple interest made in a given year, substitute real values into this formula.

$$\text{Interest} = P \times R \times T$$

First year

amount invested   interest rate   number of years   interest

$$10{,}000 \times 0.03 \times 1 = \mathbf{300}$$

Substitute the values in the formula to work out the value of the interest for the year.

invested amount   interest   total

$$10{,}000 + 300 = \mathbf{10{,}300}$$

After one year, this is the total amount of money in the saver's bank account.

Second year

result is the same

$$10{,}000 \times 0.03 \times 1 = \mathbf{300}$$

Substitute the values in the formula to work out the value of the interest for the year.

starting amount   interest   total

$$10{,}300 + 300 = \mathbf{10{,}600}$$

After two years the interest is the same as the first year, as it is only paid on the initial investment.

Compound interest

This is where interest is paid on the money invested and any interest that is earned on that money. If $10,000 is paid into a bank account with an interest rate of 0.03, then the amount will increase as follows.

△ **Compound interest formula**
To find the compound interest made in a given year, substitute values into this formula.

$$\text{Amount} = P \left(1 + R\right)^{T}$$

First year

amount invested   interest rate   number of years   total

$$10{,}000 \times \left(1 + 0.03\right)^{1} = \mathbf{10{,}300}$$

Substitute the values in the formula to work out the total for the first year.

total after first year   original amount   interest

$$10{,}300 - 10{,}000 = \mathbf{300}$$

After one year the total interest earned is the same as that earned with simple interest (see above).

Second year

number of years

$$10{,}000 \times \left(1 + 0.03\right)^{2} = \mathbf{10{,}609}$$

Substitute the values in the formula to work out the total for the second year.

total after second year   total after first year   interest

$$10{,}609 - 10{,}300 = \mathbf{309}$$

After two years there is a greater increase because interest is also earned on previous interest.

Business Finance

BUSINESSES AIM TO MAKE MONEY, AND MATH PLAYS
AN IMPORTANT PART IN ACHIEVING THIS AIM.

The aim of a business is to turn an idea
or a product into a profit, so that the
business earns more money
than it spends.

SEE ALSO
‹ 74–75 Personal finance
Pie charts   210–211 ›
Line graphs   212–213 ›

What a business does

Businesses take raw materials,
process them, and sell the end
product. To make a profit, the
business must sell its end product
at a price higher than the total
cost of the materials and the
manufacturing or production.
This example shows the basic
stages of this process using a
cake-making business.

▷ **Making cakes**
This diagram shows how
a cake-making business
processes inputs to
produce an output.

◁ **Small business**
A business can consist of
just one person or a whole
team of employees.

1

INPUTS

Inputs are raw materials that are
used in making a product. For
cake making, the inputs would
include the ingredients such as
flour, eggs, butter, and sugar.

△ **Costs**
Costs are incurred at the input stage, when
the raw materials have to be paid for. The
same costs occur every time a new batch
of cakes is made.

Revenue and profit

There is an important difference between
revenue and profit. Revenue is the money a
business makes when it sells its product. Profit
is the difference between revenue and cost—
it is the money that the business has "made."

profit is money a
business "makes"

revenue is earned by
selling final product

Profit = Revenue − Costs

costs are incurred in production,
for example, wages and rent

some costs are fixed, and the money is
spent however much of the product is
sold—so costs do not start at 0

▷ **Cost graph**
This graph shows where a business
begins to make a profit: where its
revenue is greater than its costs.

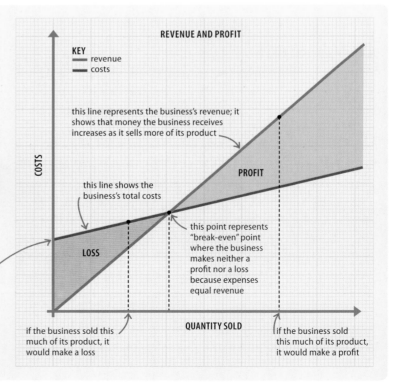

REVENUE AND PROFIT

KEY
— revenue
— costs

this line represents the business's revenue; it
shows that money the business receives
increases as it sells more of its product

this line shows the
business's total costs

PROFIT

this point represents
"break-even" point
where the business
makes neither a
profit nor a loss
because expenses
equal revenue

COSTS

LOSS

QUANTITY SOLD

if the business sold this
much of its product, it
would make a loss

if the business sold
this much of its product,
it would make a profit

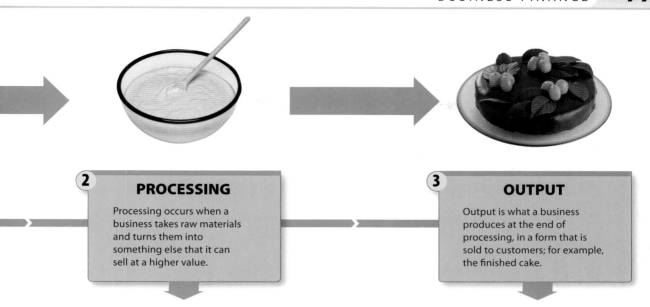

2 PROCESSING

Processing occurs when a business takes raw materials and turns them into something else that it can sell at a higher value.

△ **Costs**
Processing costs include rent, wages paid to staff, and the costs of utilities and equipment used for processing. These costs are often ongoing, long-term expenses.

3 OUTPUT

Output is what a business produces at the end of processing, in a form that is sold to customers; for example, the finished cake.

△ **Revenue**
Revenue is the money that is received by the business when it sells its output. It is used to pay off the costs. Once these are paid, the money that is left is profit.

Where the money goes

A business's revenue is not pure profit because it must pay its costs. This pie chart shows an example of where a business's revenue might be spent, and the amount left as profit.

▷ **Costs and profit pie chart**
This pie chart shows some costs that a business might have. Businesses that make different products have different expenses, which reflect the makeup of their products and the efficiency of the business. When all the costs have been paid, the money left is profit.

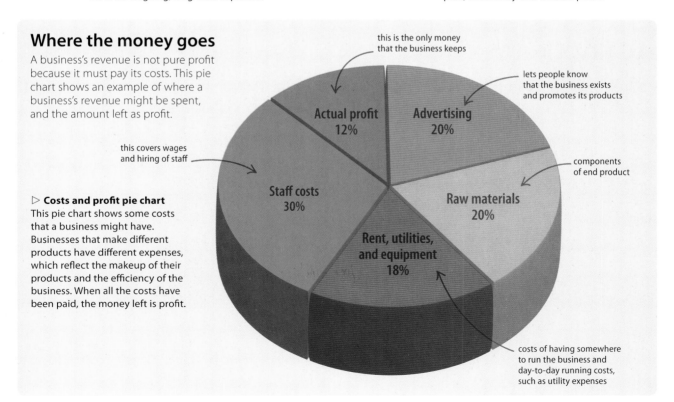

this is the only money that the business keeps

lets people know that the business exists and promotes its products

this covers wages and hiring of staff

components of end product

costs of having somewhere to run the business and day-to-day running costs, such as utility expenses

Actual profit 12%

Advertising 20%

Staff costs 30%

Raw materials 20%

Rent, utilities, and equipment 18%

Geometry

What is geometry?

GEOMETRY IS THE BRANCH OF MATHEMATICS CONCERNED
WITH LINES, ANGLES, SHAPES, AND SPACE.

Geometry has been important for thousands of years, its practical
uses include working out land areas, architecture, navigation, and
astronomy. It is also an area of mathematical study in its own right.

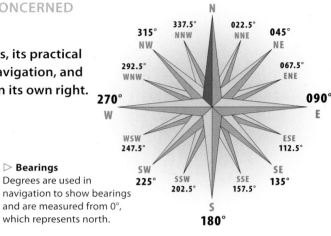

Lines, angles, shapes, and space

Geometry includes topics such as lines, angles, shapes
(in both two and three dimensions), areas, and volumes,
but also subjects like movements in space, such as
rotations and reflections, and coordinates.

▷ **Bearings**
Degrees are used in
navigation to show bearings
and are measured from 0°,
which represents north.

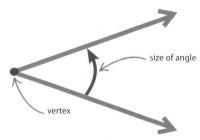

size of angle

vertex

△ **Angles**
An angle is formed when two lines meet at a
point. The size of an angle is the amount of turn
between the two lines, measured in degrees.

symbol indicates
parallel lines

△ **Parallel lines**
Lines that are parallel are the same
distance apart along their entire length,
and never meet, even if they are extended.

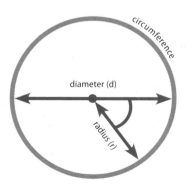

circumference

diameter (d)

radius (r)

△ **Circle**
A circle is a continuous line that is always the same
distance from a central point. The length of the
line is the circumference. The diameter runs from
one side to the other through the center. The
radius runs from the center to the circumference.

REAL WORLD
Geometry in nature

Although many people think of geometry as a purely
mathematical subject, geometric shapes and patterns are
widespread in the natural world. Perhaps the best-known
examples are the hexagonal shapes of honeycomb cells in a
beehive and of snowflakes, but there are many other examples of
natural geometry. For instance, water droplets, bubbles, and
planets are all roughly spherical. Crystals
naturally form various polyhedral shapes—
common table salt has cubic crystals,
and quartz often forms crystals in
the shape of a six-sided prism
with pyramid shaped ends.

◁ **Honeycomb cells**
Cells of honeycomb are naturally
hexagons, which can fit together
(tessellate) without leaving any
space between them.

Graphs and geometry

Graphs link geometry with other areas of mathematics. Plotting lines and shapes in graphs with coordinates makes it possible to convert them into algebraic expressions, which can then be manipulated mathematically. The reverse is also true: algebraic expressions can be shown on a graph, enabling them to be manipulated using the rules of geometry. Graphical representations of objects enables positions to be given to them, which makes it possible to apply vectors and calculate the results of movements, such as rotations and translations.

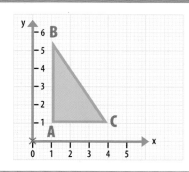

◁ **Graph**
The graph here shows a right triangle, ABC, plotted on a graph. The vertices (corners) have the coordinates A = (1, 1), B = (1, 5.5), and C = (4, 1).

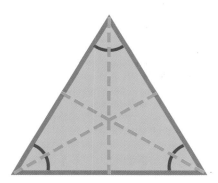

△ **Triangle**
A triangle is a three-sided, two-dimensional polygon. All triangles have three internal angles that add up to 180°.

one of four
right-angle

one of four
equal sides

△ **Square**
A square is a four-sided polygon, or quadrilateral, in which all four sides are the same length and all four internal angles are right angles (90°).

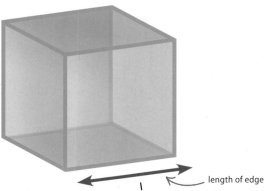

length of edge

l

△ **Cube**
A cube is a three-dimensional polygon in which all its edges are the same length. Like other rectangular solids, a cube has 6 faces, 12 edges, and 8 vertices (corners).

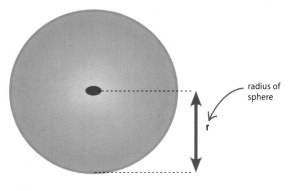

radius of sphere

r

△ **Sphere**
A sphere is a perfectly round three-dimensional shape in which every point on its surface is the same distance from the center; this distance is the radius.

Tools in geometry

MATHEMATICAL INSTRUMENTS ARE NEEDED FOR
MEASURING AND DRAWING IN GEOMETRY.

Tools used in geometry

Tools are vital to measure and construct geometric shapes
accurately. The essential tools are a ruler, a compass, and a
protractor. A ruler is used for measuring and to draw straight
lines. A compass is used to draw a whole circle or a part of a circle
(called an arc). A protractor is used to measure and draw angles.

Using a compass

A tool for drawing circles and arcs, a compass is made up of two
arms attached at one end. To use a compass, hold the arm that
ends in a point still, while pivoting the other arm, which holds a
pencil, around it. The point becomes the center of the circle.

arms of compass
can be adjusted to
length of radius

use a pencil to draw
circles and arcs

holds pencil
in place

point held
in place

tip of pencil is level
with compass point

▽ **Drawing a circle when given the radius**
Set the distance between the arms of a compass
to the given radius, then draw the circle.

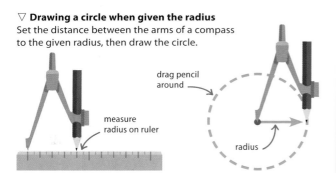

drag pencil
around

measure
radius on ruler

radius

Use a ruler to set the
arms of the compass to
the given radius.

With the compass set to the
radius, hold the point down
and drag the pencil around.

▽ **Drawing a circle when given its center and
one point on the circumference**
Put the point of the compass where the center
is marked and extend the other arm so that the
tip of the pencil touches the point on the
circumference. Then, draw the circle.

center

point on
circumference

draw a circle

radius

Set the compass to the
distance between the
two points.

Hold the point of the
compass down and draw
a circle through the point.

▽ **Drawing arcs**
Sometimes only a part of a circle—an arc—is required. Arcs
are often used as guides to construct other shapes.

center

A

radius

point on
circumference

B

hold compass
in place

A

draw arc
with pencil

B

intersection is
the same
distance
(equidistant)
from points
A and B

A

compass
held steady

B

Draw a line and mark the ends with a
point—one will be the center of the arc,
the other a point on its circumference.

Set the compass to the length of the
line—the radius of the arc—and hold it
on one of the points to draw the first arc.

Draw a second arc by holding the point
of the compass on the other point. The
intersection is equidistant from A and B.

Using a ruler

A ruler can be used to measure straight lines and the distances between any two points. A ruler is also necessary for setting the arms of a compass to a given distance.

line AB

◁ **Measuring lines**
Use a ruler to measure straight lines or the distance between any two given points.

▷ **Drawing lines**
A ruler is also used as a straight edge when drawing lines between two points.

straight line

adjust arms of compass

point of pencil marks length

◁ **Setting a compass**
Use a ruler to measure and set the width of a compass to a given radius.

Other tools

Other tools may prove useful when creating drawings and diagrams in geometry.

△ **Set square**
A set square looks like a right triangle and is used for drawing parallel lines. There are two types of set square, one has interior angles 90°, 40° and 45°, the other 90°, 60°, and 30°.

△ **Calculator**
A calculator provides a number of key options for geometry calculations. For example, functions such as Sine can be used to work out the unknown angles of a triangle.

Using a protractor

A protractor is used to measure and draw angles. It is usually made of transparent plastic, which makes it easier to place the center of the protractor over the point of the angle. When measuring an angle, always use the scale starting with zero.

outer scale is used to measure this obtuse angle

inner scale is used to measure this acute angle

▽ **Measuring angles**
Use a protractor to measure any angle formed by two lines that meet at a point.

Extend the lines if necessary to make reading easier.

Place the protractor over the angle and read the angle measurement, making sure to read up from zero.

The other scale measures the external angle.

▽ **Drawing angles**
When given the size of an angle, use a protractor to measure and draw the angle accurately.

Draw a line and mark a point on it.

Place the protractor on the line with its center over the point. Read the degrees up from zero to mark the point.

75°

Draw a line through the two points, and mark the angle.

Angles

AN ANGLE IS A FIGURE FORMED BY TWO RAYS THAT
SHARE A COMMON ENDPOINT CALLED THE VERTEX.

SEE ALSO

❮ **82–83** Tools in geometry

Straight lines **86–87** ❯

Bearings **108–109** ❯

**Angles show the amount two lines "turn" as they extend in
different directions away from the vertex. This turn is
measured in degrees, represented by the symbol °.**

Measuring angles

The size of an angle depends on the
amount of turn. A whole turn, making
one rotation around a circle, is 360°.
All other angles are less than 360°.

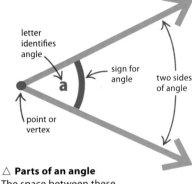

letter
identifies
angle

sign for
angle

two sides
of angle

a

point or
vertex

△ **Parts of an angle**
The space between these
two rays is the angle. An
angle can be named with
a letter, its value in
degrees, or the symbol ∠.

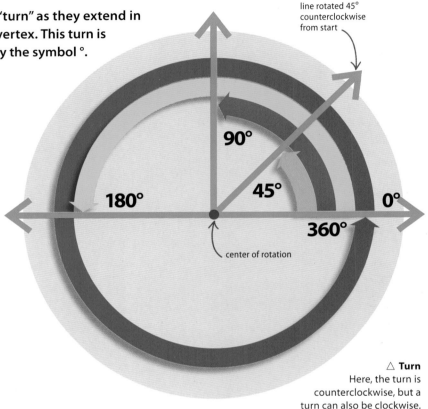

line rotated 45°
counterclockwise
from start

90°

180°

45°

0°

360°

center of rotation

△ **Turn**
Here, the turn is
counterclockwise, but a
turn can also be clockwise.

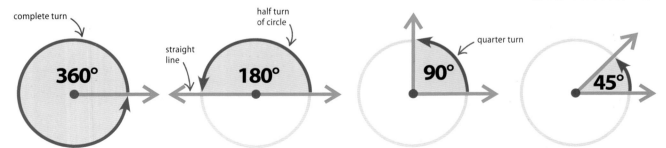

complete turn

360°

△ **Whole turn**
An angle that is a whole
turn is 360°. Such a
rotation brings both sides
of the angle back to the
starting point.

half turn
of circle

straight
line

180°

△ **Half turn**
An angle that is a half
turn is 180°. Its two sides
form a straight line. The
angle is also known as
a straight angle.

quarter turn

90°

△ **Quarter turn**
An angle that is a quarter
turn is 90°. Its two sides
are perpendicular
(L-shaped). It is also
known as a right angle.

45°

△ **Eighth turn**
An angle that is one
eighth of a whole turn is
45°. It is half of a right
angle, and eight of these
angles are a whole turn.

Types of angle

There are four important types of angle, which are shown below. They are named according to their size.

△ **Acute angle**
This angle is less than 90°.

△ **Right angle**
A right angle is 90°.

△ **Obtuse angle**
This angle is more than 90° but less than 180°.

△ **Reflex angle**
A reflex angle is more than 180°.

Naming angles

Angles can have individual names and names that reflect a shared relationship.

△ **One angle, three names**
This angle can be written as a, or as ∠ ABC, or as ∠ CBA.

△ **Complementary angles**
Any two angles that add up to 90° are complementary.

△ **Supplementary angles**
Any two angles that add up to 180° are supplementary.

Angles on a straight line

The angles on a straight line make up a half turn, so they add up to 180°. In this example, four adjacent angles add up to the 180° of a straight line.

$$a + b + c + d = 180°$$
$$20° + 40° + 90° + 30° = 180°$$

Angles at a point

The angles surrounding a point, or vertex, make up a whole turn, so they add up to 360°. In this example, five adjacent angles at the same point add up to the 360° of a complete circle.

$$a + b + c + d + e = 360°$$
$$60° + 70° + 90° + 60° + 80° = 360°$$

Straight lines

A STRAIGHT LINE IS USUALLY JUST CALLED A LINE. IT IS THE SHORTEST
DISTANCE BETWEEN TWO POINTS ON A SURFACE OR IN SPACE.

SEE ALSO
‹ 82–83 Tools in geometry
‹ 84–85 Angles
Constructions 110–113 ›

Points, lines, and planes

The most fundamental objects in geometry are points, lines,
and planes. A point represents a specific position and has no
width, height, or length. A line is one dimensional—it has
infinite length extending in two opposite directions. A plane
is a two-dimensional flat surface extending in all directions.

A ●
● B ● C

△ **Points**
A point is used to represent a precise
location. It is represented by a dot
and named with a capital letter.

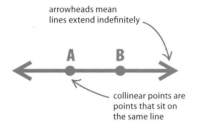

arrowheads mean
lines extend indefinitely

collinear points are
points that sit on
the same line

endpoints show
line segments
have fixed length

A

△**Lines**
A line is represented by a straight line and
arrowheads signify that it extends indefinitely
in both directions. It can be named by any two
points that it passes through—this line is AB.

△ **Line segments**
A line segment has fixed length, so it will
have endpoints rather than arrowheads. A
line segment is named by its endpoints—
this is line segment CD.

△ **Planes**
A plane is usually represented by a two-
dimensional figure and labeled with a capital
letter. Edges can be drawn, although a plane
actually extends indefinitely in all directions.

Sets of lines

Two lines on the same surface, or plane,
can either intersect—meaning they
share a point—or they can be parallel.
If two lines are the same distance apart
along their lengths and never intersect,
they are parallel.

symbol indicates
parallel lines

△ **Parallel lines**
Parallel lines are two or more lines that never
meet, even if extended. Identical arrows are
used to indicate lines that are parallel.

△ **Nonparallel lines**
Nonparallel lines are not the same distance
apart all the way along; if they are extended
they will eventually meet in a point.

transversal
crosses both
lines

transversal

△ **Transversal**
Any line that intersects two or more
other lines, each at a different point,
is called a transversal.

LOOKING CLOSER

Parallelograms

A parallelogram is a four-sided shape
with two pairs of opposite sides, both
parallel and of equal length.

△ **Parallel sides**
The sides AB and DC are parallel, as are
sides BC and AD. The sides AB and BC,
and AD and CD are not parallel—shown
by the different arrows on these lines.

Angles and parallel lines

Angles can be grouped and named according to their relationships with straight lines. When parallel lines are crossed by a transversal, it creates pairs of equal angles—each pair has a different name.

▽ **Labeling angles**
Lines AB and CD are parallel. The angles created by the intersecting transversal line are labeled with lower-case letters.

arrows indicate lines AB and CD are parallel

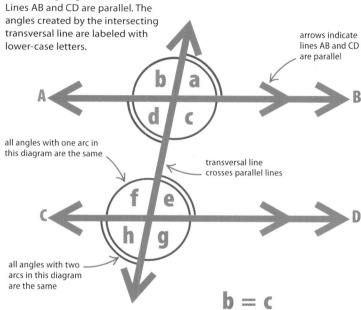

all angles with one arc in this diagram are the same

transversal line crosses parallel lines

all angles with two arcs in this diagram are the same

▷ **Vertical angles**
When two lines cross, equal angles are formed on opposite sides of the point. These angles are known as vertical angles.

b = c

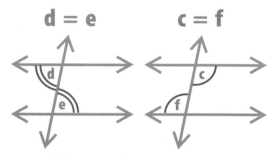

b = f   a = e

△ **Corresponding angles**
Angles in the same position in relation to the transversal line and one of a pair of parallel lines, are called corresponding angles. These angles are equal.

d = e   c = f

△ **Alternate angles**
Alternate angles are formed on either side of a transversal between parallel lines. These angles are equal.

Drawing a parallel line

Drawing a line that is parallel to an existing line requires a pencil, a ruler, and a protractor.

mark position of second line

measure this angle between the original line and the line that crosses through the point

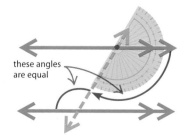

these angles are equal

Draw a straight line with a ruler. Mark a point—this will be the distance of the new, parallel line from the original line.

Draw a line through the mark, intersecting the original line. This is the transversal. Measure the angle it makes with the original line.

Measure the same angle from the transversal. Draw the new line through the mark with a ruler; this line is parallel to the original line.

Symmetry

THERE ARE TWO TYPES OF SYMMETRY—
REFLECTIVE AND ROTATIONAL.

SEE ALSO
‹ 86–87 Straight lines
Rotations   **100–101** ›
Reflections   **102–103** ›

A shape has symmetry when a line can be drawn that splits the shape exactly into two, or when it can fit into its outline in more than one way.

Reflective symmetry

A flat (two-dimensional) shape has reflective symmetry when each half of the shape on either side of a bisecting line (mirror line) is the mirror image of the other half. This mirror line is called a line of symmetry.

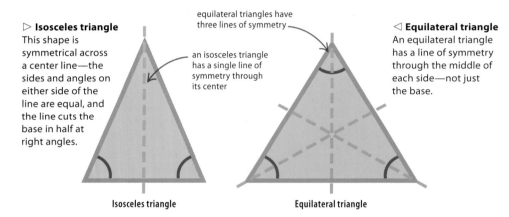

▷ **Isosceles triangle**
This shape is symmetrical across a center line—the sides and angles on either side of the line are equal, and the line cuts the base in half at right angles.

an isosceles triangle has a single line of symmetry through its center

equilateral triangles have three lines of symmetry

◁ **Equilateral triangle**
An equilateral triangle has a line of symmetry through the middle of each side—not just the base.

Isosceles triangle

Equilateral triangle

Planes of symmetry

Solid (three-dimensional) shapes can be divided using "walls" known as planes. Solid shapes have reflective symmetry when the two sides of the shape split by a plane are mirror images.

◁ **Rectangle-based pyramid**
A pyramid with a rectangular base and triangles as sides can be divided into mirror images in two ways.

▽ **Cuboid**
Formed by three pairs of rectangles, a cuboid can be divided into two symmetrical shapes in three ways.

a rectangle-based pyramid has two planes of symmetry

a cuboid has three planes of symmetry

▽ **Lines of symmetry**
These are the lines of symmetry for some flat or two-dimensional shapes. Circles have an unlimited number of lines of symmetry.

Lines of symmetry of a rectangle

Lines of symmetry of a square

Lines of symmetry of a regular pentagon

Every line through the middle of a circle is a line of symmetry

Rotational symmetry

A two-dimensional shape has rotational symmetry if it can be rotated about a point, called the center of rotation, and still exactly fit its original outline. The number of ways it fits its outline when rotated is known as its "order" of rotational symmetry.

▷ **Equilateral triangle**
An equilateral triangle has rotational symmetry of order 3—when rotated, it fits its original outline in three different ways.

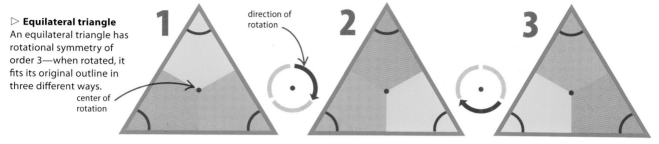

center of rotation

direction of rotation

▽ **Square**
A square has rotational symmetry of order 4—when rotated around its center of rotation, it fits its original outline in four different ways.

center of rotation

direction of rotation

Axes of symmetry

Instead of a single point as the center of rotation, a three-dimensional shape is rotated around a line known as its axis of symmetry. It has rotational symmetry if, when rotated, it fits into its original outline.

▽ **Rectangle-based pyramid**
A rectangle-based pyramid can rotate into two different positions around its axis.

a rectangle-based pyramid has one axis of rotational symmetry

▽ **Cylinder**
A cylinder can rotate into an unlimited number of positions around its vertical axis.

a cylinder has one vertical axis of rotational symmetry

▽ **Cuboid**
A cuboid can rotate into two different positions around each of its three axes.

a cuboid has three axes of rotational symmetry

Coordinates

COORDINATES GIVE THE POSITION OF A PLACE OR POINT ON A MAP OR GRAPH.

SEE ALSO	
Vectors	94–97 ❯
Linear graphs	182–185 ❯

Introducing coordinates

Coordinates come in pairs of numbers or letters, or both. They are always written in parentheses separated by a comma. The order in which coordinates are read and written is important. In this example, (E, 1), means five units, or squares on this map, to the right (along the horizontal row) and one square down, or up in some cases (the vertical column).

▽ **City Map**
A grid provides a framework for locating places on a map. Every square is identified by two coordinates. A place is found when the horizontal coordinate meets the vertical coordinate. On this city map, the horizontal coordinates are letters and the vertical coordinates are numbers. On other maps only numbers may be used.

numbers are used as vertical coordinates on this map

letters are used as horizontal coordinates on this map

Map reading

The horizontal coordinate is always given first and the vertical coordinate second. On the map below, a letter and a number are paired together to form a coordinate.

move from left to right to find the first coordinate

move from top to bottom to find the second coordinate

◁ Fire station
The coordinates of the fire station are (H, 4).

FIRST AVENUE

MAPLE SQUARE

ELM ROAD

Using coordinates

Each place of interest on this map can be found using the given coordinates. Remember when reading this map to first read across (horizontal) and then down (vertical).

◁ Cinema
Find the cinema using coordinates (B, 4). Starting at the second square on the right, move 4 squares down.

◁ Post office
The coordinates of the post office are (E, 1). Find the horizontal coordinate E then move down 1 square.

◁ Town hall
Find the town hall using coordinates (J, 5). Move 10 squares to the right, then move 5 squares down.

◁ Health club
Using the coordinates (C, 7), find the location of the health club. First, find C. Next, find 7 on the vertical column.

◁ Library
The coordinates of the library are (N, 1). Find N first then move down 1 square to locate the library.

◁ Hospital
The hospital can be found using the coordinates (G, 7). To find the horizontal coordinate of G, move 7 squares to the right. Then go down 7 squares to find the vertical coordinate 7.

◁ Fire station
Find the fire station using coordinates (H, 4). Move 8 squares to the right to find H, then move 4 squares down.

◁ School
The coordinates of the school are (L, 1). First find L, then move down 1 square to find the school.

◁ Shopping center
Using the coordinates (D, 3), find the location of the shopping center. Find D. Next, find 3 on the vertical column.

Graph coordinates

Coordinates are used to identify the positions of points on graphs, in relation to two axes—the y axis is a vertical line, and the x axis is a horizontal line. The coordinates of a point are written as its position on the x axis, followed by its position on the y axis, (x, y).

▷ **Four quadrants**
Coordinates are measured on axes, which cross at a point called the "origin." These axes create four quadrants. There are positive values on the axes above and to the right of the origin, and negative values below and to its left.

the origin

quadrant

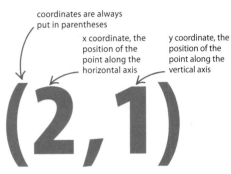

coordinates are always put in parentheses

x coordinate, the position of the point along the horizontal axis

y coordinate, the position of the point along the vertical axis

△ **Coordinates of a point**
Coordinates give the position of a point on each axis. The first number gives its position on the x axis, the second its position on the y axis.

Plotting coordinates

Coordinates are plotted on a set of axes. To plot a given point, first read along to its value on the x axis, then read up or down to its value on the y axis. The point is plotted where the two values cross each other.

$$A = (2, 2) \quad B = (-1, -3)$$
$$C = (1, -2) \quad D = (-2, 1)$$

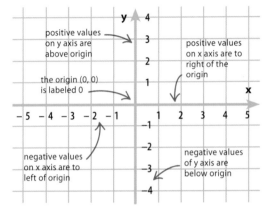

positive values on y axis are above origin

positive values on x axis are to right of the origin

the origin (0, 0) is labeled 0

negative values on x axis are to left of origin

negative values of y axis are below origin

These are four sets of coordinates. Each gives its x value first, followed by its y value. Plot the points on a set of axes.

y coordinate of A

x coordinate of A

▶ **To plot each point,** look at its x coordinate (the first number), and read along the x axis from 0 to this number. Then read up or down to its y coordinate (the second number).

Using graph paper, draw a horizontal line to form the x axis, and a vertical line for the y axis. Number the axes, with the origin separating the positive and negative values.

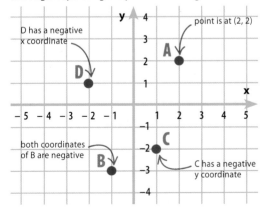

D has a negative x coordinate

point is at (2, 2)

both coordinates of B are negative

C has a negative y coordinate

▶ **Plot each point in the same way.** With negative coordinates, the process is the same, but read to the left instead of right for an x coordinate, and down instead of up for a y coordinate.

Equation of a line

Lines that pass through a set of coordinates on a pair of axes can be expressed as equations. For example, on the line of the equation $y = x + 1$, any point that lies on the line has a y coordinate that is 1 unit greater than its x coordinate.

$$y = x + 1$$

y coordinate ← → x coordinate

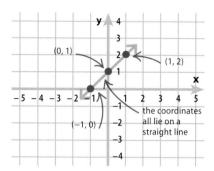

(0, 1)
(1, 2)
(−1, 0)
the coordinates all lie on a straight line

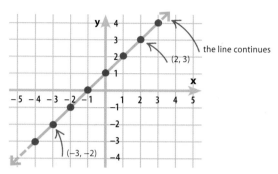

the line continues
(2, 3)
(−3, −2)

▶ **The equation of a line** can be found using only a few coordinates. This line passes through the coordinates (−1, 0), (0, 1), and (1, 2), so it is already clear what pattern the points follow.

▶ **The graph of the equation is of** all the points where the y coordinate is 1 greater than the x coordinate ($y = x + 1$). This means that the line can be used to find other coordinates that satisfy the equation.

World map

Coordinates are used to mark the position of places on the Earth's surface, using lines of latitude and longitude. These work in the same way as the x and y axes on a graph. The "origin" is the point where the Greenwich Meridian (0 for longitude) crosses the Equator (0 for latitude).

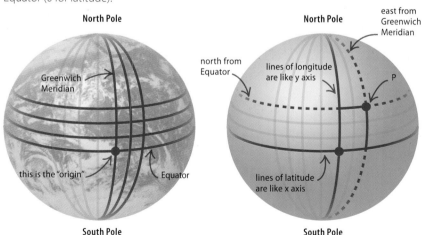

North Pole

Greenwich Meridian

this is the "origin"   Equator

South Pole

North Pole

east from Greenwich Meridian

north from Equator

lines of longitude are like y axis

P

lines of latitude are like x axis

South Pole

North Pole

P can also be shown on a map

degrees north (latitude)

Equator

degrees east (longitude)

Meridian

curved lines are flattened out into a grid

South Pole

▶ **Lines of longitude** run from the North Pole to the South Pole. Lines of latitude are at right-angles to lines of longitude. The origin is where the Equator (x axis) crosses the Greenwich Meridian (y axis).

▶ **The coordinates of a point** such as P are found by finding how many degrees East it is from the Meridian and how many degrees North it is from the Equator.

▶ **This is how** the surface of the Earth is shown on a map. The lines of latitude and longitude work as axes—the vertical lines show longitude and horizontal lines show latitude.

Vectors

A VECTOR IS A LINE THAT HAS SIZE (MAGNITUDE) AND DIRECTION.

A vector is a way to show a distance in a particular direction. It is often drawn as a line with an arrow on it. The length of the line shows the size of the vector and the arrow gives its direction.

SEE ALSO

❮ **90–93** Coordinates

Translations   **98–99** ❯

Pythagorean
Theorem   **128–129** ❯

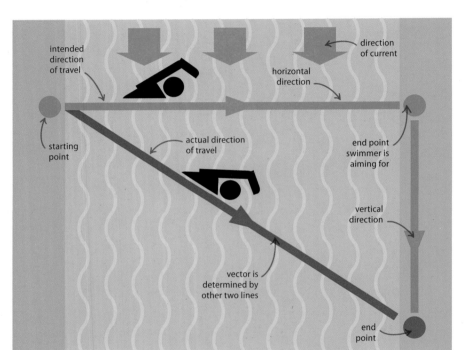

intended direction of travel

direction of current

horizontal direction

actual direction of travel

end point swimmer is aiming for

vertical direction

starting point

vector is determined by other two lines

end point

What is a vector?

A vector is a distance in a particular direction. Often, a vector is a diagonal distance, and in these cases it forms the diagonal side (hypotenuse) of a right-angled triangle (see pp.128–129). The other sides of the triangle determine the vector's length and direction. In the example on the left, a swimmer's path is a vector. The other two sides of the triangle are the distance across to the opposite shore from the starting point, and the distance down from the end point that the swimmer was aiming for to the actual end point where the swimmer reaches the shore.

◁ **Vector of a swimmer**
A man sets out to swim to the opposite shore of a river that is 30m wide. A current pushes him as he swims, and he ends up 20m downriver from where he intended. His path is a vector with dimensions 30 across and 20 down.

Expressing vectors

In diagrams, a vector is drawn as a line with an arrow on it, showing its size and direction. There are three different ways of writing vectors using letters and numbers.

$\mathbf{v} =$

A "v" is a general label for a vector, used even when its size is known. It is often used as a label in a diagram.

$\overrightarrow{\mathbf{ab}} =$

Another way of representing a vector is by giving its start and end points, with an arrow above them to show direction.

$\begin{pmatrix} 6 \\ 4 \end{pmatrix} =$

The size and direction of the vector can be shown by giving the horizontal units over the vertical units.

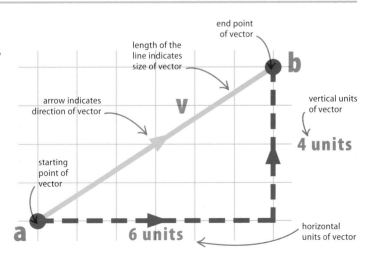

end point of vector

length of the line indicates size of vector

arrow indicates direction of vector

v

b

vertical units of vector

4 units

starting point of vector

a

6 units

horizontal units of vector

Direction of vectors

The direction of a vector is determined by whether its units are positive or negative. Positive horizontal units mean movement to the right, negative horizontal units mean left; positive vertical units mean movement up, and negative vertical units mean down.

▷ **Movement up and left**
This movement has a vector with negative horizontal units and positive vertical units.

negative horizontal units mean move left $\begin{pmatrix} -3 \\ 3 \end{pmatrix}$ positive vertical units mean move up

▷ **Movement up and right**
This movement has a vector with both sets of units positive.

positive horizontal units mean move right $\begin{pmatrix} 3 \\ 3 \end{pmatrix}$ positive vertical units mean move up

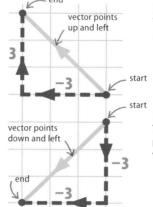

end
vector points up and left
start

end
vector points up and right
start

▷ **Movement down and left**
This movement has a vector with both sets of units negative.

negative horizontal units mean move left $\begin{pmatrix} -3 \\ -3 \end{pmatrix}$ negative vertical units mean move down

▷ **Movement down and right**
This movement has a vector with positive horizontal units and negative vertical units.

positive horizontal units mean move right $\begin{pmatrix} 3 \\ -3 \end{pmatrix}$ negative vertical units mean move down

vector points down and left
start
end

start
vector points down and right
end

Equal vectors

Vectors can be identified as equal even if they are in different positions on the same grid, as long as their horizontal and vertical units are equal.

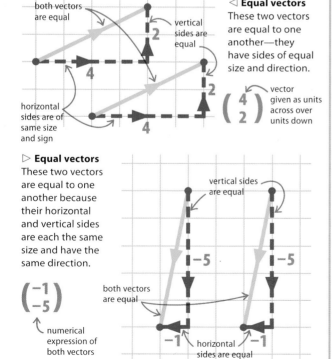

both vectors are equal

vertical sides are equal

horizontal sides are of same size and sign

◁ **Equal vectors**
These two vectors are equal to one another—they have sides of equal size and direction.

$\begin{pmatrix} 4 \\ 2 \end{pmatrix}$ vector given as units across over units down

▷ **Equal vectors**
These two vectors are equal to one another because their horizontal and vertical sides are each the same size and have the same direction.

$\begin{pmatrix} -1 \\ -5 \end{pmatrix}$
numerical expression of both vectors

vertical sides are equal

both vectors are equal

horizontal sides are equal

Magnitude of vectors

With diagonal vectors, the vector is the longest side (c) of a right triangle. Use the Pythagorean theorem to find the length of a vector from its vertical (a) and horizontal (b) units.

a in formula
vector forms longest side of right triangle, c in formula
b in formula

formula for Pythagorean theorem
$$a^2 + b^2 = c^2$$

$$(-6)^2 + 3^2 = c^2$$

$(-6)^2 = -6 \times -6 = 36$
$3^2 = 3 \times 3 = 9$

$$36 + 9 = c^2$$

c^2 is the square of vector

$$45 = c^2$$

square root of 45
c is equal to the square root of 45
$$c = \sqrt{45}$$

length of vector
$$c = \mathbf{6.7}$$

Put the vertical and horizontal units of the vector into the formula.

▽

Find the squares by multiplying each value by itself.

▽

Add the two squares. This total equals c^2 (the square of the vector).

▽

Find the square root of the total value (45) by using a calculator.

▽

The answer is the magnitude (length) of the vector.

Adding and subtracting vectors

Vectors can be added and subtracted in two ways. The first is by using written numbers to add the horizontal and vertical values. The second is by drawing the vectors end to end, then seeing what new vector is created.

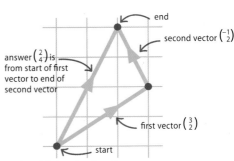

▷ **Addition**
Vectors can be added in two different ways. Both methods give the same answer.

3 + (−1) = 2
first vector
second vector
2 + 2 = 4

△ **Adding the parts**
To add vectors numerically, add the two top numbers (the horizontal values) and then the two bottom numbers (the vertical values).

Addition by drawing vectors
Draw one vector, then draw the second starting from the end point of the first. The answer is the new vector that has been created, from the start of the first vector to the end of the second.

▷ **Subtraction**
Vectors can be subtracted in two different ways. Both methods give the same answer.

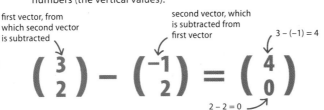

first vector, from which second vector is subtracted
second vector, which is subtracted from first vector
3 − (−1) = 4
2 − 2 = 0

△ **Subtracting the parts**
To subtract one vector from another, subtract its vertical value from the vertical value of the first vector, then do the same for the horizontal values.

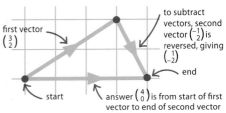

first vector $\binom{3}{2}$
to subtract vectors, second vector $\binom{-1}{2}$ is reversed, giving $\binom{1}{-2}$
end
start
answer $\binom{4}{0}$ is from start of first vector to end of second vector

△ **Subtraction by drawing vectors**
Draw the first vector, then draw the second vector reversed, starting from the end point of the first vector. The answer to the subtraction is the vector from the start point to the end point.

Multiplying vectors

Vectors can be multiplied by numbers, but not by other vectors. The direction of a vector stays the same if it is multiplied by a positive number, but is reversed if it is multiplied by a negative number. Vectors can be multiplied by drawing or by using their numerical values.

▽ **Vector a**
Vector a has −4 horizontal units and +2 vertical units. It can be shown as a written vector or a drawn vector, as shown below.

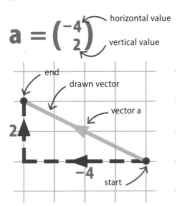

$a = \binom{-4}{2}$

horizontal value
vertical value
end
drawn vector
vector a
start

▽ **Vector a multiplied by 2**
To multiply vector a by 2 numerically, multiply both its horizontal and vertical parts by 2. To multiply it by 2 by drawing, simply extend the original vector by the same length again.

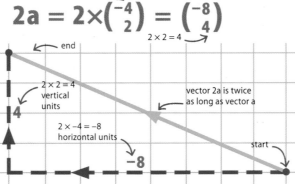

$2a = 2 \times \binom{-4}{2} = \binom{-8}{4}$

2 × −4 = −8
2 × 2 = 4
vector a
end
2 × 2 = 4 vertical units
2 × −4 = −8 horizontal units
vector 2a is twice as long as vector a
start

▽ **Vector a multiplied by −½**
To multiply vector a by −½ numerically, multiply each of its parts by −½. To multiply it by −½ by drawing, draw a vector half the length and in the opposite direction of a.

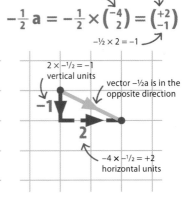

$-\frac{1}{2} a = -\frac{1}{2} \times \binom{-4}{2} = \binom{+2}{-1}$

−½ × −4 = +2
vector a
−½ × 2 = −1
2 × −½ = −1 vertical units
vector −½a is in the opposite direction
−4 × −½ = +2 horizontal units

Working with vectors in geometry

Vectors can be used to prove results in geometry. In this example, vectors are used to prove that the line joining the midpoints of any two sides of a triangle is parallel to the third side of the triangle, as well as being half its length.

First, choose 2 sides of triangle ABC, in this example AB and AC. Mark these sides as the vectors a and b. To get from B to C, go along BA and then AC, rather than BC. BA is the vector –a because it is the opposite of AB, and AC is already known (b). This means vector BC is –a + b.

$$\vec{BC} = -a + b$$

vector BC

this is negative because BA is opposite of AB

vector AB is labeled a

a

b ← vector AC is labeled b

vector BC can also be expressed like this

$-a + b$

Second, find the midpoints of the two sides that have been chosen (AB and AC). Mark the midpoint of AB as P, and the midpoint of AC as Q. This creates three new vectors: AP, AQ, and PQ. AP is half the length of vector a, and AQ is half the length of vector b.

$$\vec{AP} = \tfrac{1}{2}\vec{AB} = \tfrac{1}{2}a$$

$$\vec{AQ} = \tfrac{1}{2}\vec{AC} = \tfrac{1}{2}b$$

P is the midpoint of AB → P

$\tfrac{1}{2}a$

$\tfrac{1}{2}b$ Q ← Q is the midpoint of AC

Third, use the vectors ½a and ½b to find the length of vector PQ. To get from P to Q go along PA then AQ. PA is the vector –½a because it is the opposite of AP, and AQ is already known to be ½b. This means vector PQ is –½a + ½b.

this is half BA   this is half AC

$$\vec{PQ} = -\tfrac{1}{2}a + \tfrac{1}{2}b$$

$$\vec{PQ} = \tfrac{1}{2}\vec{BC}$$

BC is –a + b, so PQ is half BC

this is negative because BA is opposite of AB

$-\tfrac{1}{2}a$

$-\tfrac{1}{2}a + \tfrac{1}{2}b$ ← PQ is half BC

$-a + b$

$\tfrac{1}{2}b$

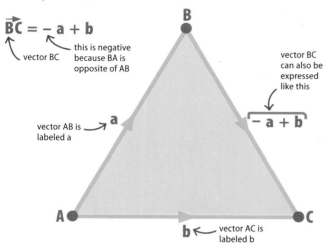

Fourth, make the proof. The vectors PQ and BC are in the same direction and are therefore parallel to each other, so the line PQ (which joins the midpoints of the sides AB and AC) must be parallel to the line BC. Also, vector PQ is half the length of vector BC, so the line PQ must be half the length of the line BC.

BC and PQ are parallel   vector BC

$-a + b$

vector PQ

$-\tfrac{1}{2}a + \tfrac{1}{2}b$

Translations

A TRANSLATION CHANGES THE POSITION OF A SHAPE.

A translation is a type of transformation. It moves an object to a new position.
The translated object is called an image, and it is exactly the same size and
shape as the original object. Translations are written as vectors.

How translations work

A translation moves an object to a new position, without making any other changes—for example to size or shape.
Here, the triangle named ABC is translated so that its image is the triangle $A_1B_1C_1$. This translation is named T_1. The
triangle $A_1B_1C_1$ is then translated again and its image is the triangle $A_2B_2C_2$. This second translation is named T_2.

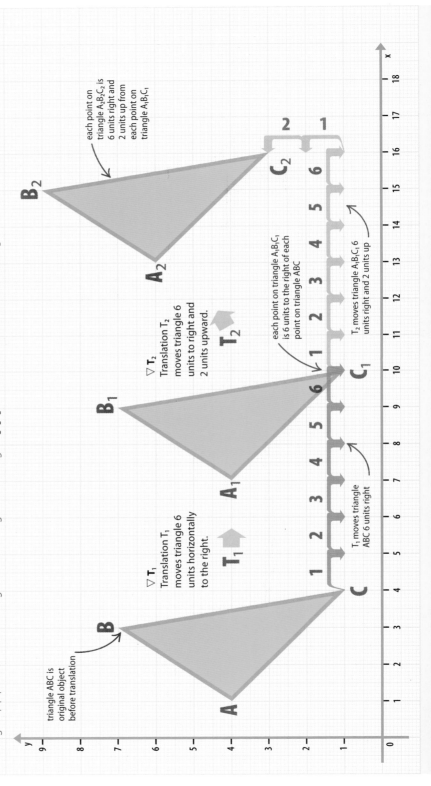

triangle ABC is
original object
before translation

▽ T_1
Translation T_1
moves triangle 6
units horizontally
to the right.

T_1

T_1 moves triangle
ABC 6 units right

each point on triangle $A_1B_1C_1$
is 6 units to the right of each
point on triangle ABC

▽ T_2
Translation T_2
moves triangle 6
units to right and
2 units upward.

T_2

T_2 moves triangle $A_1B_1C_1$ 6
units right and 2 units up

each point on
triangle $A_2B_2C_2$ is
6 units right and
2 units up from
each point on
triangle $A_1B_1C_1$

Writing translations

Translations are written as vectors. The top number shows the horizontal distance an object moves, while the bottom number shows the vertical distance moved. The two numbers are contained within a set of parentheses. Each translation can be numbered—for example, T_1, T_2, T_3—to make it clear which one is being referred to if more than one translation is shown.

translation number

distance moved horizontally

$$T_1 = \begin{pmatrix} 6 \\ 0 \end{pmatrix}$$

distance moved vertically

△ **Translation T_1**
To move triangle ABC to position $A_1B_1C_1$ each point moves 6 units horizontally, but does not move vertically. The vector is written as above.

translation number

distance moved horizontally

$$T_2 = \begin{pmatrix} 6 \\ 2 \end{pmatrix}$$

distance moved vertically

△ **Translation T_2**
To move triangle $A_1B_1C_1$ to position $A_2B_2C_2$ each point moves 6 units horizontally, then moves 2 units vertically. The vector is written as above.

Direction of translations

The numbers used to show a translation's vector are positive or negative, depending on which direction the object moved. If it moves to the right or up, it is positive; to the left or down, it is negative.

▽ **Negative translation**
The rectangle ABCD, moves down and left, so the values in its vector are negative.

this is the translation T_1

this is the original shape

moves 1 unit down

moves 3 units to left

▽ **Translation T_1**
The translation T_1, moves rectangle ABCD to the new position $A_1B_1C_1D_1$. It is written as the vector shown—both its parts are negative.

distance moved horizontally (to the left)

$$T_1 = \begin{pmatrix} -3 \\ -1 \end{pmatrix}$$

distance moved vertically (downward)

LOOKING CLOSER

Tessellations in action

A tessellation is a pattern created by using shapes to cover a surface without leaving any gaps. Two shapes can be tessellated with themselves using only translation (and no rotation)—the square and the regular hexagon. To tessellate a hexagon using translation requires 6 different translations; to tessellate a square requires 8.

translations needed

△ **Hexagons**
Each of the hexagons around the outside is a translated image of the central hexagon. The tessellation continues in the same way.

translations needed

△ **Squares**
Each of the squares around the edge is a translated image of the central square. The tessellation continues in the same way.

Rotations

A ROTATION IS A TYPE OF TRANSFORMATION THAT MOVES AN OBJECT AROUND A GIVEN POINT.

The point around which a rotation occurs is called the center of rotation, and the distance a shape turns is called the angle of rotation.

Properties of a rotation

Rotations occur around a fixed point called the center of rotation, and are measured by angles. Any point on an original object and the corresponding point on its rotated image will be exactly the same distance from the center of rotation. The center of rotation can sit inside, outside, or on the outline of an object. A rotation can be drawn, or the center and angle of an existing rotation found, using a compass, ruler, and protractor.

object—start position

direction of rotation

point is the same distance from the center of rotation as it was at the start point

▷ **Rotation around a point**
This rectangle is rotated around a point outside its outline. If it is rotated through 360°, it returns to its starting position.

angle of rotation

center of rotation

distance from center of rotation stays the same as object moves

image— end position

center of rotation is center of object

direction of rotation

angle of rotation

△ **Rotation around a point inside an object**
An object can be rotated around a point that is inside it rather than outside—this rectangle has been rotated around its center point. It will fit into its outline again if it rotates through 180°.

+ −

Positive angle of rotation

Negative angle of rotation

△ **Angle of rotation**
The angle of rotation is either positive or negative. If it is positive, the object rotates in a clockwise direction; if it is negative, it rotates counterclockwise.

Construction of a rotation

To construct a rotation, three elements of information are needed: the object to be rotated, the location of the center of rotation, and the size of the angle of rotation.

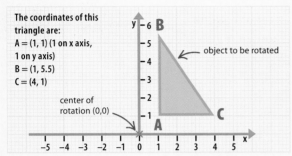

The coordinates of this triangle are:
A = (1, 1) (1 on x axis, 1 on y axis)
B = (1, 5.5)
C = (4, 1)

center of rotation (0,0)

object to be rotated

Given the position of the triangle ABC (see above) and the center of rotation, rotate the triangle –90°, which means 90° counterclockwise. The image of triangle ABC will be on the left-hand side of the y axis.

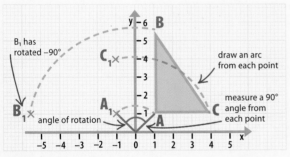

B_1 has rotated –90°

draw an arc from each point

measure a 90° angle from each point

angle of rotation

Place a compass point on the center of rotation and draw arcs counterclockwise from points A, B, and C (counterclockwise because the rotation is negative). Then, placing the center of a protractor over the center of rotation, measure an angle of 90° from each point. Mark the point where the angle meets the arc.

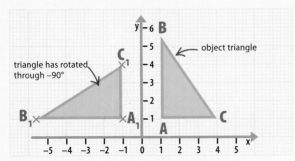

triangle has rotated through –90°

object triangle

Label the new points A_1, B_1, and C_1. Join them to form the image. Each point on the new triangle $A_1B_1C_1$ has rotated 90° counterclockwise from each point on the original triangle ABC.

Finding the angle and center of a rotation

Given an object and its rotated image, the center and angle of rotation can be found.

original triangle

image of triangle

The triangle $A_1B_1C_1$ is the image of triangle ABC after a rotation. The center and angle of rotation can be found by drawing the perpendicular bisectors (lines that cut exactly through the middle—see pp.110–111) of the lines between two sets of points, here A and A_1 and B and B_1.

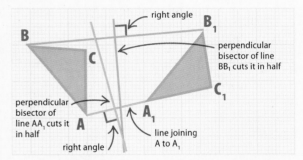

right angle

perpendicular bisector of line BB_1 cuts it in half

perpendicular bisector of line AA_1 cuts it in half

line joining A to A_1

right angle

Using a compass and a ruler, construct the perpendicular bisector of the line joining A and A_1 and the perpendicular bisector of the line that joins B and B_1. These bisectors will cross each other.

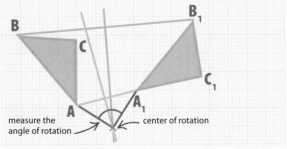

measure the angle of rotation

center of rotation

The center of rotation is the point where the two perpendicular bisectors cross. To find the angle of rotation, join A and A_1 to the center of rotation and measure the angle between these lines.

Reflections

A REFLECTION SHOWS AN OBJECT TRANSFORMED INTO ITS
MIRROR IMAGE ACROSS AN AXIS OF REFLECTION.

Properties of a reflection

Any point on an object (for example, A) and the
corresponding point on its reflected image (for
example, A_1) are on opposite sides of, and equal
distances from, the axis of reflection. The reflected
image is effectively a mirror image whose base sits
along the axis of reflection.

▽ **Reflected mountain**
The mountain on which the points
A, B, C, D, and E are marked has a
reflected image, which includes
the points A_1, B_1, C_1, D_1, and E_1.

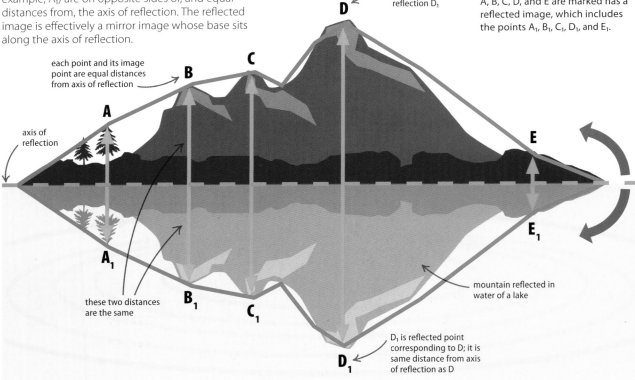

this point D has
reflection D_1

each point and its image
point are equal distances
from axis of reflection

axis of
reflection

these two distances
are the same

mountain reflected in
water of a lake

D_1 is reflected point
corresponding to D; it is
same distance from axis
of reflection as D

LOOKING CLOSER

Kaleidoscopes

A kaleidoscope creates patterns using mirrors and colored beads. The patterns are
the result of beads being reflected and then reflected again.

two mirrors

A simple kaleidoscope contains two
mirrors at right angles (90°) to each
other and some colored beads.

this is one
reflection of the
original beads

The beads are reflected in the
two mirrors, producing two reflected
images on either side.

the final
reflection, which
completes image

Each of the two reflections is
reflected again, producing another
image of the beads.

Constructing a reflection

To construct the reflection of an object it is necessary to know the position of the axis of reflection and the position of the object. Each point on the reflection will be the same distance from the axis of reflection as its corresponding point on the original. Here, the reflection of triangle ABC is drawn for the axis of reflection $y = x$ (which means that each point on the axis has the same x and y coordinates).

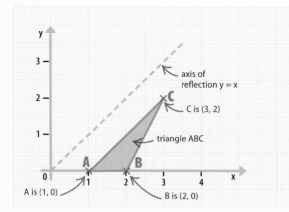

First, draw the axis of reflection. As $y = x$, this axis line crosses through the points (0, 0), (1, 1), (2, 2), (3, 3), and so on. Then draw in the object that is to be reflected—the triangle ABC, which has the coordinates (1, 0), (2, 0), and (3, 2). In each set of coordinates, the first number is the x value, and the second number is the y value.

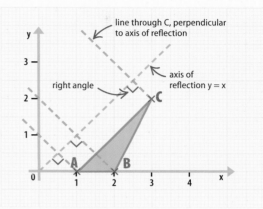

Second, draw lines from each point of the triangle ABC that are at right-angles (90°) to the axis of reflection. These lines should cross the axis of reflection and continue onward, as the new coordinates for the reflected image will be measured along them.

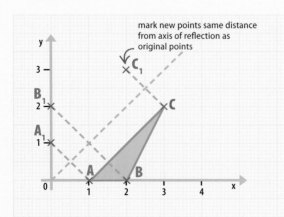

Third, measure the distance from each of the original points to the axis of reflection, then measure the same distance on the other side of the axis to find the positions of the new points. Mark each of the new points with the letter it reflects, followed by a small 1, for example A_1.

Finally, join the points A_1, B_1, and C_1 to complete the image. Each of the points of the triangle has a mirror image across the axis of reflection. Each point on the original triangle is an equal distance from the axis of reflection as its reflected point.

Enlargements

AN ENLARGEMENT IS A TRANSFORMATION OF AN OBJECT THAT
PRODUCES AN IMAGE OF THE SAME SHAPE BUT OF DIFFERENT SIZE.

Enlargements are constructed through a fixed point known as the centre
of enlargement. The image can be larger or smaller. The change in size is
determined by a number called the scale factor.

Properties of an enlargement

When an object is transformed into a larger image, the
relationship between the corresponding sides of that
object and the image is the same as the scale factor.
For example, if the scale factor is 5, the sides of the
image are 5 times bigger than those of the original.

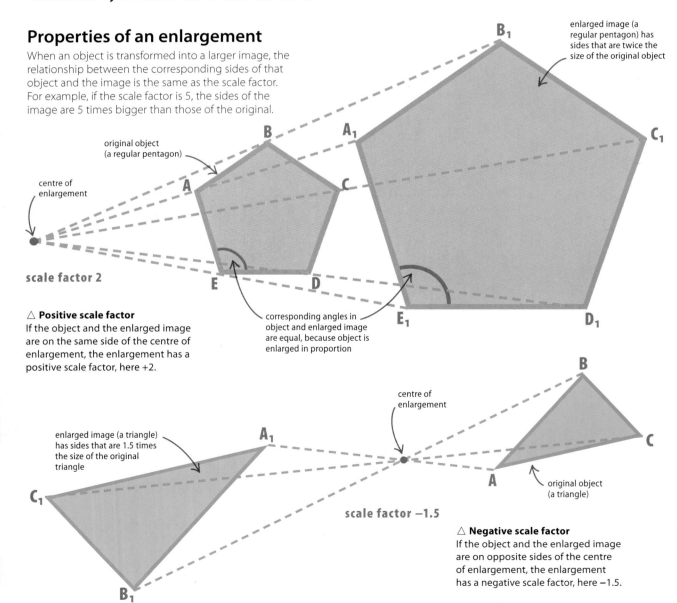

enlarged image (a
regular pentagon) has
sides that are twice the
size of the original object

original object
(a regular pentagon)

centre of
enlargement

scale factor 2

△ **Positive scale factor**
If the object and the enlarged image
are on the same side of the centre of
enlargement, the enlargement has a
positive scale factor, here +2.

corresponding angles in
object and enlarged image
are equal, because object is
enlarged in proportion

centre of
enlargement

enlarged image (a triangle)
has sides that are 1.5 times
the size of the original
triangle

scale factor −1.5

original object
(a triangle)

△ **Negative scale factor**
If the object and the enlarged image
are on opposite sides of the centre
of enlargement, the enlargement
has a negative scale factor, here −1.5.

Constructing an enlargement

An enlargement is constructed by plotting the coordinates of the object on squared (or graph) paper. Here, the quadrilateral ABCD is measured through the centre of enlargement (0, 0) with a given scale factor of 2.5.

The coordinates of this polygon are:
A (1, 1)   B (2, 3)
C (4, 2)   D (4, 1)

draw a line through each vertex (point) of shape

centre of enlargement is 0, 0

Draw the polygon ABCD using the given coordinates. Mark the centre of enlargement and draw lines from this point through each of the vertices of the shape (points where sides meet).

horizontal distance of A from centre of enlargement
vertical distance of A from centre of enlargement
x coordinate

$$A_1 = 1 \times 2.5, 1 \times 2.5 = (2.5, 2.5)$$

scale factor   y coordinate

The same principle is then applied to the other points, to work out their x and y coordinates.

$$B_1 = 2 \times 2.5, 3 \times 2.5 = (5, 7.5)$$

$$C_1 = 4 \times 2.5, 2 \times 2.5 = (10, 5)$$

$$D_1 = 4 \times 2.5, 1 \times 2.5 = (10, 2.5)$$

Then, calculate the positions of A_1, B_1, C_1, and D_1 by multiplying the horizontal and vertical distances of each point from the centre of enlargement (0, 0) by the scale factor 2.5.

B_1 is point (5, 7.5)
C_1 is point (10, 5)
A_1 is point (2.5, 2.5)
D_1 is point (10, 2.5)

Read along the x axis and the y axis to plot the vertices (points) of the enlarged image. For example, B_1 is point (5, 7.5) and C_1 is point (10, 5). Mark and label all the points A_1, B_1, C_1, and D_1.

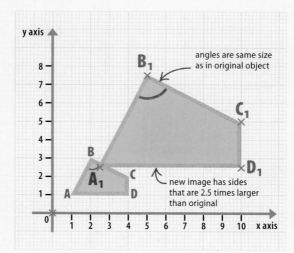

angles are same size as in original object

new image has sides that are 2.5 times larger than original

Join the new coordinates to complete the enlargement. The enlarged image is a quadrilateral with sides that are 2.5 times larger than the original object, but with angles of exactly the same size.

Scale drawings

A SCALE DRAWING SHOWS AN OBJECT ACCURATELY AT
A PRACTICAL SIZE BY REDUCING OR ENLARGING IT.

Scale drawings can be scaled down, such as a map,
or scaled up, such as a diagram of a microchip.

SEE ALSO
‹ **56–59** Ratio and proportion
‹ **104–105** Enlargements
Circles **138–139** ›

Choosing a scale

To make an accurate plan of a large object, such as a bridge, the object's measurements
need to be scaled down. To do this, every measurement of the bridge is reduced by the
same ratio. The first step in creating a scale drawing is to choose a scale—for example,
1 cm for each 10 m. The scale is then shown as a ratio, using the smallest common unit.

length (in cm)
on scale drawing

length (in cm)
of real length

symbol for ratio

◁ **Scale as a ratio**
A scale of 1 cm to 10 m
can be shown as a ratio by
using centimeters as a
common unit. There are
100 cm in a meter, so
10 × 100 cm = 1,000 cm.

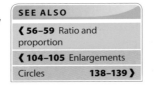

Scale:
scale shows how
lengths on bridge are
reduced in drawing

1 cm : 10 m

convert scale
to ratio of
1 cm : 1,000 cm
using centimeters
as common unit

60 m

How to make a scale drawing

In this example, a basketball court needs to be drawn to scale. The court is 30 m
long and 15 m wide. In its center is a circle with a radius of 1 m, and at either end
a semicircle, each with a radius of 5 m. To make a scale drawing, first make a rough
sketch, noting the real measurements. Next, work out a scale. Use the scale to
convert the measurements, and create the final drawing using these.

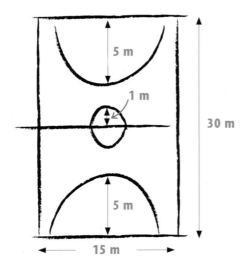

5 m

1 m

5 m

30 m

15 m

Draw a rough sketch to act as a guide, marking on it
the real measurements. Make a note of the longest
length (30 m). Based on this and the space available
for your drawing, work out a suitable scale.

Since 30 m (the longest length in the drawing) needs to fit into a
space of less than 10 cm, a convenient scale is chosen:

measurement
on drawing

1 cm : 5 m

measurement
on real court

By converting this to a ratio of 1 cm : 500 cm, it is now possible
to work out the measurements that will be used in the drawing.

real measurements changed
from meters to centimeters to
make calculation easier

scale

length for
drawing

length of court	= 3,000 cm ÷ 500	=	**6 cm**
width of court	= 1,500 cm ÷ 500	=	**3 cm**
radius of center circle =	100 cm ÷ 500	=	**0.2 cm**
radius of semicircle =	500 cm ÷ 500	=	**1 cm**

Choose a suitable scale and convert it into a ratio by using
the lowest common unit, centimeters. Next, convert the real
measurements into the same units. Divide each measurement
by the scale to find the measurements for the drawing.

squares on graph paper show measurement in cm

convert real length to centimeters (3,500 cm) and divide by converted ratio value of 1,000 to get length for drawing, in this case 3.5 cm

35 m

◁ **Scale drawing of a bridge**
Every measurement of the bridge is reduced in the same ratio. All the angles in the scale drawing are the same as those of the real bridge.

34m

110 m

measurements represent those of real bridge

50 m

▶ **Make a second rough sketch,** this time marking on the scaled measurements. This provides a guide for the final drawing.

Scale: **1 cm : 5 m**

▶ **Construct a final,** accurate scale drawing of the basketball court. Use a ruler to draw the lines, and a compass to draw the circle and semicircles.

REAL WORLD

Maps

The scale of a map varies according to the area it covers. To see a whole country such as France a scale of 1 cm : 150 km might be used. To see a town, a scale of 1 cm : 500 m is suitable.

↱ Bearings

A BEARING IS A WAY OF SHOWING A DIRECTION.

Bearings show accurate directions. They can be used to plot journeys through unfamiliar territory, where it is vital to be exact.

SEE ALSO
❮ 82–83 Tools in geometry
❮ 84–85 Angles
❮ 106–107 Scale drawings

What are bearings?

Bearings are angles measured clockwise from the compass direction north. They are usually given as three-digit whole numbers of degrees, such as 270°, but they can also use decimal numbers, such as with 247.5°. Compass directions are given in terms such as "WSW," or "west-southwest."

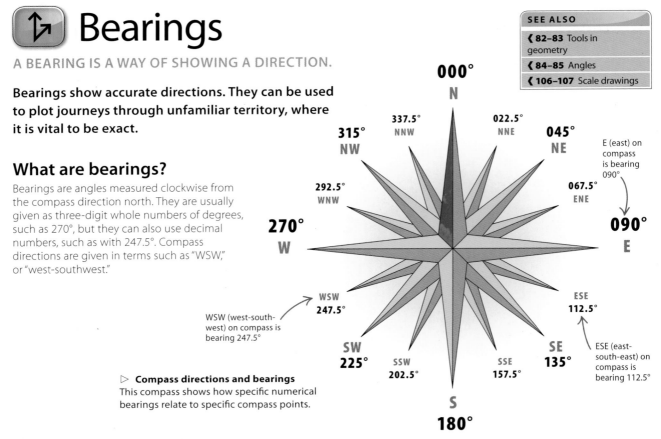

WSW (west-south-west) on compass is bearing 247.5°

E (east) on compass is bearing 090°

ESE (east-south-east) on compass is bearing 112.5°

▷ **Compass directions and bearings**
This compass shows how specific numerical bearings relate to specific compass points.

How to measure a bearing

Begin by deciding on the starting point of the journey. Place a protractor at this start or center point. Use the protractor to draw the angle of the bearing clockwise from the compass direction north.

compass direction north

bearings measured in clockwise direction

start at center point

bearing smaller than 100° has 0 as first of three digits

position of protractor for second measurement

measure angle remaining above 180°

position of protractor for first measurement

draw line at 180°, measured clockwise from north

◁ **Circle of bearings**
The start point of the journey to be plotted can be seen as the center of a circle, around which the bearings are positioned.

△ **Bearings greater than 180°**
Use the protractor to measure 180° clockwise from north. Mark the point and draw the remaining angle from 180°—in this example it is 225°.

Plotting a journey with bearings

Bearings are used to plot journeys of several direction changes. In this example, a plane flies on the bearing 290° for 300 mi, then turns to the bearing 045° for 200 mi. Plot its last leg back to the start, using a scale of 1 in for 100 mi.

SCALE
1 in : 100 mi

First, draw the bearing 290°. Set the protractor at the center and draw 180°. Draw a further 110°, giving a total of 290°.

N

center or start point

290°

draw first bearing

add 110° to bearing

measure 180°

Second, work out the distance traveled on the bearing 290°. Using the scale, the distance is 3 in, because 1 in equals 100 mi.

N

mark first part of flight

3 in

start point

actual distance

distance on scale drawing

300 ÷ 100 = 3 in

Set the protractor at the end point of the 3 in and draw a new north line. The next bearing is 045° from this north.

N   N

45°

draw second bearing of 045°

new center at end of 3 in

3 in

protractor placed at new center

start point

Work out the distance traveled on the bearing 045°. Using the scale of 1 in for every 100 mi, the distance is 200 mi.

mark second part of flight

N   N

2 in

3 in

actual distance

200 ÷ 100 = 2 in

distance on scale drawing

start point

Set the protractor at the end point of the 2 in and draw a new north line. The next bearing is found to be 150° from this latest north. This direction takes the plane back to the start point.

x = 150°

N

N   N

x

measure angle

2 in

3 in

draw last leg

start point

Finally, draw the distance traveled on the bearing 150°. Using the scale, the distance is 2.8 in, meaning the final leg of the journey is 280 mi.

y = 2.8 in

distance on scale drawing

2.8 × 100 = 280 mi

actual distance of last leg of journey

N

N   N

2 in   y

3 in

return to start point

Constructions

MAKING PERPENDICULAR LINES AND ANGLES USING
A COMPASS AND A STRAIGHT EDGE.

SEE ALSO

⟨ 82–83 Tools in geometry

⟨ 84–85 Angles

Triangles   116–117 ⟩

Congruent triangles   120–121 ⟩

An accurate geometric drawing is called a construction.

These drawings can include line segments, angles, and shapes.

The tools needed are a compass and a straight edge.

Constructing perpendicular lines

Two line segments are perpendicular when they intersect (or cross) at
90°, or right angles. There are two ways to construct a perpendicular
line—the first is to draw through a point marked on a given line
segment; the second is to use a point above or below the segment.

this angle is 90° (right angle)

intersection of two line segments

perpendicular bisector

▽ **Perpendicular bisector**
A perpendicular bisector
cuts another line segment
exactly in half, crossing
through its midpoint at right
angles, or 90°.

Using a point on the line segment

A perpendicular line can be constructed using a point marked on a line segment.
The point marked is where the two lines will intersect (cross) at right angles.

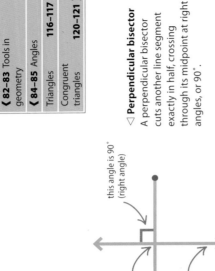

arcs must be same distance from point A

mark a point roughly halfway along the line segment

each arc will cross the line segment

mark and label points where arcs cross the line segment

▷ **Draw a line segment** and mark a point on the
segment with a letter, for example, A. Place the
point of a compass on point A, and draw two
arcs of the same distance from this point.

mark and label point where arcs cross

arcs from C and D must be same distance from point

▷ **Place the point of a compass** on point C,
and draw an arc above the line segment. Do
the same from point D. The arcs intersect
(cross) at a point, label this point E.

line segment EA is perpendicular to line CD

line segment crosses through point A

▷ **Now, draw a line segment** from
E through A. This line segment is
perpendicular (at right angles) to
the original one.

Using a point above the line

Perpendicular lines can be constructed by marking a point above the first line segment, through which the second, perpendicular, one will pass.

draw a line segment

mark point above line segment

Draw a line segment and mark a point above it. Label this point with a letter, for example, A.

draw two arcs from A

arcs from A cross line at two points

Place a compass on point A. Draw two arcs that intersect the line segment at two points. Label these points B and C.

arcs from B and C must be same distance from point A

With the compass on points B and C, draw two arcs of the same length beneath the line segment. Label the intersection of the two arcs point D.

line segment AD is perpendicular to line BC

line must cross through D

► **Now, draw a line segment** from points A to D. This is perpendicular (at right angles) to line segment BC.

Constructing a perpendicular bisector

A line that passes exactly through the midpoint of a line segment at right angles, or 90°, is called a perpendicular bisector. It can be constructed by marking points above and below the line segment.

line PQ

First, draw a line segment, and label each end point, for example P and Q.

set compass length to just over half of line PQ

draw arc from point P

Place a compass on point P and draw an arc with a distance just over half the length of line segment PQ.

keep compass at same distance

place compass on point Q

arcs from Q will cross arcs from P

Draw another arc from point Q with the compass kept at the same length. This arc will intersect the first arc at two points.

connect X and Y with straight line

line segment XY is perpendicular to segment PQ

► **Label the points** where the arcs intersect X and Y. Draw a line connecting X and Y; this is the perpendicular bisector of PQ.

Bisecting an angle

The bisector of an angle is a straight line that intersects the vertex (point) of the angle, splitting it into two equal parts. This line can be constructed by using a compass to mark points on the sides of the angle.

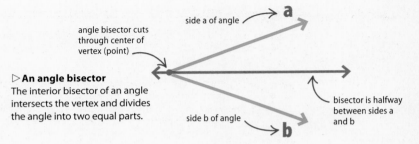

angle bisector cuts through center of vertex (point)

side a of angle

▷ An angle bisector
The interior bisector of an angle intersects the vertex and divides the angle into two equal parts.

side b of angle

bisector is halfway between sides a and b

name of angle

size of angle

vertex

First, draw an angle of any size. Label the vertex of this angle with a letter, for example, o.

arc crosses first side of angle at point a

point b is where the arc crosses second side of the angle

Draw an arc by placing the point of a compass on the vertex. Mark the points at which the arc intersects the angle's sides and label them a and b.

set compass to just over half distance it was in previous step

Place the compass on point a and draw an arc in the space between the angle's sides.

mark and label point c where two arcs cross

set compass at same length for arc a and arc b

Keep the compass set at the same length and place it on point b, and draw another arc, and then on point a. The two arcs intersect at a point, c.

line that joins vertex and point c is angle bisector

Draw a line from the vertex, o, through point c—this is the angle bisector. The angle is now split into two equal parts.

LOOKING CLOSER

Congruent triangles

Triangles are congruent if all their sides and interior angles are equal. The points that are marked when drawing an angle bisector create two congruent triangles —one above the bisector and one below.

▷ Constructing triangles
By connecting the points made after drawing a bisecting line through an angle, two congruent triangles are formed.

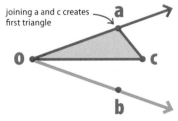

joining a and c creates first triangle

Draw a line from a to c, to make the first triangle, which is shaded red here.

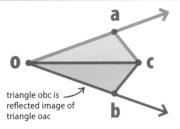

triangle obc is reflected image of triangle oac

Now, draw a line from b to c to construct the second triangle—shaded red here.

Constructing 90° and 45° angles

Bisecting an angle can be used to construct some common angles without using a protractor, for example a right angle (90°) and a 45° angle.

label end points of line

label points where arcs cross

Draw a straight line (AB). Place a compass on point A, set it to a distance just over half of the line's length, and draw an arc above and below the line.

draw arcs above and below line

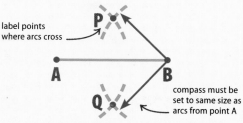

compass must be set to same size as arcs from point A

Then, draw two arcs with the compass set to the same length and placed on point B. Label the points where the arcs cross each other P and Q.

draw a line connecting P and Q

this creates a 90° angle

Draw a line from point P to point Q. This is a perpendicular bisector of the original line and it creates four 90° angles.

label the points the arc crosses

arc from o

Draw an arc from point o that crosses two lines on either side, this creates a 45° angle. Label the two points where the arc intersects the lines, f and e.

mark and label the intersecion of arcs

Keep the compass at the same length as the last arc and draw arcs from points f and e. Label the intersection of these arcs with a letter (s).

join o and S with a straight line

this creates a 45° angle

Draw a line from point o through s. This line is the angle bisector. The 90° angle is now split into two 45° angles.

Constructing 60° angles

An equilateral triangle, which has three equal sides and three 60° angles, can be constructed without a protractor.

label the line with letters

first line can be any length

Draw a line, which will form one arm of the first angle. Here the line is 2.5 cm long, but it can be any length. Mark each end of the line with a letter.

compass is set to length of first line

mark and label point where two arcs cross

Now, set the compass to the same length as the first line. Draw an arc from point A, then another from point B. Mark the point where the two arcs cross, C.

join A and C

angle is 60°

Now, draw a line to connect points A and C. Line AC is the same length as line AB. A 60° angle has been created.

Construct an equilateral triangle by drawing a third line from B to C. Each side of the triangle is equal and each internal angle of the triangle is 60°.

all internal angles are 60°

join C and B

Loci

A LOCUS (PLURAL LOCI) IS THE PATH FOLLOWED BY A POINT
THAT ADHERES TO A GIVEN RULE WHEN IT MOVES.

SEE ALSO

❮ **82–83** Tools in geometry
❮ **106–107** Scale drawings
❮ **110–113** Constructions

What is a locus?

Many familiar shapes, such as circles and straight lines, are examples of
loci because they are paths of points that conform to specific conditions.
Loci can also produce more complicated shapes. They are often used to
solve practical problems, for example pinpointing an exact location.

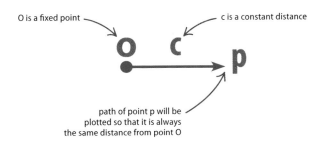

O is a fixed point

c is a constant distance

path of point p will be
plotted so that it is always
the same distance from point O

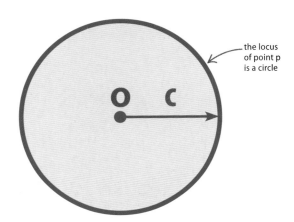

the locus
of point p
is a circle

A compass and a pencil are needed to construct this
locus. The point of the compass is held in the fixed point,
O. The arms of the compass are spread so that the
distance between its arms is the constant distance, c.

The shape drawn when turning the compass a full
rotation reveals that the locus is a circle. The center of
the circle is O, and the radius is the fixed distance
between the compass point and the pencil (c).

Working with loci

To draw a locus it is necessary to find all the points that conform to the rule
that has been specified. This will require a compass, a pencil, and a ruler. This
example shows how to find the locus of a point that moves so that its
distance from a fixed line AB is always the same.

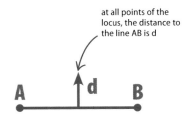

at all points of the
locus, the distance to
the line AB is d

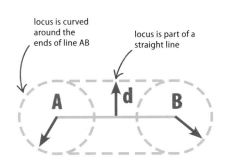

locus is curved
around the
ends of line AB

locus is part of a
straight line

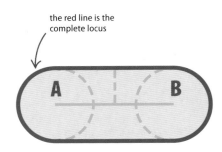

the red line is the
complete locus

Draw the line segment AB. A and B are
fixed points. Now, plot the distance of d
from the line AB.

Between points A and B, the locus is a straight
line. At the end of these lines, the locus is a
semicircle. Use a compass to draw these.

This is the completed locus.
It has the shape of a typical
athletics track.

Spiral locus

Loci can follow more complex paths. The example below follows the path of a piece of string that is wound around a cylinder, creating a spiral locus.

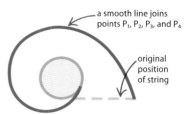

The string starts off lying flat, with point P_1 the position of the end of the string.

As the string is wound around the cylinder, the end of the string moves closer to the surface of the cylinder.

When the path of point P is plotted, it forms a spiral locus.

Using loci

Loci can be used to solve difficult problems. Suppose two radio stations, A and B, share the same frequency, but are 200 km apart. The range of their transmitters is 150 km. The area where the ranges of the two transmitters overlap, or interference, can be found by showing the locus of each transmitter and using a scale drawing (see pp.106–107).

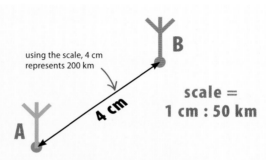

using the scale, 4 cm represents 200 km

scale =
1 cm : 50 km

To find the area of interference, first choose a scale, then draw the reach of each transmitter. An appropriate scale for this example is 1 cm : 50 km.

everyone inside, and on, the locus can receive station A

using the scale, 3 cm represents 150 km

this arc represents a section of the locus of all points that are 150 km away from transmitter A

this area is where the signals from the transmitters cross over

everyone inside, and on, the locus can receive station B

this arc is a section of the locus of all points that are 150 km from B

Construct the reception area for radio station A. Draw the locus of a point that is always 150 km from station A. The scale gives 150 km = 3 cm, so draw an arc with a radius of 3cm, with A as the center.

Construct the reception area for radio station B. This time draw an arc with the compass set to 3cm, with B as the center. The interference occurs in the area where the two paths overlap.

△ Triangles

A TRIANGLE IS A POLYGON WITH THREE ANGLES AND THREE SIDES.

A triangle has three sides and three interior angles. A vertex (plural vertices) is the point where two sides of a triangle meet. A triangle has three vertices.

Introducing triangles

A triangle is a three-sided polygon. The base of a triangle can be any one of its three sides, but it is usually the bottom one. The longest side of a triangle is opposite the largest angle. The shortest side of a triangle is opposite the smallest angle. The three interior angles of a triangle add up to 180°.

A

shortest side

longest side

▲ABC

B

biggest angle

smallest angle

C

△ **Labeling a triangle**
A capital letter is used to identify each vertex. A triangle with vertices A, B, and C is known as △ABC. The symbol "△" can be used to represent the word triangle.

vertex the point where two sides meet

perimeter the length of the outside frame

side one of three sides

angle the amount of turn between two straight lines about a fixed point

base side on which a triangle "rests"

Types of triangles

There are several types of triangles, each with specific features, or properties. A triangle is classified according to the length of its sides or the size of its angles.

equal sides are shown by a dash or double dash

◁ **Equilateral triangle**
A triangle with three equal sides and three equal angles, each of which measures 60°.

equal angles are shown as an arc or double arc

◁ **Isosceles triangle**
A triangle with two equal sides. The angles opposite these sides are also equal.

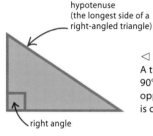

hypotenuse (the longest side of a right-angled triangle)

◁ **Right triangle**
A triangle with an angle of 90° (a right angle). The side opposite the right angle is called the hypotenuse.

right angle

angle more than 90°

◁ **Obtuse triangle**
A triangle with one angle that measures more than 90°.

all of the angles and sides are different

◁ **Scalene triangle**
A triangle with three sides of different length, and three angles of different size.

Interior angles of a triangle

A triangle has three interior angles at the points where each side meets. These angles always add up to 180°. If rearranged and placed together on a straight line, the interior angles would still add up to 180°, because a straight angle always measures 180°.

$$a + b + c = 180°$$

Proving that the angle sum of a triangle is 180°

Adding a parallel line produces two types of relationships between angles that help prove that the interior sum of a triangle is 180°.

Draw a triangle, then add a line parallel to one side of the triangle, starting at its base, to create two new angles.

▶ **Corresponding angles** are equal and alternate angles are equal; angles c, a, and b sit on a straight line so together add up to 180°.

parallel line

new angles

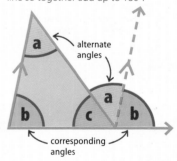

alternate angles

corresponding angles

Exterior angles of a triangle

In addition to having three interior angles a triangle also has three exterior angles. Exterior angles are found by extending each side of a triangle. The exterior angles of any triangle add up to 360°.

$$x + y + z = 360°$$

each exterior angle of a triangle is equal to the sum of the two opposite interior angles, so y = p + q

opposite interior angle (to y)

opposite interior angle (to y)

Constructing triangles

DRAWING (CONSTRUCTING) TRIANGLES REQUIRES A COMPASS,
A RULER, AND A PROTRACTOR.

SEE ALSO

‹ 82–83 Tools in geometry
‹ 110–113 Constructions
‹ 114–115 Loci

To construct a triangle, not all the measurements for its sides
and angles are required, as long as some of the measurements
are known in the right combination.

What is needed?

A triangle can be constructed from just a few of its measurements, using a
combination of the tools mentioned above, and its unknown measurements
can be found from the result. A triangle can be constructed when the
measurements of all three sides (SSS) are known, when two angles and the
side in between are known (ASA), or when two sides and the angle between
them are known (SAS). In addition, knowing either the SSS, the ASA, or the
SAS measurements of two triangles will reveal whether they are the same size
(congruent)—if the measurements are equal, the triangles are congruent.

REAL WORLD

Using triangles for 3-D graphics

3-D graphics are common in films, computer
games, and the internet. What may be surprising
is that they are created using triangles. An object is
drawn as a series of basic shapes, which are then
divided into triangles. When the shape of the
triangles is changed, the object appears to move.
Each triangle is colored to bring the object to life.

▷ **Computer animation**
To create movement, a
computer calculates the new
shape of millions of shapes.

Constructing a triangle when three sides are known (SSS)

If the measurements of the three sides are given, for example, **5 cm**, **4 cm**, and **3 cm**, it is
possible to construct a triangle using a ruler and a compass, following the steps below.

▷ **Draw the baseline,** using the longest length.
Label the ends A and B. Set the compass to the
second length, 4 cm. Place the point of the
compass on A and draw an arc.

place compass point here
set compass to 4 cm
draw an arc with compass set at 4 cm

▷ **Set the compass** to the third length,
3 cm. Place the point of the compass on B
and draw another arc. Mark the spot where
the arcs intersect (cross) as point C.

draw an arc with compass set at 3 cm
point where two arcs cross is third point of triangle
set compass to 3 cm
place point of compass here

▷ **Join the points** to complete the triangle. Now
use a protractor to find out the measurements
of the angles. These will add up to 180°
(90° + 53° + 37° = 180°).

use protractor to measure angles

Constructing a triangle when two angles and one side are known (AAS)

A triangle can be constructed when the two angles, for example, **73°** and **38°**, are given, along with the length of the side that falls between them, for example, **5 cm**.

draw line from A at 73° angle

73°

measure first given angle from baseline

5 cm

A   B

Draw the baseline of the triangle, here 5 cm. Label the ends A and B. Place the protractor over point A and measure the first angle, 73°. Draw a side of the triangle from A.

point where two lines cross is third point of triangle

C

measure second given angle from baseline

73°   **38°**

5 cm

A   B

Place the protractor over point B and mark 38°. Draw another side of the triangle from B. Point C is where the two new lines meet.

because interior angles of triangles add up to 180°, work out angle C by subtracting known angles from 180°:
180° – 73° – 38° = 69°

use ruler to measure sides

C

3.3 cm   **69°**   **5.1 cm**

73°   **38°**

5 cm

A   B

Join the points to complete the triangle. Calculate the unknown angle, and use a ruler to measure the two unknown sides.

Constructing a triangle when two sides and the angle in between are known (SAS)

Using the measurements for two of a triangle's sides, for example, **5 cm** and **4.5 cm**, and the angle between them, for example **50°**, it is possible to construct a triangle.

draw line at 50° from baseline

50°

measure given angle between two sides from baseline

5 cm

A   B

Draw the baseline, using the longest length. Label the ends A and B. Place the protractor over point A and mark 50°. Draw a line from A that runs through 50°. This line will be the next side of the triangle.

point C is where arc and line meet

C

4.5 cm

50°

5 cm

A   B

Set the compass to the second length, 4.5 cm. Place the compass on point A and draw an arc. Point C is found when the arc intersects the line through point A.

measure unknown side with ruler

measure unknown angles with protractor

C

71°   **4.5 cm**   **4 cm**

50°   **59°**

5 cm

A   B

Join the points to complete the triangle. Use a protractor to measure the unknown angles and a ruler to measure the length of the unknown side.

Congruent triangles

TRIANGLES THAT ARE EXACTLY THE SAME SHAPE AND SIZE.

SEE ALSO

❮ **98–99** Translations
❮ **100–101** Rotations
❮ **102–103** Reflections

Identical triangles

Two or more triangles are congruent if their sides are the same length and their corresponding interior angles are the same size. In addition to sides and angles, all other properties of congruent triangles are the same, for example, area. Like other shapes, congruent triangles can be translated, rotated, and reflected, so they may appear different, even though they remain the same size and have identical angles.

this angle is same size as angle with three arcs on ▲PQR

this angle is same size as angle with one arc on ▲ABC

this side is same length as side with three dashes on ▲PQR

this side is same length as side with two dashes on ▲PQR

▲PQR

▲ABC

this angle is same size as angle with two arcs on ▲PQR

ROTATION

reflecting an object creates a mirror image of it

REFLECTION

△ **Congruent triangles**
The triangle on the right is how the triangle on the left would appear if rotated clockwise through 180° and reflected.

this side is same length as side with one dash on ▲PQR

How to tell if triangles are congruent

It is possible to tell if two triangles are congruent without knowing the lengths of all of the sides or the sizes of all of the angles—knowing just three measurements will do. There are four groups of measurements.

▷ **Side, side, side (SSS)**
When all three sides of a triangle are the same as the corresponding three sides of another triangle, the two triangles are congruent.

▷ **Angle, angle, side (AAS)**
When two angles and any one side of a triangle are equal to two angles and the corresponding side of another triangle, the two triangles are congruent.

▷ **Side, angle, side (SAS)**
When two sides and the angle between them (called the included angle) of a triangle are equal to two sides and the included angle of another triangle, the two triangles are congruent.

▷ **Right angle, hypotenuse, side (RHS)**
When the hypotenuse and one other side of a right triangle are equal to the hypotenuse and one side of another right triangle, the two triangles are congruent.

Proving an isosceles triangle has two equal angles

An isosceles triangle has two equal sides. Drawing a perpendicular line helps prove that it has two equal angles too.

line through point B is perpendicular (at right angles) to line AC

equal sides

right angle

right angle

congruent triangles

Draw a line perpendicular (at right angles) to the base of an isosceles triangle. This creates two new right triangles. They are congruent—identical in every way.

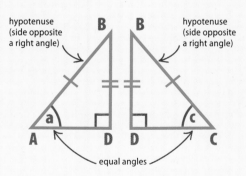

hypotenuse (side opposite a right angle)

hypotenuse (side opposite a right angle)

equal angles

The perpendicular line is common to both triangles. The two triangles have equal hypotenuses, another pair of equal sides, and right angles. The triangles are congruent (RHS) so angles "a" and "c" are equal.

Area of a triangle

AREA IS THE COMPLETE SPACE INSIDE A TRIANGLE.

SEE ALSO
⟨ **116–117** Triangles
Area of a circle **142–143** ⟩
Formulas **177–179** ⟩

What is area?

The area of a shape is the amount of space that fits inside its outline, or perimeter. It is measured in squared units, such as cm². If the length of the base and vertical height of a triangle are known, these values can be used to find the area of the triangle, using a simple formula, which is shown below.

$$\text{area} = \frac{1}{2} \times \text{base} \times \text{vertical height}$$

this is the formula for finding the area of a triangle

area is the space inside a triangle's frame

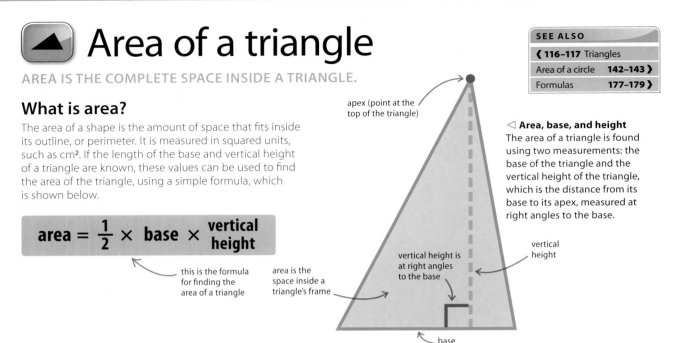

apex (point at the top of the triangle)

◁ **Area, base, and height**
The area of a triangle is found using two measurements: the base of the triangle and the vertical height of the triangle, which is the distance from its base to its apex, measured at right angles to the base.

vertical height is at right angles to the base

vertical height

base

Base and vertical height

Finding the area of a triangle requires two measurements, the base and the vertical height. The side on which a triangle "sits" is called the base. The vertical height is a line formed at right angles to the base from the apex. Any one of the three sides of a triangle can act as the base in the area formula.

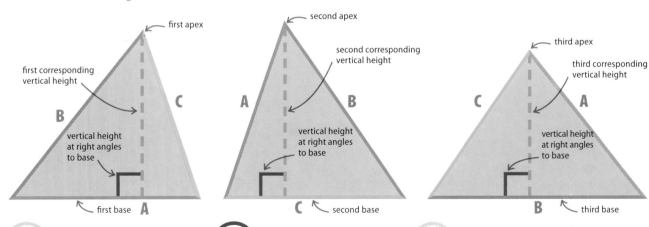

first apex

first corresponding vertical height

B

C

vertical height at right angles to base

first base A

second apex

second corresponding vertical height

A

B

vertical height at right angles to base

C second base

third apex

third corresponding vertical height

C A

vertical height at right angles to base

B third base

△ **First base**
The area of the triangle can be found using the orange side (A) as the "base" needed for the formula. The corresponding vertical height is the distance from the base of the triangle to its apex (highest point).

△ **Second base**
Any one of the triangle's three sides can act as its base. Here the triangle is rotated so that the green side (C) is its base. The corresponding vertical height is the distance from the base to the apex.

△ **Third base**
The triangle is rotated again, so that the purple side (B) is its base. The corresponding vertical height is the distance from the base to the apex. The area of the triangle is the same, whichever side is used as the base in the formula.

Finding the area of a triangle

To calculate the area of a triangle, substitute the given values for the base and vertical height into the formula. Then work through the multiplication shown by the formula (½ × base × vertical height).

Why the formula works

By adjusting the shape of a triangle, it can be converted into a rectangle. This process makes the formula for a triangle easier to understand.

Draw any triangle and label its base and vertical height.

▷ **An acute-angled triangle**
The base of this triangle is 6 cm and its vertical height is 3 cm. Find the area of the triangle using the formula.

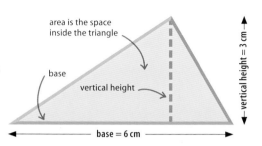

area is the space inside the triangle

base

vertical height

vertical height = 3 cm

base = 6 cm

First, write down the formula for the area of a triangle.

$$\text{area} = \frac{1}{2} \times \text{base} \times \text{vertical height}$$

Then, substitute the lengths that are known into the formula.

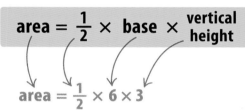

$$\text{area} = \frac{1}{2} \times 6 \times 3$$

Work through the multiplication in the formula to find the answer. In this example, ½ × 6 × 3 = 9. Add the units of area to the answer, here cm².

area is measured in squared units

$$\text{area} = 9 \text{ cm}^2$$

line through the midpoint of vertical height

base

Draw a line through the midpoint of the vertical height that is parallel to the base.

vertical height can be measured outside the triangle as long as it is the distance between the base and the apex

area is the space inside the triangle

▷ **An obtuse triangle**
The base of this triangle is 3 cm and its vertical height is 4 cm. Find the area of the triangle using the formula. The formula and the steps are the same for all types of triangles.

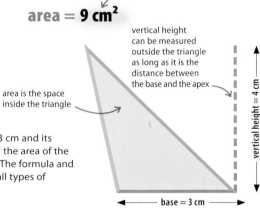

vertical height = 4 cm

base = 3 cm

base

This creates two new triangles. These can be rotated around the triangle to form a rectangle. This has exactly the same area as the original triangle.

First, write down the formula for the area of a triangle.

$$\text{area} = \frac{1}{2} \times \text{base} \times \text{vertical height}$$

Then, substitute the lengths that are known into the formula.

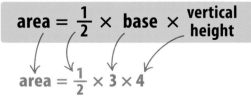

$$\text{area} = \frac{1}{2} \times 3 \times 4$$

Work through the multiplication to find the answer, and add the appropriate units of area.

½ × 3 × 4 = 6

area is measured in squared units

$$\text{area} = 6 \text{ cm}^2$$

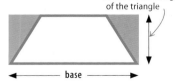

½ the vertical height of the triangle

base

The original triangle's area is found using the formula for the area of a rectangle (b × h). Both shapes have the same base; the rectangle's height is ½ the height of the triangle. This gives the area of the triangle formula: ½ × base × vertical height.

Finding the base of a triangle using the area and height

The formula for the area of a triangle can also be used to find the length of the base, if the area and height are known. Given the area and height of the triangle, the formula needs to be rearranged to find the length of the triangle's base.

First, write down the formula for the area of a triangle. The formula states that the area of a triangle is equal to ½ multiplied by the length of the base, multiplied by the height.

▼

Substitute the known values into the formula. Here the values of the area (12cm²) and the height (3cm) are known.

▼

Simplify the formula as far as possible, by multiplying the ½ by the height. This answer is 1.5.

▼

Make the base the subject of the formula by rearranging it. In this example both sides are divided by 1.5.

▼

Work out the final answer by dividing 12 (area) by 1.5. In this example, the answer is 8cm.

Finding the vertical height of a triangle using the area and base

The formula for area of a triangle can also be used to find its height, if the area and base are known. Given the area and the length of the base of the triangle, the formula needs to be rearranged to find the height of the triangle.

First, write down the formula. This shows that the area of a triangle equals ½ multiplied by its base, multiplied by its height.

▼

Substitute the known values into the formula. Here the values of the area (8cm²) and the base (4cm) are known.

▼

Simplify the equation as far as possible, by multiplying the ½ by the base. In this example, the answer is 2.

▼

Make the height the subject of the formula by rearranging it. In this example both sides are divided by 2.

▼

Work out the final answer by dividing 8 (the area) by 2 (½ the base). In this example the answer is 4cm.

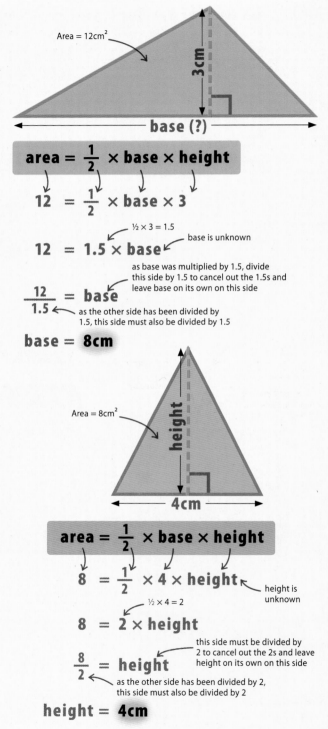

Area = 12cm²

3cm

base (?)

$$\text{area} = \frac{1}{2} \times \text{base} \times \text{height}$$

$$12 = \frac{1}{2} \times \text{base} \times 3$$

½ × 3 = 1.5
base is unknown

$$12 = 1.5 \times \text{base}$$

as base was multiplied by 1.5, divide this side by 1.5 to cancel out the 1.5s and leave base on its own on this side

$$\frac{12}{1.5} = \text{base}$$

as the other side has been divided by 1.5, this side must also be divided by 1.5

base = **8cm**

Area = 8cm²

height

4cm

$$\text{area} = \frac{1}{2} \times \text{base} \times \text{height}$$

$$8 = \frac{1}{2} \times 4 \times \text{height}$$

height is unknown

½ × 4 = 2

$$8 = 2 \times \text{height}$$

this side must be divided by 2 to cancel out the 2s and leave height on its own on this side

$$\frac{8}{2} = \text{height}$$

as the other side has been divided by 2, this side must also be divided by 2

height = **4cm**

Similar triangles

TWO TRIANGLES THAT ARE EXACTLY THE SAME SHAPE BUT NOT
THE SAME SIZE ARE CALLED SIMILAR TRIANGLES.

SEE ALSO

❮ **56–59** Ratio and proportion
❮ **104–105** Enlargements
❮ **116–117** Triangles

What are similar triangles?

Similar triangles are made by making bigger or smaller copies of a triangle—a transformation known as enlargement. Each of the triangles have equal corresponding angles, and corresponding sides that are in proportion to one another, for example each side of triangle ABC below is twice the length of each side on triangle $A_2B_2C_2$. There are four different ways to check if a pair of triangles are similar (see p.126), and if two triangles are known to be similar, their properties can be used to find the lengths of missing sides.

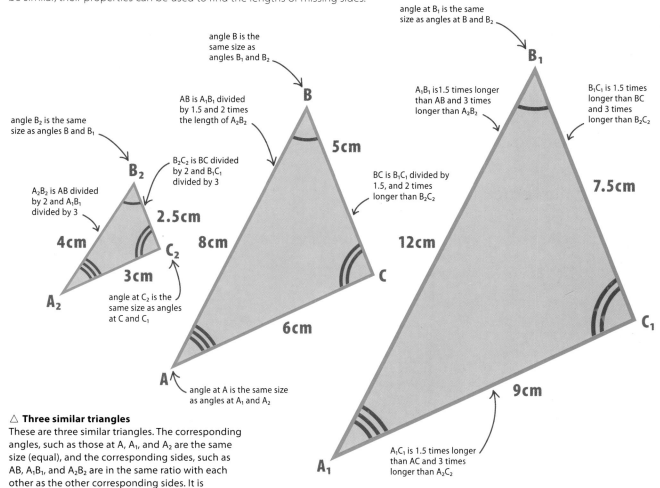

angle at B_1 is the same size as angles at B and B_2

angle B is the same size as angles B_1 and B_2

A_1B_1 is1.5 times longer than AB and 3 times longer than A_2B_2

B_1C_1 is 1.5 times longer than BC and 3 times longer than B_2C_2

AB is A_1B_1 divided by 1.5 and 2 times the length of A_2B_2

5cm

angle B_2 is the same size as angles B and B_1

B_2C_2 is BC divided by 2 and B_1C_1 divided by 3

BC is B_1C_1 divided by 1.5, and 2 times longer than B_2C_2

7.5cm

A_2B_2 is AB divided by 2 and A_1B_1 divided by 3

2.5cm

4cm

3cm

8cm

12cm

angle at C_2 is the same size as angles at C and C_1

6cm

9cm

angle at A is the same size as angles at A_1 and A_2

A_1C_1 is 1.5 times longer than AC and 3 times longer than A_2C_2

△ **Three similar triangles**
These are three similar triangles. The corresponding angles, such as those at A, A_1, and A_2 are the same size (equal), and the corresponding sides, such as AB, A_1B_1, and A_2B_2 are in the same ratio with each other as the other corresponding sides. It is possible to check this by dividing each side of one triangle by the corresponding side of another triangle – if the answers are all equal, the sides are in proportion to each other.

WHEN ARE TWO TRIANGLES SIMILAR?

It is possible to see if two triangles are similar without measuring every angle and every side. This can be done by looking at the following corresponding measurements for both triangles: two angles, all three sides, a pair of sides with an angle between them, or if the triangles are right triangles, the hypotenuse and another side.

Angle, angle AA

When two angles of one triangle are equal to two angles of another triangle then all the corresponding angles are equal in pairs, so the two triangles are similar.

$$U = U_1$$
$$V = V_1$$

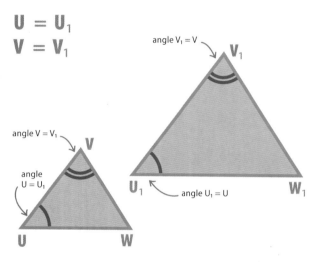

angle $V_1 = V$

angle $V = V_1$

angle $U = U_1$

angle $U_1 = U$

Side, angle, side (S) A (S)

When two triangles have two pairs of corresponding sides that are in the same ratio and the angles between these two sides are equal, the two triangles are similar.

$$\frac{PR}{P_1R_1} = \frac{PQ}{P_1Q_1} \quad \text{and} \quad P = P_1$$

PQ is in proportion with P_1Q_1

P_1Q_1 is in proportion with PQ

angle at $P = P_1$

PR is in proportion with P_1R_1

angle at $P_1 = P$

P_1R_1 is in proportion with PR

Side, side, side (S) (S) (S)

When two triangles have three pairs of corresponding sides that are in the same ratio, then the two triangles are similar.

$$\frac{AB}{A_1B_1} = \frac{AC}{A_1C_1} = \frac{BC}{B_1C_1}$$

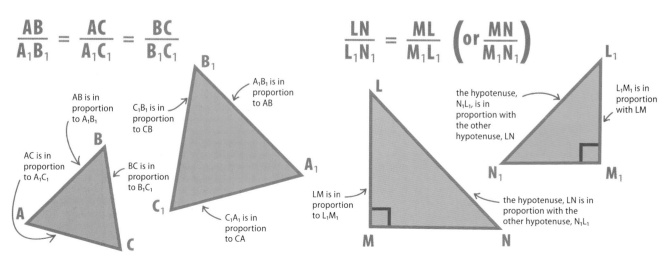

AB is in proportion to A_1B_1

C_1B_1 is in proportion to CB

A_1B_1 is in proportion to AB

AC is in proportion to A_1C_1

BC is in proportion to B_1C_1

C_1A_1 is in proportion to CA

Right-angle, hypotenuse, side R (H) (S)

If the ratio between the hypotenuses of two right triangles is the same as the ratio between another pair of corresponding sides, then the two triangles are similar.

$$\frac{LN}{L_1N_1} = \frac{ML}{M_1L_1} \left(\text{or} \frac{MN}{M_1N_1} \right)$$

the hypotenuse, N_1L_1, is in proportion with the other hypotenuse, LN

L_1M_1 is in proportion with LM

LM is in proportion to L_1M_1

the hypotenuse, LN is in proportion with the other hypotenuse, N_1L_1

MISSING SIDES IN SIMILAR TRIANGLES

The proportional relationships between the sides of similar triangles can be used to find the value of sides that are missing, if the lengths of some of the sides are known.

▷ **Similar triangles**
Triangles ABC and ADE are similar (AA). The missing values of AD and BC can be found using the ratios between the known sides.

Finding the length of BC

To find the length of BC, use the ratio between BC and its corresponding side DE, and the ratio between a pair of sides where both the lengths are known – AE and AC.

Write out the ratios between the two pairs of sides, each with the longer side above the shorter side. These ratios are equal.

$$\frac{DE}{BC} = \frac{AE}{AC}$$

Substitute the values that are known into the ratios. The numbers can now be rearranged to find the length of BC.

$$\frac{3}{BC} = \frac{4.5}{2.5}$$

Finding the length of AD

To find the length of AD, use the ratio between AD and its corresponding side AB, and the ratio between a pair of sides where both the lengths are known – AE and AC.

Write out the ratios between the two pairs of sides, each with the longer side above the shorter side. These ratios are equal.

$$\frac{AD}{AB} = \frac{AE}{AC}$$

Substitute the values that are known into the ratios. The numbers can now be rearranged to find the length of AD.

AD is the unknown

$$\frac{AD}{3} = \frac{4.5}{2.5}$$

Rearrange the equation to isolate AD. In this example this is done by multiplying both sides of the equation by 3.

multiply both sides by 3

$$AD = 3 \times \frac{4.5}{2.5}$$

multiply by 3 to isolate AD

Rearrange the equation to isolate BC. This may take more than one step. First multiply both sides of the equation by BC.

multiply both sides by BC   multiply both sides by BC

$$3 = \frac{4.5}{2.5} \times BC$$

Then rearrange the equation again. This time multiply both sides of the equation by 2.5.

multiply both sides by 2.5

$$3 \times 2.5 = 4.5 \times BC$$

multiply both sides by 2.5

BC can now be isolated by rearranging the equation one more time – divide both sides of the equation by 4.5.

divide both sides by 4.5

$$BC = \frac{3 \times 2.5}{4.5}$$

divide both sides by 4.5

Do the multiplication to find the answer, and add the units to the answer that has been found. This is the length of AD.

$$AD = \mathbf{5.4cm}$$

Do the multiplication to find the answer, add the units, and round to a sensible number of decimal places.

1.6666.... is rounded to 2 decimal places

$$BC = \mathbf{1.67cm}$$

Pythagorean Theorem

THE PYTHAGOREAN THEOREM IS USED TO FIND THE LENGTH OF
MISSING SIDES IN RIGHT TRIANGLES.

If the lengths of two sides of a right triangle are known, the length
of the third side can be worked out using **Pythagorean Theorem.**

What is the Pythagorean Theorem?

The basic principle of the Pythagorean Theorem is
that squaring the two smaller sides of a right
triangle (multiplying each side by itself) and
adding the results will equal the square of the
longest side. The idea of "squaring" each side can
be shown literally. On the right, a square on each
side shows how the biggest square has the same
area as the other two squares put together.

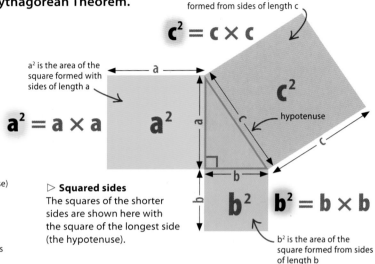

c^2 is the area of the square
formed from sides of length c

$$c^2 = c \times c$$

a^2 is the area of the
square formed with
sides of length a

$$a^2 = a \times a$$

hypotenuse

$$b^2 = b \times b$$

b^2 is the area of the
square formed from sides
of length b

▷ **Squared sides**
The squares of the shorter
sides are shown here with
the square of the longest side
(the hypotenuse).

side a   side b   side c (hypotenuse)

$$a^2 + b^2 = c^2$$

formula shows that side a squared plus
side b squared equals side c squared

If the formula is used with values substituted for the sides a, b, and c, the
Pythagorean Theorem can be shown to be true. Here the length of c
(the hypotenuse) is 5, while the lengths of a and b are 4 and 3.

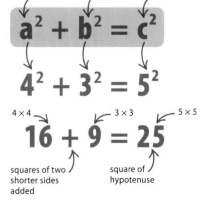

a is 4   b is 3   c is 5

$$a^2 + b^2 = c^2$$

$$4^2 + 3^2 = 5^2$$

4 × 4   3 × 3   5 × 5

$$16 + 9 = 25$$

squares of two
shorter sides
added

square of
hypotenuse

△ **Pythagoras in action**
In the equation the squares of the two
shorter sides (4 and 3) added together
equal the square of the hypotenuse
(5), proving that the Pythagorean
Theorem works.

each side of square
is 4 cm long

4 cm

16 cm²

4 cm

5 cm

25 cm²

5 cm

each side of square
is 5 cm long

area of larger
square is 5^2 (or
5 × 5), which is
25 smaller squares

3 cm

3 cm

9 cm²

each side of square
is 3 cm long

area of larger square
is 4^2 (or 4 × 4), which
is 16 smaller squares

area of larger square is 3^2
(or 3 × 3), which is 9
smaller squares

Find the value of the hypotenuse

The Pythagorean Theorem can be used to find the value of the length of the longest side (the hypotenuse) in a right triangle when the lengths of the two shorter sides are known. This example shows how this works, if the two known sides are 3.5 cm and 7.2 cm in length.

7.2 cm

3.5 cm

c (hypotenuse)

missing side length

$$a^2 + b^2 = c^2$$

First, take the formula for the Pythagorean Theorem.

one side · · · other side · · · hypotenuse missing

$$3.5^2 + 7.2^2 = c^2$$

Substitute the values given into the formula, in this example, 3.5 and 7.2.

3.5 × 3.5 equals · · · 7.2 × 7.2 equals

$$12.25 + 51.84 = c^2$$

Calculate the squares of each of the triangle's known sides by multiplying them.

12.25 + 51.84 equals

$$64.09 = c^2$$

Add these answers together to find the square of the hypotenuse.

sign means square root

$$\sqrt{64.09} = \sqrt{c^2}$$

the square root of 64.09 is the same as the square root of c^2

Use a calculator to find the square root of 64.09. This gives the length of side c.

The square root is the length of the hypotenuse.

answer rounded to the hundredths place

$$c = \mathbf{8.01\ cm}$$

Find the value of another side

The theorem can be rearranged to find the length of either of the two sides of a right triangle that are not the hypotenuse. The length of the hypotenuse and one other side must be known. This example shows how this works with a side of 5 cm and a hypotenuse of 13 cm.

this side is known

5 cm

b

missing side length

this side is known

13 cm (hypotenuse)

$$a^2 + b^2 = c^2$$

To calculate the length of side b, take the formula for the Pythagorean Theorem.

known side · · · hypotenuse

$$5^2 + b^2 = 13^2$$

unknown side

Substitute the values given into the formula. In this example, 5 and 13.

unknown side is now result of equation

$$13^2 - 5^2 = b^2$$

hypotenuse now at start of formula

Rearrange the equation by subtracting 5^2 from each side. This isolates b^2 on one side because $5^2 - 5^2$ cancels out.

$$169 - 25 = b^2$$

13 × 13 equals · · · 5 × 5 equals

Calculate the squares of the two known sides of the triangle.

$$144 = b^2$$

Subtract these squares to find the square of the unknown side.

sign means square root

$$\sqrt{144} = \sqrt{b^2}$$

the square root of 144 is the same as the square root of b^2

Find the square root of 144 for the length of the unknown side.

The square root is the length of side b.

length of missing side

$$b = \mathbf{12\ cm}$$

Quadrilaterals

A QUADRILATERAL IS A FOUR-SIDED POLYGON.
"QUAD" MEANS FOUR AND "LATERAL" MEANS SIDE.

SEE ALSO
❮ 84–85 Angles
❮ 86–87 Straight lines
Polygons   134–137 ❯

Introducing quadrilaterals

A quadrilateral is a two-dimensional shape with four straight sides, four vertices (points where the sides meet), and four interior angles. The interior angles of a quadrilateral always add up to 360°. An exterior angle and its corresponding interior angle always add up to 180° because they form a straight line. There are several types of quadrilaterals, each with different properties.

vertex, one of four vertices

one of four sides

diagonal

one of four interior angles

interior angle

line extends to form exterior angle

interior and exterior angle add up to 180°

△ **Interior angles**
If a single diagonal line is drawn from any one corner to the opposite corner, the quadrilateral is divided into two triangles. The sum of the interior angles of any triangle is 180°, so the sum of the interior angles of a quadrilateral is 2 × 180°.

▽ **Types of quadrilaterals**
Each type of quadrilateral is grouped and named according to its properties. There are regular and irregular quadrilaterals. A regular quadrilateral has equal sides and angles, whereas an irregular quadrilateral has sides and angles of different sizes.

START

? Are all the interior angles right angles?
| YES | NO |

? Are all the sides the same length?
| YES | NO |

? Are the opposite angles equal?
| YES | NO |

? Are two of the sides parallel?
| YES | NO |

? Are all the sides the same length?
| YES | NO |

? Are there adjacent sides of the same length?
| YES | NO |

SQUARE   RECTANGLE   RHOMBUS   PARALLELOGRAM   TRAPEZOID   KITE   IRREGULAR

PROPERTIES OF QUADRILATERALS

Each type of quadrilateral has its own name and a number of unique properties. Knowing just some of the properties of a shape can help distinguish one type of quadrilateral from another. Six of the more common quadrilaterals are shown below with their respective properties.

Square

A square has four equal angles (right angles) and four sides of equal length. The opposite sides of a square are parallel. The diagonals bisect—cut into two equal parts—each other at 90° (right angles).

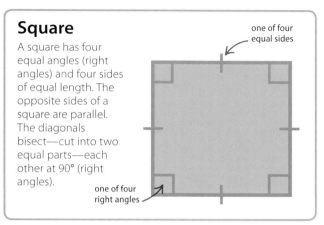

one of four equal sides

one of four right angles

Rectangle

A rectangle has four right angles and two pairs of opposite sides of equal length. Adjacent sides are not of equal length. The opposite sides are parallel and the diagonals bisect each other.

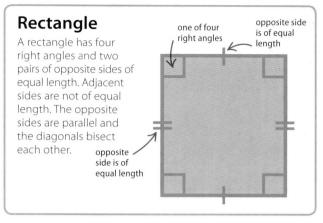

one of four right angles

opposite side is of equal length

opposite side is of equal length

Rhombus

All sides of a rhombus are of equal length. The opposite angles are equal and the opposite sides are parallel. The diagonals bisect each other at right angles.

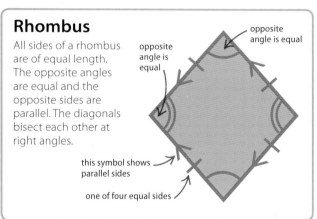

opposite angle is equal

opposite angle is equal

this symbol shows parallel sides

one of four equal sides

Parallelogram

The opposite sides of a parallelogram are parallel and are of equal length. Adjacent sides are not of equal length. The opposite angles are equal and the diagonals bisect each other in the center of the shape.

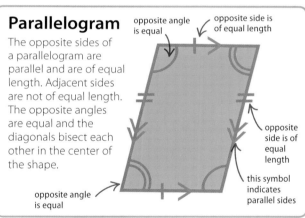

opposite angle is equal

opposite side is of equal length

opposite side is of equal length

this symbol indicates parallel sides

opposite angle is equal

Trapezoid

A trapezoid, also known as a trapezium, has one pair of opposite sides that are parallel. These sides are not equal in length.

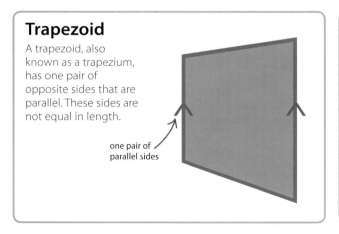

one pair of parallel sides

Kite

A kite has two pairs of adjacent sides that are equal in length. Opposite sides are not of equal length. It has one pair of opposite angles that are equal and another pair of angles of different values.

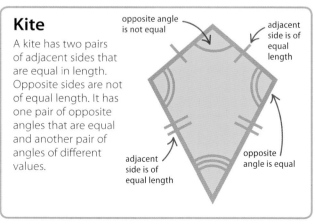

opposite angle is not equal

adjacent side is of equal length

adjacent side is of equal length

opposite angle is equal

FINDING THE AREA OF QUADRILATERALS

Area is the space inside the frame of a two-dimensional shape. Area is measured in square units, for example, cm². Formulas are used to calculate the areas of many types of shapes. Each type of quadrilateral has a unique formula for calculating its area.

Finding the area of a square

The area of a square is found by multiplying its length by its width. Because its length and width are equal in size, the formula is the square of a side.

one of four right angles

one of four equal sides

side

side = 5.2 cm

5.2 cm

this means side × side

$$area = side^2$$

units of area, square centimeters

$$5.2 \times 5.2 = 27.04 \ cm^2$$

△ **Multiply sides**
In this example, each of the four sides measures 5.2 cm. To find the area of this square, multiply 5.2 by 5.2.

Finding the area of a rectangle

The area of a rectangle is found by multiplying its base by its height.

this side is the same length as the side opposite

one of four right angles

height = 26 m

this side is the same length as the side opposite

base = 35 m

formula can also be written length × width (l × w)

$$area = base \times height$$

units of area, square meters

$$35 \times 26 = 910 \ m^2$$

△ **Multiply base by height**
The height (or width) of this rectangle is 26 m, and its base (or length) measures 35 m. Multiply these two measurements together to find the area.

Finding the area of a rhombus

The area of a rhombus is found by multiplying the length of its base by its vertical height. The vertical height, also known as the perpendicular height, is the vertical distance from the top (vertex) of a shape to the base opposite. The vertical height is at right angles to the base.

▷ **Vertical height**
Finding the area of a rhombus depends on knowing its vertical height. In this example, the vertical height measures 8 cm and its base is 9 cm.

vertical height = 8 cm

B   C

one of four equal sides

A   D

base = 9 cm

formula can also be written area = bh

$$area = base \times vertical \ height$$

$$9 \times 8 = 72 \ cm^2$$

Finding the area of a parallelogram

Like the area of a rhombus, the area of a parallelogram is found by multiplying the length of its base by its vertical height.

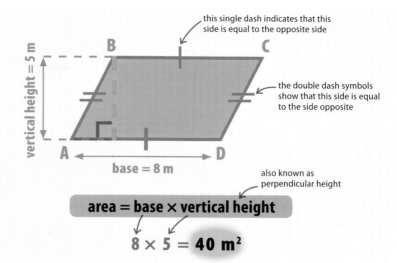

this single dash indicates that this side is equal to the opposite side

the double dash symbols show that this side is equal to the side opposite

vertical height = 5 m

base = 8 m

also known as perpendicular height

▷ **Multiply base by vertical height**
It is important to remember that the slanted side, AB, is not the vertical height. This formula only works if the vertical height is used.

$$\text{area} = \text{base} \times \text{vertical height}$$

$$8 \times 5 = 40 \text{ m}^2$$

Proving the opposite angles of a rhombus are equal

Creating two pairs of isosceles triangles by dividing a rhombus along two diagonals helps prove that the opposite angles of a rhombus are equal. An isosceles triangle has two equal sides and two equal angles.

one of four equal sides

angle U is equal to angle W

angle W is equal to angle U

angle X is equal to angle V

angle V is equal to angle X

All the sides of a rhombus are equal in length. To show this a dash is used on each side.

Divide the rhombus along a diagonal to create two isosceles triangles. Each triangle has a pair of equal angles.

Dividing along the other diagonal creates another pair of isosceles triangles.

Proving the opposite sides of a parallelogram are parallel

Creating a pair of congruent triangles by dividing a parallelogram along two diagonals helps prove that the opposite sides of a parallelogram are parallel. Congruent triangles are the same size and shape.

opposite side is equal

opposite side is equal

angle BCA is equal to angle CAD

congruent triangle

angle BAC is equal to angle ACD

congruent triangle

one of two pairs of parallel sides

Opposites sides of a parallelogram are equal in length. To show this a dash and a double dash are used.

The triangles ABC and ADC are congruent. Angle BCA = CAD, and because these are alternate angles, BC is parallel to AD.

The triangles are congruent, so angle BAC = ACD; because these are alternate angles, DC is parallel to AB.

Polygons

A CLOSED TWO-DIMENSIONAL SHAPE OF THREE OR MORE SIDES.

Polygons range from simple three-sided triangles and four-sided squares to more complicated shapes such as trapezoids and dodecagons. Polygons are named according to the number of sides and angles they have.

What is a polygon?

A polygon is a closed two-dimensional shape formed by straight lines that connect end to end at a point called a vertex. The interior angles of a polygon are usually smaller than the exterior angles, although the reverse is possible. Polygons with an interior angle of more than 180° are called concave.

▷ **Parts of a polygon**
Regardless of shape, all polygons are made up of the same parts—sides, vertices (connecting points), and interior and exterior angles.

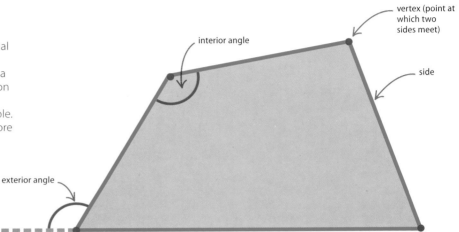

vertex (point at which two sides meet)

interior angle

side

exterior angle

Describing polygons

There are several ways to describe polygons. One is by the regularity or irregularity of their sides and angles. A polygon is regular when all of its sides and angles are equal. An irregular polygon has at least two sides or two angles that are different.

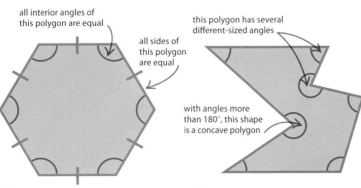

all interior angles of this polygon are equal

all sides of this polygon are equal

this polygon has several different-sized angles

with angles more than 180°, this shape is a concave polygon

△ **Regular**
All the sides and all the angles of regular polygons are equal. This hexagon has six equal sides and six equal angles, making it regular.

△ **Irregular**
In an irregular polygon, all the sides and angles are not the same. This heptagon has many different-sized angles, making it irregular.

LOOKING CLOSER

Equal angles or equal sides?

All the angles and all the sides of a regular polygon are equal—in other words, the polygon is both equiangular and equilateral. In certain polygons, only the angles (equiangular) or only the sides (equilateral) are equal.

◁ **Equiangular**
A rectangle is an equiangular quadrilateral. Its angles are all equal, but not all its sides are equal.

all angles the same

◁ **Equilateral**
A rhombus is an equilateral quadrilateral. All its sides are equal, but all its angles are not.

all sides the same

Naming polygons

Regardless of whether a polygon is regular or irregular, the number of sides it has always equals the number of its angles. This number is used in naming both kinds of polygons. For example, a polygon with six sides and angles is called a hexagon because "hex" is the prefix used to mean six. If all of its sides and angles are equal, it is known as a regular hexagon; if not, it is called an irregular hexagon.

Triangle
3
Sides and angles

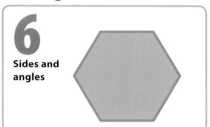

Quadrilateral
4
Sides and angles

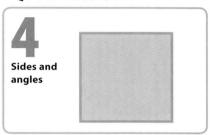

Pentagon
5
Sides and angles

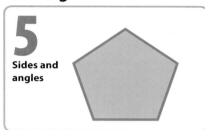

Hexagon
6
Sides and angles

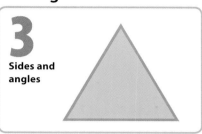

Heptagon
7
Sides and angles

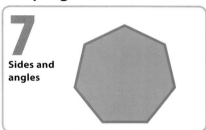

Octagon
8
Sides and angles

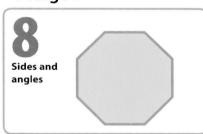

Nonagon
9
Sides and angles

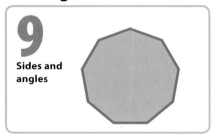

Decagon
10
Sides and angles

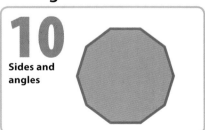

Hendecagon
11
Sides and angles

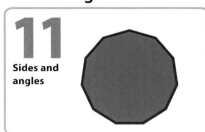

Dodecagon
12
Sides and angles

Pentadecagon
15
Sides and angles

Icosagon
20
Sides and angles

PROPERTIES OF A POLYGON

There are an unlimited number of different polygons that can be drawn using straight lines. However, they all share some important properties.

Convex or concave

Regardless of how many angles a polygon has, it can be classified as either concave or convex. This difference is based on whether a polygon's interior angles are over 180° or not. A convex polygon can be easily identified because at least one its angles is over 180°.

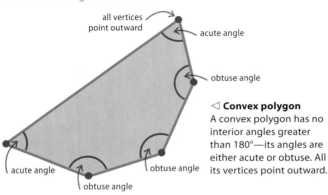

all vertices point outward

acute angle

obtuse angle

acute angle

obtuse angle

obtuse angle

◁ **Convex polygon**
A convex polygon has no interior angles greater than 180°—its angles are either acute or obtuse. All its vertices point outward.

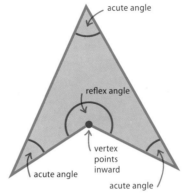

acute angle

reflex angle

vertex points inward

acute angle

acute angle

◁ **Concave polygon**
At least one angle of a concave polygon is over 180°. This type of angle is known as a reflex angle. The vertex of the reflex angle points inward, toward the center of the shape.

Interior angle sum of polygons

The sum of the interior angles of both regular and irregular convex polygon depends on the number of sides the polygon has. The sum of the angles can be worked out by dividing the polygon into triangles.

convex quadrilateral

diagonal splits shape into two triangles

This quadrilateral is convex—all of its angles are smaller than 180°. The sum of its interior angles can be found easily, by breaking the shape down into triangles. This can be done by drawing in a diagonal line that connects two vertices that are not next to one another.

interior angles of triangle 1 add up to 180°

interior angles of triangle 2 add up to 180°

1

2

▷ **A quadrilateral can be split** into two triangles. The sum of the angles of each triangle is 180°, so the sum of the angles of the quadrilateral is the sum of the angles of the two triangles added together: 2 × 180° = 360°.

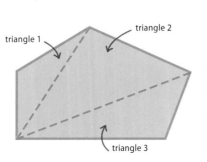

triangle 1

triangle 2

triangle 3

◁ **Irregular pentagon**
This pentagon can be split up into three triangles. The sum of its interior angles is the sum of the angles of the three triangles: 3 × 180° = 540°.

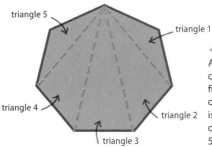

triangle 5

triangle 1

triangle 4

triangle 2

triangle 3

◁ **Regular heptagon**
A heptagon (7 sides) can be split up into five triangles. The sum of its interior angles is the sum of the angles of the five triangles: 5 × 180° = 900°.

A formula for the interior angle sum

The number of triangles a convex polygon can be split up into is always 2 fewer than the number of its sides. This means that a formula can be used to find the sum of the interior angles of any convex polygon.

$$\text{Sum of interior angles} = (n - 2) \times 180°$$

5 sides

number of sides

$$(5 - 2) \times 180°$$
$$= 540°$$

sum of its interior angles

each angle is 108°

◁ **Regular pentagon**
The interior angles of a regular pentagon add up to 540°. Because a regular polygon has equal angles and sides, each angle can be found by dividing by the number of angles: 540° ÷ 5 = 108°.

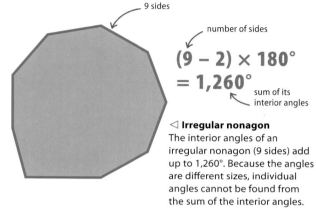

9 sides

number of sides

$$(9 - 2) \times 180°$$
$$= 1,260°$$

sum of its interior angles

◁ **Irregular nonagon**
The interior angles of an irregular nonagon (9 sides) add up to 1,260°. Because the angles are different sizes, individual angles cannot be found from the sum of the interior angles.

Sum of exterior angles of a polygon

Imagine walking along the exterior of a polygon. Start at one vertex, and facing the next, walk toward it. At the next vertex, turn the number of degrees of the exterior angle until facing the following vertex, and repeat until you have been around all the vertices. In walking around the polygon, you will have turned a complete circle, or 360°. The exterior angles of any polygon always add up to 360°.

exterior angles add up to 360° (60 × 6 = 360)

each sector is an equilateral triangle

center

central angles of equilateral triangles are equal to exterior angles

the exterior angles add up to 360° (58 + 57 + 90 + 70 + 85 = 360)

the exterior angles of an irregular polygon are not all the same

△ **Irregular pentagon**
The exterior angles of a polygon, regardless of whether it is regular or irregular add up to 360°. Another way to think about this is that, added together, the exterior angles of a polygon would form a complete circle.

△ **Regular hexagon**
The size of the exterior angles of a regular polygon can be found by dividing 360° by the number of sides the polygon has. A regular hexagon's central angles (formed by splitting the shape into 6 equilateral triangles) are the same as the exterior angles.

Circles

A CIRCLE IS A CLOSED CURVED LINE SURROUNDING A CENTER POINT. EVERY POINT OF THIS CURVED LINE IS OF EQUAL DISTANCE FROM THE CENTER POINT.

SEE ALSO

❮ **82–83** Tools in geometry

Circumference and diameter **140–141** ❯

Area of a circle **142–143** ❯

Properties of a circle

A circle can be folded into two identical halves, which means that it possesses "reflective symmetry" (see p.88). The line of this fold is one of the most important parts of a circle—its diameter. A circle may also be rotated about its center and still fit into its own outline, giving it a "rotational symmetry" about its center point.

circumference the distance around the circle

segment the space between a chord and an arc

chord a straight line linking two points on the circumference

diameter a line that cuts a circle exactly in half

center point of circle

sector the space enclosed by two radii

radius distance from edge to center

area the total space covered by the circle

arc a section of the circumference

tangent a line that touches the circle at one point

▷ **A circle divided**
This diagram shows the many different parts of a circle. Many of these parts will feature in formulas over the pages that follow.

Parts of a circle

A circle can be measured and divided in various ways. Each of these has a specific name and character, and they are all shown below.

Radius
Any straight line from the center of a circle to its circumference. The plural of radius is radii.

Diameter
Any straight line that passes through the center from one side of a circle to the other.

Chord
Any straight line linking two points on a circle's circumference, but not passing through its center.

Segment
The smaller of the two parts of a circle created when divided by a chord.

Circumference
The total length of the outside edge (perimeter) of a circle.

Arc
Any section of the circumference of a circle.

Sector
A "slice" of a circle, similar to the slice of a pie. It is enclosed by two radii and an arc.

Area
The amount of space inside a circle's circumference.

Tangent
A straight line that touches the circle at a single point.

How to draw a circle

Two instruments are needed to draw a circle—a compass and a pencil. The point of the compass marks the center of the circle and the distance between the point and the pencil attached to the compass forms the circle's radius. A ruler is needed to measure the radius of the circle correctly.

"x" stands for distance in inches between compass point and pencil or length of radius

x in

use ruler to set length of radius

Set the compass. First, decide what the radius of the circle is, and then use a ruler to set the compass at this distance.

keep moving pencil around to complete circle

center of circle

Decide where the center of the circle is and then hold the point of the compass firmly in this place. Then put the pencil on the paper and move the pencil around to draw the circumference of the circle.

radius

x in

circumference

The completed circle has a radius that is the same length as the distance that the compass was originally set to.

Circumference and diameter

THE DISTANCE AROUND THE EDGE OF A CIRCLE IS CALLED THE CIRCUMFERENCE; THE DISTANCE ACROSS THE MIDDLE IS THE DIAMETER.

All circles are similar because they have exactly the same shape. This means that all their measurements, including the circumference and the diameter, are in proportion to each other.

The number pi

The ratio between the circumference and diameter of a circle is a number called pi, which is written π. This number is used in many of the formulas associated with circles, including the formulas for the circumference and diameter.

symbol for pi

$$\Pi \approx 3.14$$

value to 2 decimal places

◁ **The value of pi**
The numbers after the decimal point in pi go on for ever and in an unpredictable way. It starts 3.1415926 but is usually given to two decimal places.

Circumference (C)

The circumference is the distance around the edge of a circle. A circle's circumference can be found using the diameter or radius and the number pi. The diameter is always twice the length of the radius.

circumference — π is a constant — radius

$$C = 2\pi r$$

circumference — π is a constant — diameter

$$C = \pi d$$

◁ **Formulas**
There are two circumference formulas. One uses diameter and the other uses radius.

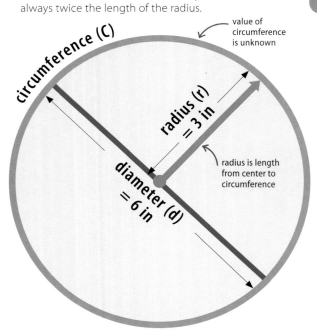

circumference (C)

value of circumference is unknown

radius (r) = 3 in

radius is length from center to circumference

diameter (d) = 6 in

△ **Finding the circumference**
The length of a circle's circumference can be found if the length of the diameter is known, in this example the diameter is 6 in long.

The formula for circumference shows that the circumference is equal to pi multiplied by the diameter of the circle.

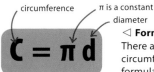

$$C = \pi d$$

d is the same as 2 × r, the formula can also be written C=2πr

Substitute known values into the formula for circumference. Here, the radius of the circle is known to be 3 in.

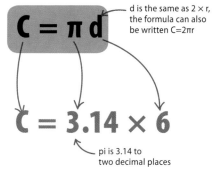

$$C = 3.14 \times 6$$

pi is 3.14 to two decimal places

Multiply the numbers to find the length of the circumference. Round the answer to a suitable number of decimal places.

$$C = 18.8 \text{ in}$$

18.84 is rounded to one decimal place

Diameter (d)

The diameter is the distance across the middle of a circle. It is twice the length of the radius. A circle's diameter can be found by doubling the length of its radius, or by using its circumference and the number pi in the formula shown below. The formula is a rearranged version of the formula for the circumference of a circle.

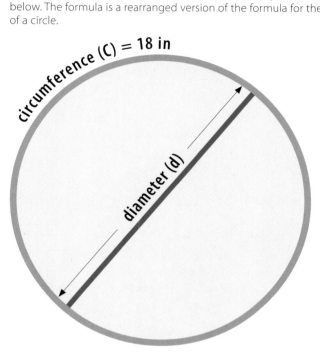

△ **Finding the diameter**
This circle has a circumference of 18 in. Its diameter can be found using the formula given above.

circumference (C) = 18 in

diameter (d)

diameter   circumference

$$d = \dfrac{C}{\pi}$$

π is a constant

The formula for diameter shows that the length of the diameter is equal to the length of the circumference divided by the number pi.

Substitute known values into the formula for diameter. In the example shown here, the circumference of the circle is 18 in.

$$d = \dfrac{18}{\pi}$$

Divide the circumference by the value of pi, 3.14, to find the length of the diameter.

$$d = \dfrac{18}{3.14}$$

more accurate to use π button on a calculator

Round the answer to a suitable number of decimal places. In this example, the answer is given to two decimal places.

$$d = 5.73 \text{ in}$$

the answer is given to two decimal places

LOOKING CLOSER

Why π ?

All circles are similar to one another. This means that corresponding lengths in circles, such as their diameters and circumferences, are always in proportion to each other. The number π is found by dividing the circumference of a circle by its diameter—any circle's circumference divided by its diameter always equals π—it is a constant value.

▷ **Similar circles**
As all circles are enlargements of each other, their diameters (d1, d2) and circumferences (C1, C2) are always in proportion to one another.

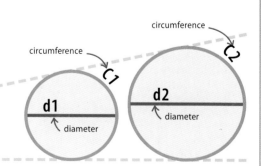

circumference

circumference

C1

C2

d1

d2

diameter

diameter

0

Area of a circle

THE AREA OF A CIRCLE IS THE AMOUNT OF SPACE ENCLOSED
INSIDE ITS PERIMETER (CIRCUMFERENCE).

SEE ALSO
❮ 138–139 Circles
❮ 140–141 Circumference and diameter
Formulas   177–179 ❯

The area of a circle can be found by using the measurements
of either the radius or the diameter of the circle.

Finding the area of a circle

The area of a circle is measured in square units. It can be found
using the radius of a circle (r) and the formula shown below. If the
diameter is known but the radius is not, the radius can be found
by dividing the diameter by 2.

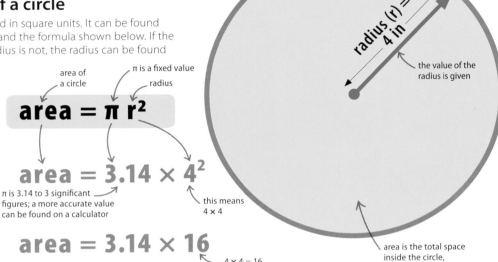

edge of circle is circumference

radius (r) = 4 in

the value of the radius is given

area is the total space inside the circle, shown in yellow

In the formula for the area of
a circle, πr^2 means π (pi) ×
radius × radius.

area of a circle

π is a fixed value

radius

$$\text{area} = \pi\, r^2$$

Substitute the known values
into the formula; in this
example, the radius is 4 in.

$$\text{area} = 3.14 \times 4^2$$

π is 3.14 to 3 significant
figures; a more accurate value
can be found on a calculator

this means
4 × 4

Multiply the radius by itself
as shown—this makes the last
multiplication simpler.

$$\text{area} = 3.14 \times 16$$

4 × 4 = 16

Make sure the answer is in
the right units (in^2 here) and
round it to a suitable number.

$$\text{area} = 50.24\ in^2$$

answer is
50.24 exactly

LOOKING CLOSER

Why does the formula for the area of a circle work?

The formula for the area of a circle
can be proved by dividing a circle
into segments, and rearranging the
segments into a rectangular shape. The
formula for the area of a rectangle is
simpler than that of the area for a
circle—it is just height × width. The
rectangular shape's height is simply the
length of a circle segment, which is the
same as the radius of the circle.
The width of the rectangular shape is
half of the total segments, equivalent
to half the circumference of the circle.

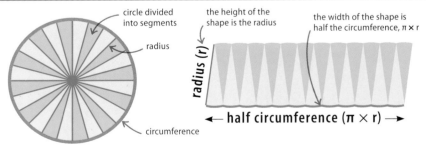

circle divided into segments

radius

circumference

the height of the shape is the radius

the width of the shape is half the circumference, $\pi \times r$

radius (r)

← half circumference ($\pi \times r$) →

Split any circle up into equal
segments, making them as
small as possible.

Lay the segments out in a rectangular shape. The
area of a rectangle is height × width, which in this case
is radius × half circumference, or $r \times \pi r$, which is πr^2.

Finding area using the diameter

The formula for the area of a circle usually uses the radius, but the area can also be found if the diameter is given.

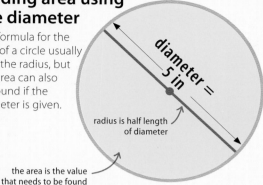

radius is half length of diameter

the area is the value that needs to be found

The formula for the area of a circle is always the same, whatever values are known.

$$area = \pi r^2$$

Substitute the known values into the formula—the radius is half the diameter—2.5 in this example.

$$area = 3.14 \times 2.5^2$$

the radius is half the diameter: $5 \div 2 = 2.5$

π is 3.14 to 3 significant figures

Multiply the radius by itself (square it) as shown by the formula—this makes the last multiplication simpler.

$$area = 3.14 \times 6.25$$

$2.5 \times 2.5 = 6.25$

19.6349... is rounded to 2 decimal places

Make sure the answer is in the right units, in² here, and round it to a suitable number.

$$area = \mathbf{19.63 \ in^2}$$

Finding the radius from the area

The formula for area of a circle can also be used to find the radius of a circle if its area is given.

find the radius r

$$area = 13 \ in^2$$

The formula for the area of a circle can be used to find the radius if the area is known.

$$area = \pi r^2$$

Substitute the known values into the formula— here the area is 13 in².

$$13 = 3.14 \times r^2$$

divide this side by 3.14

r² was multiplied by 3.14, so divide by 3.14 to isolate r²

$$\frac{13}{3.14} = r^2$$

Rearrange the formula so r² is on its own on one side: divide both sides by 3.14.

r² is shown first

Round the answer, and switch the sides so that the unknown, r², is shown first.

$$r^2 = 4.14$$

4.1380... is rounded to 2 decimal places

Find the square root of the last answer in order to find the value of the radius.

$$\sqrt{r^2} = \sqrt{4.14}$$

2.0342... is rounded to 2 decimal places

Make sure the answer is in the right units (in here) and round it to a suitable number.

$$r = \mathbf{2.03 \ in}$$

LOOKING CLOSER

Areas of compound shapes

When two or more different shapes are put together, the result is called a compound shape. The area of a compound shape can be found by adding the areas of the parts of the shape. In this example, the two different parts are a semicircle, and a rectangle. The total area is 1,414 in² (area of the semicircle, which is ½ × πr², half the area of a circle) + 5,400 in² (the area of the rectangle) = 6,814 in².

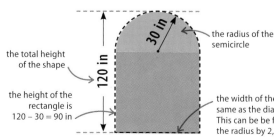

the total height of the shape

120 in

the height of the rectangle is 120 – 30 = 90 in

30 in

the radius of the semicircle

◁ **Compound shapes**
This compound shape consists of a semicircle and a rectangle. Its area can be found using only the two measurements given here.

the width of the rectangle is the same as the diameter of the circle. This can be be found by multiplying the radius by 2, 30 × 2 = 60 in.

⊘ Angles in a circle

THE ANGLES IN A CIRCLE HAVE A NUMBER OF SPECIAL PROPERTIES.

SEE ALSO
❮ **84–85** Angles
❮ **116–117** Triangles
❮ **138–139** Circles

If angles are drawn to the center and the circumference from the same two points on the circumference, the angle at the center is twice the angle at the circumference.

Subtended angles

Any angle within a circle is "subtended" from two points on its circumference—it "stands" on the two points. In both of these examples, the angle at point R is the angle subtended, or standing on, points P and Q. Subtended angles can sit anywhere within the circle.

▷ **Subtended angles**
These circles show how a point is subtended from two other points on the circle's circumference to form an angle. The angle at point R is subtended from points P and Q.

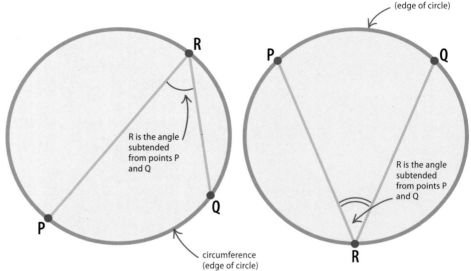

circumference (edge of circle)

R is the angle subtended from points P and Q

circumference (edge of circle)

R is the angle subtended from points P and Q

Angles at the center and at the circumference

When angles are subtended from the same two points to both the center of the circle and to its circumference, the angle at the center is always twice the size of the angle formed at the circumference. In this example, both angles R at the circumference and O at the center are subtended from the same points, P and Q.

$$\text{angle at center} = 2 \times \text{angle at circumference}$$

▷ **Angle property**
The angles at O and R are both subtended by the points P and Q at the circumference. This means that the angle at O is twice the size of the angle at R.

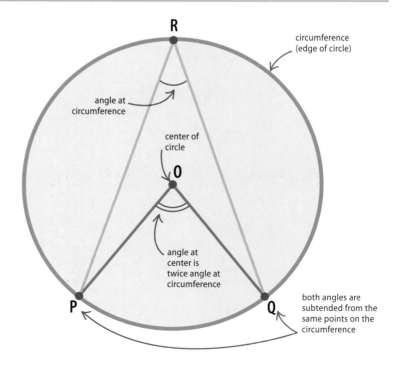

circumference (edge of circle)

angle at circumference

center of circle

angle at center is twice angle at circumference

both angles are subtended from the same points on the circumference

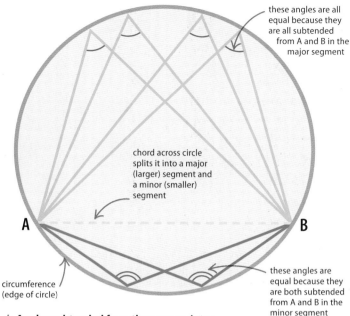

these angles are all equal because they are all subtended from A and B in the major segment

chord across circle splits it into a major (larger) segment and a minor (smaller) segment

circumference (edge of circle)

these angles are equal because they are both subtended from A and B in the minor segment

△ **Angles subtended from the same points**
Angles at the circumference subtended from the same two points in the same segment are equal. Here the angles marked with one red line are equal, as are the angles marked with two red lines.

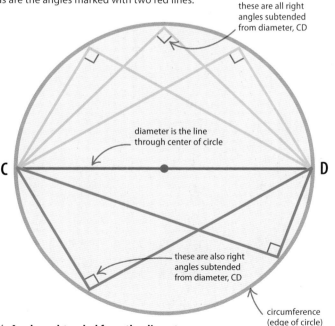

these are all right angles subtended from diameter, CD

diameter is the line through center of circle

these are also right angles subtended from diameter, CD

circumference (edge of circle)

△ **Angles subtended from the diameter**
Any angle at the circumference that is subtended from two points either side of the diameter is equal to 90°, which is a right angle.

Proving angle rules in circles

Mathematical rules can be used to prove that the angle at the center of a circle is twice the size of the angle at the circumference when both the angles are subtended from the same points.

R, P, and Q are 3 points on the circumference

Draw a circle and mark any 3 points on its circumference, for example, P, Q, and R. Mark the center of the circle, in this example it is O.

center

angle R subtended from P and Q

Draw straight lines from R to P, R to Q, O to P, and O to Q. This creates two angles, one at R (the circumference of the circle) and one at O (the center of the circle). Both are subtended from points P and Q.

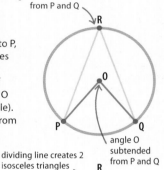

angle O subtended from P and Q

dividing line creates 2 isosceles triangles

Draw a line from R through O, to the other side of the circle. This dividing line creates two isosceles triangles. Isosceles triangles have 2 sides and 2 angles that are the same. In this case, two sides of triangles POR and QOR are formed from 2 radii of the circle.

the angle at O is twice the angle at R

For one triangle the two angles on its base are equal, and labeled A. The exterior angle of this triangle is the sum of the opposite interior angles (A and A), or 2A. Looking at both triangles, it is clear that the angle at O (the center) is twice the angle at R (the circumference).

2A

Chords and cyclic quadrilaterals

A CHORD IS A STRAIGHT LINE JOINING ANY TWO POINTS ON THE CIRCUMFERENCE
OF A CIRCLE. A CYCLIC QUADRILATERAL HAS FOUR CHORDS AS ITS SIDES.

Chords vary in length—the diameter of a circle is also its longest chord. Chords of
the same length are always equal distances from the center of the circle. The corners
of a cyclic quadrilateral (four-sided shape) touch the circumference of a circle.

SEE ALSO

❰ **130–133** Quadrilaterals

❰ **138–139** Circles

Chords

A chord is a straight line across a circle.
The longest chord of any circle is its
diameter because the diameter crosses a
circle at its widest point. The perpendicular
bisector of a chord is a line that passes
through its center at right angles (90°) to it.
The perpendicular bisector of any chord
passes through the center of the circle. The
distance of a chord to the center of a circle
is found by measuring its perpendicular
bisector. If two chords are equal lengths they
will always be the same distance from the
center of the circle.

all chords touch
the circumference
at two points

these two chords are equal
lengths, so they are equal
distances from the center
of the circle

center of circle

diameter is the longest
chord; it passes
through the center

distance of chord from
the center is found
by measuring its
perpendicular bisector

right angle

chord

this is perpendicular
bisector of chord

circumference
(edge) of circle

▷ **Chord properties**
This circle shows four chords. Two
of these chords are equal in length.
The longest chord is the diameter,
and one is shown on the right with
its perpendicular bisector (a line
that cuts it in half at right angles).

LOOKING CLOSER

Intersecting chords

When two chords cross, or "intersect," they gain
an interesting property: the two parts of one
chord, either side of where it is split, multiply to
give the same value as the answer found by
multiplying the two parts of the other chord.

▷ **Crossing chords**
This circle shows two chords, which
cross one another (intersect). One
chord is split into parts A and B, the
other into parts C and D.

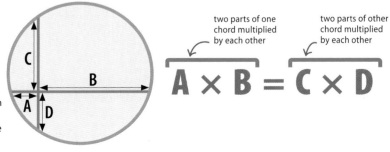

two parts of one
chord multiplied
by each other

two parts of other
chord multiplied
by each other

$$A \times B = C \times D$$

Finding the center of a circle

Chords can be used to find the center of a circle. To do this, draw any two chords across the circle. Then find the midpoint of each chord, and draw a line through it that is at right angles to that chord (this is a perpendicular bisector). The center of the circle is where these two lines cross.

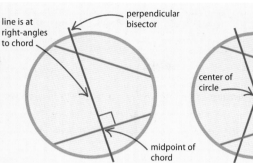

First, draw any two chords across the circle of which the center needs to be found.

▶ **Then measure the midpoint** of one of the chords, and draw a line through the midpoint at right-angles (90°) to the chord.

▶ **Do the same** for the other chord. The center of the circle is the point where the two perpendicular lines cross.

Cyclic quadrilaterals

Cyclic quadrilaterals are four-sided shapes made from chords. Each corner of the shape sits on the circumference of a circle. The interior angles of a cyclic quadrilateral add up to 360°, as they do for all quadrilaterals. The opposite interior angles of a cyclic quadrilateral add up to 180°, and their exterior angles are equal to the opposite interior angles.

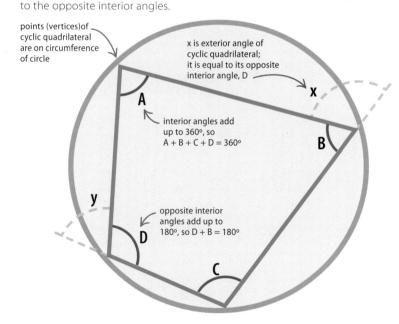

points (vertices) of cyclic quadrilateral are on circumference of circle

x is exterior angle of cyclic quadrilateral; it is equal to its opposite interior angle, D

interior angles add up to 360°, so A + B + C + D = 360°

opposite interior angles add up to 180°, so D + B = 180°

$$A + B + C + D = 360°$$

△ **Interior angle sum**
The interior angles of a cyclic quadrilateral always add up to 360°. Therefore, in this example A + B + C + D = 360°.

$$A + C = 180°$$
$$B + D = 180°$$

△ **Opposite angles**
Opposite angles in a cyclic quadrilateral always add up to 180°. In this example, A + C = 180° and B + D = 180°.

exterior angle opposite to angle B

$$y = B$$

exterior angle opposite to angle D

$$x = D$$

△ **Angles in a cyclic quadrilateral**
The four interior angles of this cyclic quadrilateral are A, B, C, and D. Two of the four exterior angles are x and y.

△ **Exterior angles**
Exterior angles in cyclic quadrilaterals are equal to the opposite interior angles. Therefore, in this example, y = B and x = D.

Tangents

A TANGENT IS A STRAIGHT LINE THAT TOUCHES THE CIRCUMFERENCE (EDGE) OF A CIRCLE AT A SINGLE POINT.

SEE ALSO
⟨ **110–113** Constructions
⟨ **128–129** Pythagorean Theorem
⟨ **138–139** Circles

What are tangents?

A tangent is a line that extends from a point outside a circle and touches the edge of the circle in one place, the point of contact. The line joining the centre of the circle to the point of contact is a radius, at right-angles (90º) to the tangent. From a point outside the circle there are two tangents to the circle.

▷ **Tangent properties**
The lengths of the two tangents from a point outside a circle to their points of contact are equal.

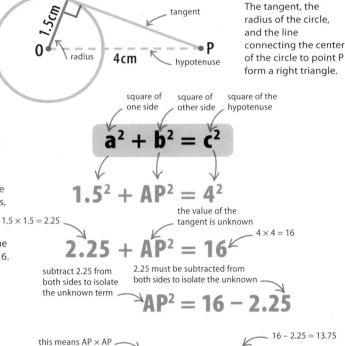

point of contact

circumference

right angle

right angle

radius that touches tangent at point of contact is at right-angles to tangent

tangent

tangent

point outside the circle

tangent

point of contact

Finding the length of a tangent

A tangent is at right-angles to the radius at the point of contact, so a right triangle can be created using the radius, the tangent, and a line between them, which is the hypotenuse of the triangle. Pythagorean theorem can be used to find the length of any one of the three sides of the right triangle, if two sides are known.

A

1.5cm

0

radius

4cm

tangent

P

hypotenuse

◁ **Find the tangent**
The tangent, the radius of the circle, and the line connecting the center of the circle to point P form a right triangle.

Pythagorean theorem shows that the square of the hypotenuse (side facing the right-angle) of a right triangle is equal to the the sum of the two squares of the other sides of the triangle.

square of one side   square of other side   square of the hypotenuse

$$a^2 + b^2 = c^2$$

Subsitute the known numbers into the formula. The hypotenuse is side OP, which is 4cm, and the other known length is the radius, which is 1.5cm. The side not known is the tangent, AP.

$$1.5^2 + AP^2 = 4^2$$

the value of the tangent is unknown

Find the squares of the two known sides by multiplying the value of each by itself. The square of 1.5 is 2.25, and the square of 4 is 16. Leave the value of the unknown side, AP² as it is.

$1.5 \times 1.5 = 2.25$

$4 \times 4 = 16$

$$2.25 + AP^2 = 16$$

subtract 2.25 from both sides to isolate the unknown term

2.25 must be subtracted from both sides to isolate the unknown

Rearrange the equation to isolate the unknown variable. In this example the unknown is AP², the tangent. It is isolated by subtracting 2.25 from both sides of the equation.

$$AP^2 = 16 - 2.25$$

Carry out the subtraction on the right-hand side of the equation. The value this creates, 13.75, is the squared value of AP, which is the length of the missing side.

this means AP × AP

$16 - 2.25 = 13.75$

$$AP^2 = 13.75$$

this is the sign for a square root

Find the square root of both sides of the equation to find the value of AP. The square root of AP² is just AP. Use a calculator to find the square root of 13.75.

the square root of AP² is just AP

$$AP = \sqrt{13.75}$$

3.708... is rounded to 2 decimal places

Find the square root of the value on the right, and round the answer to a suitable number of decimal places. This is the length of the missing side.

$$AP = 3.71cm$$

Constructing tangents

To construct a tangent accurately requires a compass and a straight edge. This example shows how to construct two tangents between a circle with center O and a given point outside the circle, in this case, P.

draw circle
center point of circle
mark point outside circle

Draw a circle using a compass, and mark the center O. Also, mark another point outside the circle and label it (in this case P). Construct two tangents to the circle from the point.

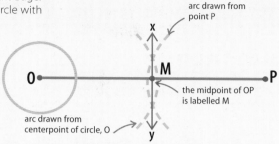

arc drawn from point P
the midpoint of OP is labelled M
arc drawn from centerpoint of circle, O

▷ **Draw a line between O and P,** then find its midpoint. Set a compass to just over half OP, and draw two arcs, one from O and one from P. Join the two points where the arcs cross with a straight line (xy). The midpoint is where xy crosses OP.

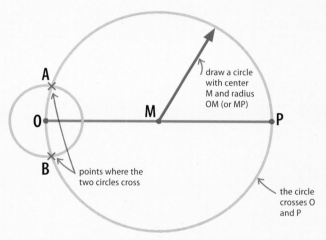

draw a circle with center M and radius OM (or MP)
points where the two circles cross
the circle crosses O and P

▷ **Set the compass** to distance OM (or MP which is the same length), and draw a circle with M as its center. Mark the two points where this new circle intersects (crosses) the circumference of the original circle as A and B.

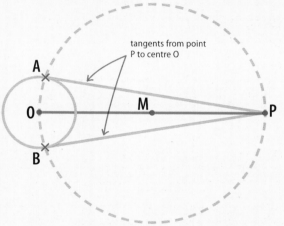

tangents from point P to centre O

▷ **Finally, join each point** where the circles intersect (cross), A and B, with point P. These two lines are the tangents from point P to the circle with center O. The two tangents are equal lengths.

Tangents and angles

Tangents to circles have some special angle properties. If a tangent touches a circle at B, and a chord, BC, is drawn across the circle from B, an angle is formed between the tangent and the chord at B. If lines (BD and CD) are drawn to the circumference from the ends of the chord, they create an angle at D that is equal to angle B.

▷ **Tangents and chords**
The angle formed between the tangent and the chord is equal to the angle formed at the circumference if two lines are drawn from either end of the chord to meet at a point on the circumference.

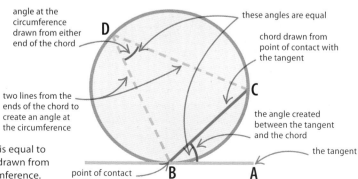

angle at the circumference drawn from either end of the chord
these angles are equal
chord drawn from point of contact with the tangent
two lines from the ends of the chord to create an angle at the circumference
the angle created between the tangent and the chord
the tangent
point of contact

Arcs

AN ARC IS A SECTION OF A CIRCLE'S CIRCUMFERENCE. ITS LENGTH CAN
BE FOUND USING ITS RELATED ANGLE AT THE CENTER OF THE CIRCLE.

SEE ALSO

❮ **56–59** Ratio and proportion

❮ **138–139** Circles

❮ **140–141** Circumference and diameter

What is an arc?

An arc is a part of the circumference of a circle. The length
of an arc is in proportion with the size of the angle made
at the center of the circle when lines are drawn from each
end of the arc. If the length of an arc is unknown, it can
be found using the circumference and this angle. When a
circle is split into two arcs, the bigger is called the "major"
arc, and the smaller the "minor" arc.

angle created at the center
when two lines are drawn from
the ends of the major arc

minor arc

major arc

angle created at
the center when
two lines are drawn
from the ends of
the minor arc

formula for finding
the length of an arc

$$\frac{\text{arc length}}{\text{circumference}} = \frac{\text{angle at center}}{360°}$$

total length of circle's edge

360° in a circle

▷ **Arcs and angles**
This diagram shows two
arcs: one major, one
minor, and their angles
at the center of the circle.

Finding the length of an arc

The length of an arc is a proportion of the whole
circumference of the circle. The exact proportion is
the ratio between the angle formed from each end of
the arc at the center of the circle, and 360°, which is the
total number of degrees around the central point. This
ratio is part of the formula for the length of an arc.

120°

◁ **Find the arc length**
This circle has a circumference of
10 cm. Find the length of the arc
that forms an angle of 120° at the
center of the circle.

circumference is 10cm

Take the formula for finding the length of an arc.
The formula uses the ratios between arc length and
circumference, and between the angle at the center
of the circle and 360° (total number of degrees).

$$\frac{\text{arc length}}{\text{circumference}} = \frac{\text{angle at center}}{360°}$$

Substitute the numbers that are known into the
formula. In this example, the circumference is
known to be 10 cm, and the angle at the center of
the circle is 120°; 360° stays as it is.

$$\frac{\text{arc length}}{10} = \frac{120}{360}$$

this side has been multiplied by
10 to leave arc length on its own
(÷10 × 10 cancels out)

this side has also been
multiplied by 10
because what is done
to one side must be
done to the other

Rearrange the equation to isolate the unknown
value—the arc length—on one side of the equals
sign. In this example the arc length is isolated by
multiplying both sides by 10.

$$\text{arc length} = \frac{10 \times 120}{360}$$

Multiply 10 by 120 and divide the answer by 360 to
get the value of the arc length. Then round the
answer to a suitable number of decimal places.

3.333... is rounded to
2 decimal places

$$C = 3.33\text{cm}$$

Sectors

A SECTOR IS A SLICE OF A CIRCLE'S AREA. ITS AREA CAN BE FOUND
USING THE ANGLE IT CREATES AT THE CENTER OF THE CIRCLE.

SEE ALSO

❮ **56–59** Ratio and proportion

❮ **138–139** Circles

❮ **140–141** Circumference and diameter

What is a sector?

A sector of a circle is the space between two radii and one arc. The area of a sector depends on the size of the angle between the two radii at the center of the circle. If the area of a sector is unknown, it can be found using this angle and the area of the circle. When a circle is split into two sectors, the bigger is called the "major" sector, and the smaller the "minor" sector.

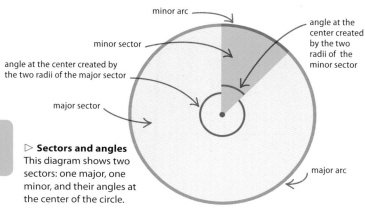

minor arc

angle at the center created by the two radii of the minor sector

minor sector

angle at the center created by the two radii of the major sector

major sector

major arc

$$\frac{\text{area of sector}}{\text{area of circle}} = \frac{\text{angle at center}}{360°}$$

formula for finding the area of a sector

▷ **Sectors and angles**
This diagram shows two sectors: one major, one minor, and their angles at the center of the circle.

Finding the area of a sector

The area of a sector is a proportion, or part, of the area of the whole circle. The exact proportion is the ratio of the angle formed between the two radii that are the edges of the sector and 360º. This ratio is part of the formula for the area of a sector.

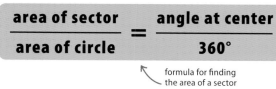

45°

angle formed by sector

the area of the circle is 7 cm²

◁ **Find the sector area**
This circle has an area of 7 cm². Find the area of the sector that forms a 45° angle at the center of the circle.

Take the formula for finding the area of a sector. The formula uses the ratios between the area of a sector and the area of the circle, and between the angle at the center of the circle and 360º.

$$\frac{\text{area of sector}}{\text{area of circle}} = \frac{\text{angle at center}}{360°}$$

total number of degrees in circle

Substitute the numbers that are known into the formula. In this example, the area is known to be 7 cm², and the angle at the center of the circle is 45º. The total number of degrees in a circle is 360º.

$$\frac{\text{area of sector}}{7} = \frac{45}{360}$$

Rearrange the equation to isolate the unknown value—the area of the sector—on one side of the equals sign. In this example, this is done by multiplying both sides by 7.

this side has been multiplied by 7 to leave the area of a sector on its own (÷7 ×7 cancels out)

this side has also been multiplied by 7

$$\text{area of sector} = \frac{45 \times 7}{360}$$

Multiply 45 by 7 and divide the answer by 360 to get the area of the sector. Round the answer to a suitable number of decimal places.

0.875 is rounded to 2 decimal places

$$C = 0.88 \text{ cm}^2$$

Solids

A SOLID IS A THREE-DIMENSIONAL SHAPE.

Solids are objects with three dimensions: width, length, and height. They also have surface areas and volumes.

Prisms

Many common solids are polyhedrons—three-dimensional shapes with flat surfaces and straight edges. Prisms are a type of polyhedron made up of two parallel shapes of exactly the same shape and size, which are connected by faces. In the example to the right, the parallel shapes are pentagons, joined by rectangular faces. Usually a prism is named after the shape of its ends (or bases), so a prism whose parallel shapes are rectangles is known as a rectangular prism. If all its edges are equal sizes, it is called a cube.

edge
a line where surfaces meet

height
distance from top to bottom

width
horizontal distance at right angles to length

▷ **A prism**
The cross section of this prism is a pentagon (a shape with five sides), so it is called a pentagonal prism.

◁ **Volume**
The amount of space that a solid occupies is called its volume.

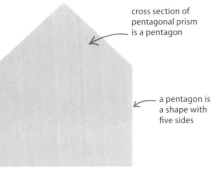

cross section of pentagonal prism is a pentagon

a pentagon is a shape with five sides

△ **Cross section**
A cross section is the shape made when an object is sliced from top to bottom.

this net forms a shape with seven faces

cross section

cut out net and fold along edges to construct

◁ **Surface area**
The surface area of a solid is the total area of its net —a two-dimensional shape, or plan, that forms the solid if it is folded up.

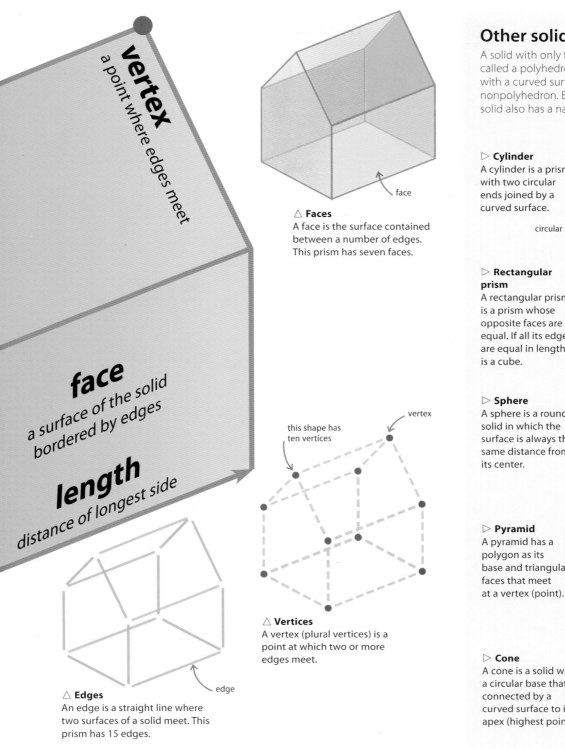

vertex
a point where edges meet

face
a surface of the solid
bordered by edges

length
distance of longest side

△ **Faces**
A face is the surface contained
between a number of edges.
This prism has seven faces.

face

△ **Vertices**
A vertex (plural vertices) is a
point at which two or more
edges meet.

this shape has
ten vertices

vertex

△ **Edges**
An edge is a straight line where
two surfaces of a solid meet. This
prism has 15 edges.

edge

Other solids

A solid with only flat surfaces is
called a polyhedron and a solid
with a curved surface is called a
nonpolyhedron. Each common
solid also has a name of its own.

▷ **Cylinder**
A cylinder is a prism
with two circular
ends joined by a
curved surface.

circular end

this face is equal in
size to its opposite

▷ **Rectangular
prism**
A rectangular prism
is a prism whose
opposite faces are
equal. If all its edges
are equal in length, it
is a cube.

▷ **Sphere**
A sphere is a round
solid in which the
surface is always the
same distance from
its center.

vertex

▷ **Pyramid**
A pyramid has a
polygon as its
base and triangular
faces that meet
at a vertex (point).

apex

▷ **Cone**
A cone is a solid with
a circular base that is
connected by a
curved surface to its
apex (highest point).

Volumes

THE AMOUNT OF SPACE WITHIN A THREE-DIMENSIONAL SHAPE.

SEE ALSO

❰ **28–29** Units of measurement

❰ **152–153** Solids

Surface area of solids   **156–157** ❱

Solid space

When measuring volume, unit cubes, also called cubic units, are used, for example, cm³ and m³. An exact number of unit cubes fits neatly into some types of three-dimensional shapes, also known as solids, such as a cube, but for most solids, for example, a cylinder, this is not the case. Formulas are used to find the volumes of solids. Finding the area of the base, or the cross section, of a solid is the key to finding its volume. Each solid has a different cross-section.

▷ **Unit cubes**
A unit cube has sides that are of equal size. A 1 cm cube has a volume of $1 \times 1 \times 1$ cm, or 1 cm³. The space within a solid can be measured by the number of unit cubes that can fit inside. This cuboid has a volume of $3 \times 2 \times 2$ cm, or 12 cm³.

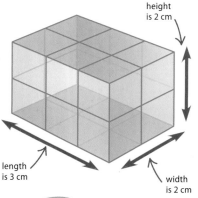

height is 2 cm

length is 3 cm

width is 2 cm

Finding the volume of a cylinder

A cylinder is made up from a rectangle and two circles. Its volume is found by multiplying the area of a circle with the length, or height, of the cylinder.

$$\text{volume} = \pi \times r^2 \times l$$

formula for finding volume of a cylinder

The formula for the volume of a cylinder uses the formula for the area of a circle multiplied by the length of the cylinder.

equals 3.14

or $r \times r$

$$\text{area} = \pi \times r^2$$

formula for finding area of a circle

$$3.14 \times 3.8 \times 3.8 = \mathbf{45\ cm^2}$$

area of cross section, given to 2 significant figures

First, find the area of the cylinder's cross-section using the formula for finding the area of a circle. Insert the values given on the illustration of the cylinder below.

$$\text{volume} = \text{area} \times \text{length}$$

$$45 \times 12 = \mathbf{544\ cm^3}$$

Next, multiply the area by the length of the cylinder to find its volume.

▷ **Circular cross-section**
The base of a cylinder is a circle. When a cylinder is sliced widthwise, the circles created are identical, so a cylinder is said to have a circular cross-section.

LENGTH = 12 cm

RADIUS = 3.8 cm

area of a cross section

Volume of a rectangular prism

A rectangular prism has six flat sides and all of its faces are rectangles. Multiply the length by the width by the height to find the volume of a rectangular prism.

formula also written
$v = l \times w \times h$, or $v = lwh$

volume = length × width × height

$$4.3 \times 2.2 \times 1.7 = \textbf{16 cm}^3$$

answer rounded to 2 significant figures

▷ **Multiply lengths of the sides**
This rectangular prism has a length of 4.3 cm, a width of 2.2 cm, and a height of 1.7 cm. Multiply these measurements to find its volume.

WIDTH = 2.2 cm

LENGTH = 4.3 cm

HEIGHT = 1.7 cm

Finding the volume of a cone

Multiply the distance from the tip of the cone to the center of its base (the vertical height) with the area of its base (the area of a circle), then multiply by ⅓.

also called the perpendicular height

volume $= \dfrac{1}{3} \times \pi \times r^2 \times$ **vertical height**

$$\dfrac{1}{3} \times 3.14 \times 2 \times 2 \times 4.3 = \textbf{18 cm}^3$$

answer rounded to 2 significant figures

▷ **Using the formula**
To find the volume of this cone, multiply together ⅓, π, the radius squared, and the vertical height.

VERTICAL HEIGHT = 4.3 cm

RADIUS = 2 cm

Finding the volume of a sphere

The radius is the only measurement needed to find the volume of a sphere. This sphere has a radius of 2.5 cm.

multiply radius by itself twice

volume $= \dfrac{4}{3} \times \pi \times r^3$

$$\dfrac{4}{3} \times 3.14 \times 2.5 \times 2.5 \times 2.5 = \textbf{65 cm}^3$$

answer rounded to 2 significant figures

▷ **Using the formula**
To find the volume of this sphere, multiply together ⁴/₃, π, and the radius cubed (the radius multiplied by itself twice).

RADIUS = 2.5 cm

Surface area of solids

SURFACE AREA IS THE SPACE OCCUPIED BY A SHAPE'S OUTER SURFACES.

For most solids, surface area can be found by adding together the areas of its faces. The sphere is the exception, but there is an easy formula to use.

Surfaces of shapes

For all solids with straight edges, surface area can be found by adding together the areas of all the solid's faces. One way to do this is to imagine taking apart and flattening out the solid into two-dimensional shapes. It is then straightforward to work out and add together the areas of these shapes. A diagram of a flattened and opened out shape is known as its net.

▷ **Cylinder**
A cylinder has two flat faces and a curved surface. To create its net, the flat surfaces are separated and the curved surface opened up.

radius is the length from center of circle to its perimeter

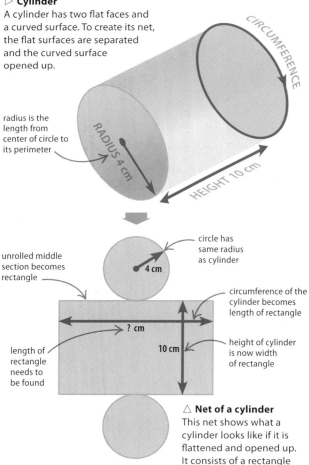

unrolled middle section becomes rectangle

circle has same radius as cylinder

4 cm

circumference of the cylinder becomes length of rectangle

? cm

10 cm

height of cylinder is now width of rectangle

length of rectangle needs to be found

△ **Net of a cylinder**
This net shows what a cylinder looks like if it is flattened and opened up. It consists of a rectangle and two circles.

Finding the surface area of a cylinder

Breaking the cylinder down into its component parts creates a rectangle and two circles. To find the total surface area, work out the area of each of these and add them together.

formula for area of circle

area of circle

$$\text{Area} = \pi \times r^2$$

$$3.14 \times 4 \times 4 = \mathbf{50.24 \ cm^2}$$

The area of the circles can be worked out using the known radius and the formula for the area of a circle. π (pi) is usually shortened to 3.14, and area is always expressed in square units.

formula for circumference

circumference of cylinder

$$\text{Circumference} = 2 \times \pi \times r$$

$$2 \times 3.14 \times 4 = \mathbf{25.12 \ cm}$$

Before the area of the rectangle can be found, it is necessary to work out its width—the circumference of the cylinder. This is done using the known radius and the formula for circumference.

length of rectangle = circumference of cylinder

width of rectangle = height of cylinder

area of rectangle

$$25.12 \times 10 = \mathbf{251.2 \ cm^2}$$

The area of the rectangle can now be found by using the formula for the area of a rectangle (length × width).

surface area of cylinder

$$50.24 + 50.24 + 251.2 = \mathbf{351.68 \ cm^2}$$

The surface area of the cylinder is found by adding together the areas of the three shapes that make up its net—two circles and a rectangle.

Finding the surface area of a rectangular prism

A rectangular prism is made up of three different pairs of rectangles, here labeled A, B, and C. The surface area is the sum of the areas of all its faces.

WIDTH 4.9 cm

LENGTH 12.3 cm   HEIGHT 3 cm

△ **Net of a rectangular prism**
The net is made up of three different pairs of rectangles.

To find the area of rectangle A, multiply together the rectangular prism's height and width.

▽

To find the area of rectangle B, multiply together the rectangular prism's length and width.

▽

To find the area of rectangle C, multiply together the rectangular prism's height and length.

▽

The surface area of the rectangular prism is the total of the areas of its sides—twice area A, added to twice area B, added to twice area C.

Area of A = height × width

$3 \times 4.9 =$ **14.7 cm²**

Area of B = length × width

$12.3 \times 4.9 =$ **60.27 cm²**

Area of C = height × length

$3 \times 12.3 =$ **36.9 cm²**

parentheses used to separate operations

$$(2 \times A) + (2 \times B) + (2 \times C)$$

$(2 \times 14.7) + (2 \times 60.27) + (2 \times 36.9)$

$=$ **223.74 cm²**

Finding the surface area of a cone

A cone is made up of two parts—a circular base and a cone shape. Formulas are used to find the areas of the two parts, which are then added together to give the surface area.

slant height

Area = π × r × h

surface area of cone without base

$3.14 \times 3.9 \times 9 =$ **110.21 cm²**

formula for area of a circle

π × r²

surface area of base

$3.14 \times 3.9 \times 3.9 =$ **47.76 cm²**

total surface area of cone

$110.21 + 47.76 =$ **157.97 cm²**

▷ **Cone**
Find the surface area of a cone by using formulas to find the area of the cone shape and the area of the base, and adding the two.

To find the area of the cone, multiply π by the radius and slant length.

▽

To find the area of the base, use the formula for the area of a circle, π × r² .

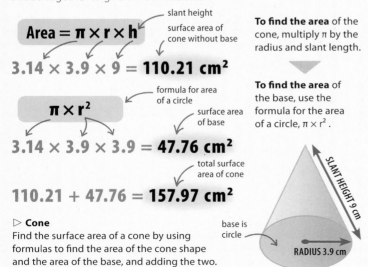

SLANT HEIGHT 9 cm

base is circle

RADIUS 3.9 cm

Finding the surface area of a sphere

Unlike many other solid shapes, a sphere cannot be unrolled or unfolded. Instead, a formula is used to find its surface area.

Area = 4 × π × r²

formula for the surface area of a sphere

$4 \times 3.14 \times 17 \times 17$

$=$ **3,629.84 cm²**

▷ **Sphere**
The formula for the surface area of a sphere is the same as 4 times the formula for the area of a circle (πr²). This means that the surface area of a sphere is equal to the surface area of 4 circles with the same radius.

RADIUS 17 cm

Trigonometry

What is trigonometry?

TRIGONOMETRY DEALS WITH THE RELATIONSHIPS BETWEEN THE
SIZES OF ANGLES AND LENGTHS OF SIDES IN TRIANGLES.

SEE ALSO
❮ **56–59** Ratio and proportion
❮ **125–127** Similar triangles

Corresponding triangles

Trigonometry uses comparisons of the lengths of the sides of
similar right triangles (which have the same shape but different
sizes) to find the sizes of unknown angles and sides. This
diagram shows the Sun creating shadows of a person and a
building, which form two similar triangles. By measuring the
shadows, the height of the person, which is known, can be
used to find the height of the building, which is unknown.

▽ **Similar triangles**
The shadows the sun makes
of the person and the
building create two
corresponding triangles.

the Sun's rays
create shadows of
the person and the
building

the Sun

height of the
building,
which is
unknown

h

the height of
the person

the length of the
person's shadow

6 ft

the length of
the building's
shadow

the length of
the person's
shadow

9 ft

250 ft

▷ **The ratio between** corresponding sides of similar triangles
is equal, so the building's height divided by the person's
height equals the length of the building's shadow divided by
the length of the person's shadow.

▷ **Substitute the values** from the diagram into this
equation. This leaves only one unknown—the height
of the building (h)—which is found by rearranging
the equation.

▷ **Rearrange the equation** to leave h (the height of the
building) on its own. This is done by multiplying both
sides of the equation by 6, then canceling out the two
6s on the left side, leaving just h.

▷ **Work out the right side** of the equation to find the
value of h, which is the height of the building.

$$\frac{\text{height of building}}{\text{height of person}} = \frac{\text{length of building's shadow}}{\text{length of person's shadow}}$$

the value of h is
unknown

$$\frac{h}{6} = \frac{250}{9}$$

whatever is done to one
side of the equation
must be done to the
other, so this side must
also be multiplied by 6

this side has been
multiplied by 6 to
cancel out the ÷ 6
and isolate h

$$h = \frac{250}{9} \times 6$$

the answer is
rounded to 2
decimal places

$$h = 166.67 \text{ ft}$$

Using formulas in trigonometry

TRIGONOMETRY FORMULAS CAN BE USED TO WORK OUT THE
LENGTHS OF SIDES AND SIZES OF ANGLES IN TRIANGLES.

SEE ALSO

‹ 56–59 Ratio and proportion

‹ 125–127 Similar triangles

Finding missing sides **162–163 ›**

Finding missing angles **164–165 ›**

Right triangles

The sides of these triangles are called the hypotenuse, opposite, and adjacent. The hypotenuse is always the side opposite the right angle. The names of the other two sides depend on where they are in relation to the particular angle specified.

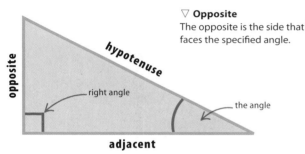

▽ **Opposite**
The opposite is the side that faces the specified angle.

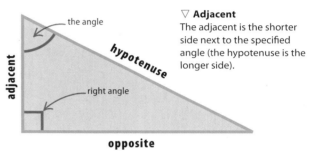

▽ **Adjacent**
The adjacent is the shorter side next to the specified angle (the hypotenuse is the longer side).

Trigonometry formulas

There are three basic formulas used in trigonometry. "A" stands in for the angle that is being found (this may also sometimes be written as θ). The formula to use depends on the sides of the triangle that are known.

$$\sin A = \frac{\text{opposite}}{\text{hypotenuse}}$$

△ **The sine formula**
The sine formula is used when the lengths of the opposite and hypotenuse are known.

$$\cos A = \frac{\text{adjacent}}{\text{hypotenuse}}$$

△ **The cosine formula**
The cosine formula is used when the lengths of the adjacent and hypotenuse are known.

$$\tan A = \frac{\text{opposite}}{\text{adjacent}}$$

△ **The tangent formula**
The tangent formula is used when the lengths of the opposite and adjacent are known.

Using a calculator

The values of sine, cosine, and tangent are set for each angle. Calculators have buttons that retrieve these values. Use them to find the sine, cosine, or tangent of a particular angle.

△ **Sine, cosine, and tangent**
Press the sine, cosine, or tangent button then enter the value of the angle to find its sine, cosine, or tangent.

 then

△ **Inverse sine, cosine, and tangent**
Press the shift button, then the sin, cosine, or tangent button, then enter the value of the sine, cosine, or tangent to find the inverse (the angle in degrees).

Finding missing sides

GIVEN AN ANGLE AND THE LENGTH OF ONE SIDE OF A RIGHT
TRIANGLE, THE OTHER SIDES CAN BE FOUND.

The trigonometry formulas can be used to find a length in a right triangle
if one angle (other than the right angle) and one other side are known. Use
a calculator to find the sine, cosine, or tangent of an angle.

Which formula?

The formula to use depends on what information is known. Choose the
formula that contains the known side as well as the side that needs to be
found. For example, use the sine formula if the length of the hypotenuse
is known, one angle other than the right angle is known, and the length
of the side opposite the given angle needs to be found.

▽ **Calculator buttons**
These calculator buttons
recall the value of sine,
cosine, and tangent for any
value entered.

this is the
sine button

this is the
cosine button

this is the
tangent button

$$\sin A = \frac{\text{opposite}}{\text{hypotenuse}}$$

△ **The sine formula**
This formula is used if one angle, and
either the side opposite it or the
hypotenuse are given.

$$\cos A = \frac{\text{adjacent}}{\text{hypotenuse}}$$

△ **The cosine formula**
Use this formula if one angle and
either the side adjacent to it or the
hypotenuse are known.

$$\tan A = \frac{\text{opposite}}{\text{adjacent}}$$

△ **The tangent formula**
This formula is used if one angle
and either the side opposite it or
adjacent to it are given.

Using the sine formula

In this right triangle, one angle other than
the right angle is known, as is the length
of the hypotenuse. The length of the side
opposite the angle is missing and needs to
be found.

missing length

hypotenuse
is side opposite
right angle

7 cm (hypotenuse)

x (opposite)

37°

use this angle
in calculation

Choose the right formula—
because the hypotenuse is
known and the value for the
opposite side is what needs to
be found, use the sine formula.

Substitute the known values
into the sine formula.

Rearrange the formula to make
the unknown (x) the subject by
multiplying both sides by 7.

Use a calculator to find the
value of sin 37°—press the sin
button then enter 37.

Round the answer to a
suitable size.

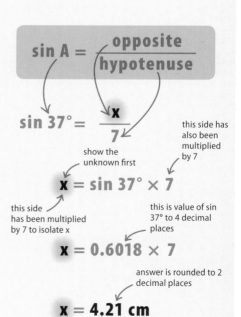

$$\sin A = \frac{\text{opposite}}{\text{hypotenuse}}$$

$$\sin 37° = \frac{x}{7}$$

show the
unknown first

this side has
also been
multiplied
by 7

$$x = \sin 37° \times 7$$

this side
has been multiplied
by 7 to isolate x

this is value of sin
37° to 4 decimal
places

$$x = 0.6018 \times 7$$

answer is rounded to 2
decimal places

$$x = 4.21 \text{ cm}$$

Using the cosine formula

In this right triangle, one angle other than the right angle is known, as is the length of the side adjacent to it. The hypotenuse is the missing side that needs to be found.

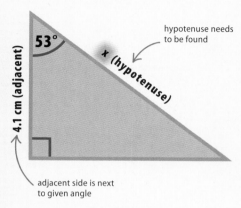

hypotenuse needs to be found

53°

x (hypotenuse)

4.1 cm (adjacent)

adjacent side is next to given angle

Choose the right formula—because the side adjacent to the angle is known and the value of the hypotenuse is missing, use the cosine formula.

Substitute the known values into the formula.

Rearrange to make x the subject of the equation—first multiply both sides by x.

Divide both sides by cos 53° to make x the subject of the equation.

Use a calculator to find the value of cos 53°—press the cos button then enter 53.

Round the answer to a suitable size.

$$\cos A = \frac{\text{adjacent}}{\text{hypotenuse}}$$

$$\cos 53° = \frac{4.1}{x}$$

this side has also been multiplied by x

$$\cos 53° \times x = 4.1$$

this side has been multiplied by x

this side has also been multiplied by x, leaving 4.1 on its own

$$x = \frac{4.1}{\cos 53°}$$

this side has been divided by cos 53° to isolate x

this side has also been divided by cos 53°

$$x = \frac{4.1}{0.6018}$$

value of cos 53° is rounded to 4 decimal places

$$x = 6.81 \text{ cm}$$

answer is rounded to 2 decimal places

Using the tangent formula

In this right triangle, one angle other than the right angle is known, as is the length of the side adjacent to it. Find the length of the side opposite the angle.

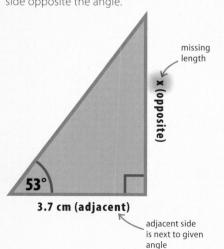

missing length

x (opposite)

53°

3.7 cm (adjacent)

adjacent side is next to given angle

Choose the right formula—since the side adjacent to the angle given are known and the opposite side is sought, use the tangent formula.

Substitute the known values into the tangent formula.

Rearrange to make x the subject by multiplying both sides by 3.7.

Use a calculator to find the value of tan 53° – press the tan button then enter 53.

Round the answer to a suitable size.

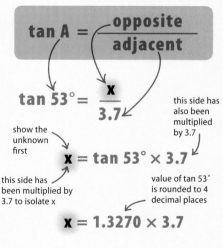

$$\tan A = \frac{\text{opposite}}{\text{adjacent}}$$

$$\tan 53° = \frac{x}{3.7}$$

this side has also been multiplied by 3.7

show the unknown first

$$x = \tan 53° \times 3.7$$

this side has been multiplied by 3.7 to isolate x

value of tan 53° is rounded to 4 decimal places

$$x = 1.3270 \times 3.7$$

$$x = 4.91 \text{ cm}$$

the answer is rounded to 2 decimal places

Finding missing angles

IF THE LENGTHS OF TWO SIDES OF A RIGHT TRIANGLE ARE KNOWN,
ITS MISSING ANGLES CAN BE FOUND.

SEE ALSO

❮ **72–73** Using a calculator

❮ **160** What is
trigonometry?

❮ **162–163** Finding missing
sides

Formulas   **177–179** ❯

To find the missing angles in a right triangle, the inverse sine, cosine, and
tangent are used. Use a calculator to find these values.

Which formula?

Choose the formula that contains the pair of sides that are
given in an example. For instance, use the sine formula if the
lengths of the hypotenuse and the side opposite the unknown
angle are known, and the cosine formula if the lengths of the
hypotenuse and the side next to the angle are given.

▽ **Calculator functions**
To find the inverse values of sine, cosine,
and tangent, press shift before sine,
cosine, or tangent.

$$\sin^{-1} \qquad \cos^{-1} \qquad \tan^{-1}$$

SHIFT then **sin** **cos** **tan**

this is the   this is the   this is the
sine button   cosine button   tangent button

$$\sin A = \frac{\text{opposite}}{\text{hypotenuse}}$$

△ **The sine formula**
Use the sine formula if the lengths of the
hypotenuse and the side opposite the
missing angle are known.

$$\cos A = \frac{\text{adjacent}}{\text{hypotenuse}}$$

△ **The cosine formula**
Use the cosine formula if the lengths of the
hypotenuse and the side adjacent (next to)
to the missing angle are known.

$$\tan A = \frac{\text{opposite}}{\text{adjacent}}$$

△ **The tangent formula**
Use the tangent formula if the lengths of
the sides opposite and adjacent to the
missing angle are known.

Using the sine formula

In this right triangle the hypotenuse and the side opposite angle A
are known. Use the sine formula to find the size of angle A.

side opposite
angle to be found

right angle

4.5 cm (opposite)

7.7 cm (hypotenuse)

hypotenuse is side
opposite right angle

A

this is the missing
angle

Choose the right formula—in
this example the hypotenuse
and the side opposite the
missing angle, A, are known,
so use the sine formula.

▼

Substitute the known values
into the sine formula.

▼

Work out the value of sin A
by dividing the opposite side
by the hypotenuse.

▼

Find the value of the angle by
using the inverse sine function
on a calculator.

▼

Round the answer to a
suitable size. This is the value
of the missing angle.

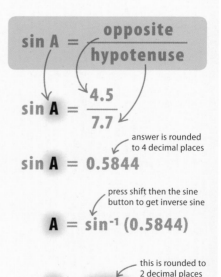

$$\sin A = \frac{\text{opposite}}{\text{hypotenuse}}$$

$$\sin A = \frac{4.5}{7.7}$$

answer is rounded
to 4 decimal places

$$\sin A = 0.5844$$

press shift then the sine
button to get inverse sine

$$A = \sin^{-1}(0.5844)$$

this is rounded to
2 decimal places

$$A = 35.76°$$

Using the cosine formula

In this right triangle the hypotenuse and the side adjacent to
angle A are known. Use the cosine formula to find the size of
angle A.

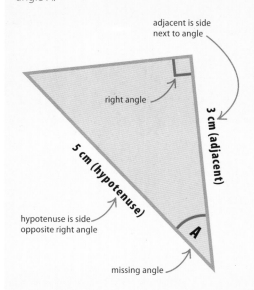

adjacent is side
next to angle

right angle

3 cm (adjacent)

5 cm (hypotenuse)

hypotenuse is side
opposite right angle

A

missing angle

Choose the right formula. In
this example the hypotenuse and
the side adjacent to the mssing
angle, A, are known, so use the
cosine formula.

$$\cos A = \frac{\text{adjacent}}{\text{hypotenuse}}$$

Substitute the known values
into the formula.

$$\cos A = \frac{3}{5}$$

Work out the value of cos A by
dividing the adjacent side by the
length of the hypotenuse.

$$\cos A = 0.6$$

Find the value of the angle by
using the inverse cosine function on
a calculator.

press shift then
cosine button to get
inverse cosine

$$A = \cos^{-1}(0.6)$$

Round the answer to a suitable size.
This is the value of the missing angle.

answer is
rounded to 2
decimal places

$$A = 53.13°$$

Using the tangent formula

In this right triangle the sides opposite and adjacent to angle A
are known. Use the tangent formula to find the size of angle A.

hypotenuse is
side opposite
right angle

side opposite
missing
angle

6 cm (opposite)

missing angle

right angle

A

4.5 cm (adjacent)

adjacent is side next
to angle

Choose the right formula—here
the sides opposite and adjacent to
the missing angle, A, are known,
so use the tangent formula.

$$\tan A = \frac{\text{opposite}}{\text{adjacent}}$$

Substitute the known values into
the tangent formula.

$$\tan A = \frac{6}{4.5}$$

answer rounded to
1 decimal place

Work out the value of tan A
by dividing the opposite by
the adjacent.

$$\tan A = 1.3$$

press shift then
tangent button to
get inverse tangent

Find the value of the angle by
using the inverse tangent function
on a calculator.

$$A = \tan^{-1}(1.3)$$

answer is rounded to
2 decimal places

Round the answer to a suitable size.
This is the value of the missing angle.

$$A = 52.43°$$

Algebra

What is algebra?

ALGEBRA IS A BRANCH OF MATHEMATICS IN WHICH LETTERS AND SYMBOLS ARE USED TO REPRESENT NUMBERS AND THE RELATIONSHIPS BETWEEN NUMBERS.

Algebra is widely used in maths, in sciences such as physics, as well as in other areas, such as economics. Formulas for solving a wide range of problems are often given in algebraic form.

Using letters and symbols

Algebra uses letters and symbols. Letters usually represent numbers, and symbols represent operations, such as addition and subtraction. This allows relationships between quantities to be written in a short, generalized way, eliminating the need to give individual specific examples containing actual values. For instance, the volume of a rectangular solid can be written as lwh (which means length × width × height), enabling the volume of any cuboid to be found once its dimensions are known.

boths sides must be balanced (equal) at all times

◁ **Balancing**
Both sides of an equation must always be balanced. For example, in the equation a + b = c + d, if a number is added to one side, it must be added to the other side to keep the equation balanced.

TERM
The parts of an algebraic expression that are separated by symbols for operations, such as + and −. A term can be a number, a variable, or a combination of both

OPERATION
A procedure carried out on the terms of an algebraic expression, such as addition, subtraction, multiplication, and division

VARIABLE
An unknown number or quantity represented by a letter

$$2 + \; ? \; b$$

EXPRESSION
An expression is a statement written in algebraic form, 2 + b in the example above. An expression can contain any combination of numbers, letters, and symbols (such as + for addition)

△ **Algebraic equation**
An equation is a mathematical statement that two things are equal. In this example, the left side (2 + b) is equal to the right side (8).

REAL WORLD
Algebra in everyday life

Although algebra may seem abstract, with equations consisting of strings of symbols and letters, it has many applications in everyday life. For example, an equation can be used to find out the area of something, such as a tennis court.

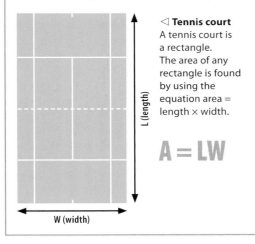

◁ **Tennis court**
A tennis court is a rectangle. The area of any rectangle is found by using the equation area = length × width.

L (length)

W (width)

$$A = LW$$

EQUALS
The equals sign means that the two sides of the equation balance each other

CONSTANT
A number with a value that is always the same

THE ANSWER IS:
b = 6

BASIC RULES OF ALGEBRA
Like other areas of maths, algebra has rules that must be followed to get the correct answer. For example, one rule is about the order in which operations must be done.

Addition and subtraction
Terms can be added together in any order in algebra. However, when subtracting, the order of the terms must be kept as it was given.

$$a + b \qquad = \qquad b + a$$

△ **Two terms**
When adding together two terms, it is possible to start with either term.

$$(a + b) + c \qquad = \qquad a + (b + c)$$

△ **Three terms**
As with adding two terms, three terms can be added together in any order.

Multiplication and division
Multiplying terms in algebra can be done in any order, but when dividing the terms must be kept in the order they were given.

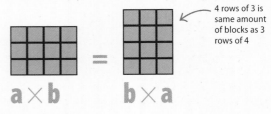

4 rows of 3 is same amount of blocks as 3 rows of 4

$$a \times b \qquad b \times a$$

△ **Two terms**
When multiplying together two terms, the terms can be in any order.

$$a \times (b \times c) \qquad b \times (a \times c) \qquad c \times (a \times b)$$

△ **Three terms**
Multiplication of three terms can be done in any order.

Sequences

A SEQUENCE IS A SERIES OF NUMBERS WRITTEN AS A LIST
THAT FOLLOWS A PARTICULAR PATTERN, OR "RULE."

SEE ALSO

❰ 36–39 Powers and roots
❰ 168–169 What is algebra?
Working with expressions   172–173 ❱
Formulas   177–179 ❱

Each number in a sequence is called a "term." The value of any term
in a sequence can be worked out by using the rule for that sequence.

The terms of a sequence

The first number in a sequence is the first
term, the second number in a sequence
is the second term, and so on.

rule for this sequence is each term
equals previous term plus 2

fifth term
is 10

▷ **A basic sequence**
For this sequence, the rule is that
each term is the previous term
with 2 added to it.

first term
is 2

dots show
sequence
continues

+2   +2   +2   +2

$$2, \quad 4, \quad 6, \quad 8, \quad 10, \quad \ldots$$

1st term   2nd term   3rd term   4th term   5th term

Finding the "nth" value

The value of a particular term can be found without
writing out the entire sequence up until that point
by writing the rule as an expression and then using
this expression to work out the term.

▷ **The rule as an expression**
Knowing the expression, which
is 2n in this example, helps find
the value of any term.

2n

expression used to
find value of term—
1 is substituted for n
in 1st term, 2 in 2nd
term, and so on

means 2 × n   substitute 1 for n
$$2n = 2 \times 1 = 2$$

$$2n = 2 \times 2 = 4$$

$$2n = 2 \times 41 = 82$$

$$2n = 2 \times 1{,}000 = 2{,}000$$

1st term

2nd term

41st term

1,000th term

To find the first term,
substitute 1 for n.

To find the second term,
substitute 2 for n.

To find the 41st term,
substitute 41 for n.

For the 1,000th term, substitute
1,000 for n. The term here is 2,000.

In the example below, the expression is 4n − 2. Knowing this, the rule
can be shown to be: each term is equal to the previous term plus 4.

+4   +4   +4   +4

$$2, \quad 6, \quad 10, \quad 14, \quad 18, \quad \ldots$$

1st term 2nd term 3rd term 4th term 5th term

sum of 14 and 4

expression here is 4
multiplied by n, minus 2

4n−2

value of term

$$4n - 2 = 4 \times 1 - 2 = 2$$

$$4n - 2 = 4 \times 2 - 2 = 6$$

$$4n - 2 = (4 \times 1{,}000{,}000) - 2 = 3{,}999{,}998$$

1st term

2nd term

1,000,000th term

To find the first term,
substitute 1 for n.

To find the second term,
substitute 2 for n.

For the 1,000,000th term, substitute
1,000,000 for n. The term here is 3,999,998.

IMPORTANT SEQUENCES

Some sequences have rules that are slightly more complicated; however, they can be very significant. Two examples of these are square numbers and the Fibonacci sequence.

Square numbers

A square number is found by multiplying a whole number by itself. These numbers can be drawn as squares. Each side is the length of a whole number, which is multiplied by itself to make the square number.

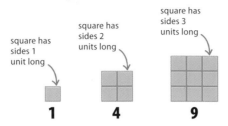

square has sides 1 unit long

square has sides 2 units long

square has sides 3 units long

square has sides 4 units long

square has sides 5 units long

1   **4**   **9**   **16**   **25**

Fibonacci sequence

The Fibonacci sequence is a widely recognized sequence, appearing frequently in nature and architecture. The first two terms of the sequence are both 1, then after this each term is the sum of the two terms that came before it.

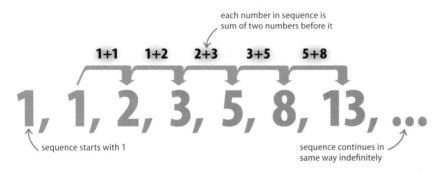

each number in sequence is sum of two numbers before it

1+1   1+2   2+3   3+5   5+8

1, 1, 2, 3, 5, 8, 13, ...

sequence starts with 1

sequence continues in same way indefinitely

REAL WORLD

Fibonacci and nature

Evidence of the Fibonacci sequence is found everywhere, including in nature. The sequence forms a spiral (see below) and it can be seen in the spiral of a shell (as shown here) or in the arrangement of the seeds in a sunflower. It is named after Leonardo Fibonacci, an Italian mathematician.

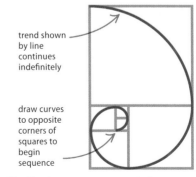

How to draw a Fibonacci spiral

A spiral can be drawn using the numbers in the Fibonacci sequence, by drawing squares with sides as long as each term in the sequence, then drawing a curve to touch the opposite corners of these squares.

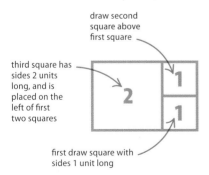

draw second square above first square

third square has sides 2 units long, and is placed on the left of first two squares

first draw square with sides 1 unit long

each new square has sides that are total length of all that came before

continue to add squares counterclockwise, so they all fit together

trend shown by line continues indefinitely

draw curves to opposite corners of squares to begin sequence

First, draw a square that is 1 unit long by 1 unit wide. Draw an identical one above it, then a square with sides 2 units long next to the 1 unit squares. Each square represents a term of the sequence.

Keep drawing squares that represent the terms of the Fibonacci sequence, adding them in a counterclockwise direction. This diagram shows the first six terms of the sequence.

Finally, draw curves to touch the opposite corners of each square, starting at the center and working outward counterclockwise. This curve is a Fibonacci spiral.

2ab Working with expressions

AN EXPRESSION IS A COLLECTION OF SYMBOLS, SUCH AS X AND Y, AND
OPERATIONS, SUCH AS + AND −. IT CAN ALSO CONTAIN NUMBERS.

SEE ALSO

⟨ 168–169
What is algebra?

Formulas   177–179 ⟩

Expressions are important and occur everywhere in mathematics. They can
be simplified to as few parts as possible, making them easier to understand.

Like terms in an expression

Each part of an expression is called a "term." A term can be a number, a symbol, or a number with
a symbol. Terms with the same symbols are "like terms" and it is possible to combine them.

x is symbol

like terms

+ is operation

$$2x + 2y - 4y + 3x$$

like terms

◁ **Identifying like terms**
The terms 2x and 3x are like terms
because they both contain the symbol x.
Terms 2y and −4y are also like terms
because each contains the symbol y.

Simplifying expressions involving addition and subtraction

When an expression is made up of a number of terms that are to be added or subtracted, there
are a number of important steps that need to be followed in order to simplify it.

▷ **Write down the expression**
Before simplifying the
expression, write it out in a line
from left to right.

$$3a - 5b + 6b - 2a + 3b - 7b$$

▷ **Group the like terms**
Then group the like terms
together, keeping the
operations as they are.

$$3a - 2a - 5b + 6b + 3b - 7b$$

like terms   like terms

▷ **Work out the result**
The next step is to work
out the result of each
like term.

3a − 2a = 1a → $1a - 3b$ ← −5b + 6b + 3b − 7b = −3b

▷ **Simplify the result**
Further simplify the result
by removing any 1s in front
of symbols.

term 1a always
written as a → $a - 3b$

Simplifying expressions involving multiplication

To simplify an expression that involves terms linked by multiplication signs, the individual numbers and symbols first need to be separated from each other.

simplified expression written without multiplication signs

$$6a \times 2b \quad\Rightarrow\quad 6 \times a \times 2 \times b \quad\Rightarrow\quad 12 \times ab = \mathbf{12ab}$$

▶ **The term 6a** means $6 \times a$. Similarly, the term 2b means $2 \times b$.

▶ **Separate the expression** into the individual numbers and symbols involved.

▶ **The product of** multiplying 6 and 2 is 12, and that of multiplying a and b is ab. The simplified expression is 12ab.

Simplifying expressions involving division

To simplify an expression involving division, look for any possible cancellation. This means looking to divide all terms of the expression by the same number or letter.

q^2 means $q \times q$

this means $2 \times q$

divide 6 by 2, leaving 3

divide q by q, leaving 1

3pq divided by 1 is simply 3pq

$$6pq^2 \div 2q \quad\Rightarrow\quad \frac{6 \times p \times q \times q}{2 \times q} \quad\Rightarrow\quad \frac{\overset{3}{\cancel{6}} \times p \times q \times \cancel{q}}{\underset{1}{\cancel{2}} \times \underset{1}{\cancel{q}}} \quad\Rightarrow\quad \frac{3pq}{1} = \mathbf{3pq}$$

same as ÷

divide 2 by 2, leaving 1

divide q by q, leaving 1

▶ **Any chance to** cancel the expression down makes it smaller and easier to understand.

▶ **Both terms** (top and bottom) are canceled down by dividing them by 2 and q.

▶ **Canceling down by** dividing each term equally makes the expression smaller.

Substitution

Once the value of each symbol in an expression is known, for example that $y = 2$, the overall value of the expression can be found. This is called "substituting" the values in the expression or "evaluating" the expression.

Substitute the values in the expression $2x - 2y - 4y + 3x$ if

$$x = 1 \quad \text{and} \quad y = 2$$

L = LENGTH

W = WIDTH

◁ **Substituting values**
The formula for the area of a rectangle is length × width. Substituting 5 in for the length and 8 in for the width, gives an area of 5 in × 8 in = 40 in².

like terms

grouped terms are easier to substitute

substitute 1 for x

answer is −7

$$2x - 2y - 4y + 3x \quad\Rightarrow\quad 5x - 6y \quad\Rightarrow\quad \begin{array}{l} 5x = 5 \times 1 = 5 \\ -6y = -6 \times 2 = -12 \end{array} \quad\Rightarrow\quad 5 - 12 = \mathbf{-7}$$

like terms

substitute 2 for y

▶ **Group like terms** together to simplify the expression.

▶ **The expression** has now been simplified.

▶ **Now substitute** the given values for x and y.

▶ **The final answer** is shown to be −7.

2(a + 2) Expanding and factorizing expressions

SEE ALSO

❮ **172–173** Working with expressions

Quadratic expressions **176** ❯

THE SAME EXPRESSION CAN BE WRITTEN IN DIFFERENT WAYS—MULTIPLIED OUT (EXPANDED) OR GROUPED INTO ITS COMMON FACTORS (FACTORIZED).

How to expand an expression

The same expression can be written in a variety of ways, depending on how it will be used. Expanding an expression involves multiplying all the parts it contains (terms) and writing it out in full.

first term is multiplied by number

second term is multiplied by number

$4 \times a = 4a$ $4 \times 3 = 12$

$$4(a + 3) = 4 \times a + 4 \times 3 = 4a + 12$$

number outside is multiplied by each number inside

sign between terms remains the same

▶ **To expand an expression** with a number outside a parenthesis, multiply all the terms inside the parenthesis by that number.

▶ **Multiply each term** inside the parenthesis by the number outside. The sign between the two terms (letters and numbers) remains the same.

▶ **Simplify the resulting terms** to show the expanded expression in its final form. Here, $4 \times a$ is simplified to $4a$ and 4×3 to 12.

Expanding multiple parentheses

To expand an expression that contains two parentheses, each part of the first one is multiplied by each part of the second parenthesis. To do this, split up the first (blue) parenthesis into its parts. Multiply the second (yellow) parenthesis by the first part and then by the second part of the first parenthesis.

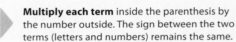

second parenthesis multiplied by first part of first parenthesis

$3x \times 2y = 6xy$ $3x \times 3 = 9x$ $1 \times 2y = 2y$ $1 \times 3 = 3$

$$(3x + 1)(2y + 3) = 3x(2y + 3) + 1(2y + 3) = 6xy + 9x + 2y + 3$$

first parenthesis   second parenthesis

second parenthesis multiplied by second term of first parenthesis

these signs remain

▶ **To expand an expression** of two parentheses, multiply all the terms of the second by all the terms of the first.

▶ **Break down the first parenthesis** into its terms. Multiply the second parenthesis by each term from the first in turn.

▶ **Simplify the resulting terms** by carrying out each multiplication. The signs remain the same.

Squaring a parenthesis

Squaring a parenthesis simply means multiplying a parenthesis by itself. Write it out as two parentheses next to each other, and then multiply it to expand as shown above.

parenthesis means multiply

$x \times x = x^2$ $x \times -3 = -3x$ $-3 \times x = -3x$ $-3 \times -3 = 9$

$$(x - 3)^2 = (x - 3)(x - 3) = x(x - 3) - 3(x - 3) = x^2 - 3x - 3x + 9 = x^2 - 6x + 9$$

multiply second parenthesis by first part of first one

sign remains the same

multiply second parenthesis by second part of first parenthesis

▶ **To expand a squared parenthesis,** first write the expression out as two parentheses next to each other.

▶ **Split the first parenthesis** into its terms and multiply the second parenthesis by each term in turn.

▶ **Simplify the resulting terms,** making sure to multiply their signs correctly. Finally, add or subtract like terms (see pp.172–173) together.

How to factorize an expression

Factorizing an expression is the opposite of expanding an expression. To do this, look for a factor (number or letter) that all the terms (parts) of the expression have in common. The common factor can then be placed outside a parenthesis enclosing what is left of the other terms.

4 is common to both 4b and 12 (because they can both be divided by 4)

this is the same as 12

both b and 3 are not common to both parts so they go inside the parenthesis

place 4 outside parenthesis

remaining factors go inside parenthesis

$$4b + 12$$

this means $4 \times b$

$$4 \times b + 4 \times 3$$

$$4(b + 3)$$

parenthesis means multiply

To factorize an expression, look for any letter or number (factor) that all its parts have in common.

In this case, 4 is a common factor of both 4b and 12, because both can be divided by 4. Divide each by 4 to find the remaining factors of each part. These go inside the parenthesis.

Simplify the expression by placing the common factor (4) outside a parenthesis. The other two factors are placed inside the parenthesis.

Factorizing more complex expressions

Factorizing can make it simpler to understand and write complex expressions with many terms. Find the factors that all parts of the expression have in common.

3×3

$3 \times 3 \times x \times x \times x \times y = 9x^2y$

$x \times x$

3×5

$3 \times 5 \times x \times y \times y = 15xy^2$

$x \times y^2$

$2 \times 3 \times 3 \times x \times y \times y \times y = 18xy^3$

$y \times y$

$$9x^2y + 15xy^2 + 18xy^3$$

all 3 terms multiplied

To factorize an expression write out the factors of each part, for example, y^2 is $y \times y$. Look for the numbers and letters that are common to all the factors.

common factor of x variables

common factor of numbers

common factor of y variables

$$3xy$$

All the parts of the expressions contain the letters x and y, and can be factorized by the number 3. These factors are combined to produce one common factor.

3xy is common factor of all parts of the expression

$9x^2y \div 3xy = 3x$

$15xy^2 \div 3xy = 5y$

$18xy^3 \div 3xy = 6y^2$

$$3xy(3x + 5y + 6y^2)$$

Set the common factor (3xy) outside a set of parentheses. Inside, write what remains of each part when divided by it.

LOOKING CLOSER

Factorizing a formula

The formula for finding the surface area (see pp.156–157) of a shape can be worked out using known formulas for the areas of its parts. The formula can look daunting, but it can be made much easier to use by factorizing it.

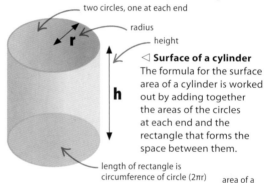

two circles, one at each end

radius

height

r

h

◁ **Surface of a cylinder**
The formula for the surface area of a cylinder is worked out by adding together the areas of the circles at each end and the rectangle that forms the space between them.

length of rectangle is circumference of circle (2πr)

area of rectangle is length (2πr) height (h)

area of a circle is πr², for 2 circles it is 2πr²

$$2\pi rh + 2\pi r^2$$

To find the formula for the surface area of a cylinder, add together the formulas for the areas of its parts.

2πr is common to both expressions

means multiply by

h and r are not common to both terms so they sit inside the parenthesis

$$2\pi r (h + r)$$

To make the formula easier to use, simplify it by identifying the common factor, in this case 2πr, and setting it outside the parentheses.

Quadratic expressions

A QUADRATIC EXPRESSION CONTAINS AN UNKNOWN TERM (VARIABLE) SQUARED, SUCH AS X^2.

SEE ALSO

❮ **174–175** Expanding and factorizing expressions

Factorizing quadratic equations **190–191** ❯

An expression is a collection of mathematical symbols, such as x and y, and operations, such as + and −. A quadratic expression typically contains a squared variable (x^2), a number multiplied by the same variable (x), and a number.

What is a quadratic expression?

A quadratic expression is usually given in the form $ax^2 + bx + c$, where a is the multiple of the squared term x^2, b is the multiple of x, and c is the number. The letters a, b, and c all stand for different positive or negative numbers.

a can be any number, including 1

squared term listed first

term multiplied by x listed next

number listed last

◁ **Quadratic expression**
The standard form of a quadratic expression is one with squared term (x^2) listed first, terms multiplied by x listed second, and the number listed last.

From two parentheses to a quadratic expression

Some quadratic expressions can be factorized to form two expressions within parentheses, each containing a variable (x) and an unknown number. Conversely, multiplying out these expressions gives a quadratic expression.

Multiplying two expressions in parentheses means multiplying every term of one parenthesis with every term of the other. The final answer will be a quadratic equation.

To multiply the two parentheses, split one of the parentheses into its terms. Multiply all the terms of the second parenthesis first by the x term and then by the numerical term of the first parenthesis.

Multiplying both terms of the second parenthesis by each term of the first in turn results in a squared term, two terms multiplied by x, and two numerical terms multiplied together.

Simplify the expression by adding the x terms. This means adding the numbers together inside parentheses and multiplying the result by an x outside.

Looking back at the original quadratic expression, it is possible to see that the numerical terms are added to give b, and multiplied to give c.

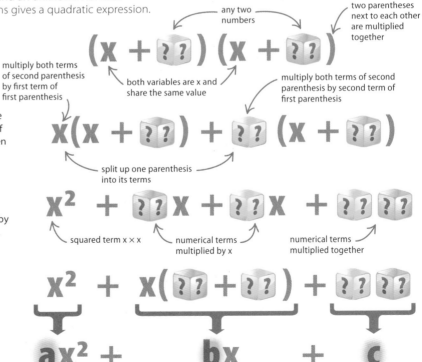

any two numbers

two parentheses next to each other are multiplied together

multiply both terms of second parenthesis by first term of first parenthesis

both variables are x and share the same value

multiply both terms of second parenthesis by second term of first parenthesis

split up one parenthesis into its terms

squared term x × x

numerical terms multiplied by x

numerical terms multiplied together

number terms are added to give b

number terms are multiplied to give c

Formulas

IN MATHS, A FORMULA IS BASICALLY A "RECIPE" FOR FINDING THE VALUE OF ONE THING (THE SUBJECT) WHEN OTHERS ARE KNOWN.

SEE ALSO
❮ **74–75** Personal finance
❮ **172–173** Working with expressions
Solving equations **180–181** ❯

A formula usually has a single subject and an equals sign, together with an expression written in symbols that indicates how to find the subject.

Introducing formulas

The recipe that makes up a formula can be simple or complicated. However, formulas usually have three basic parts: a single letter at the beginning (the subject); an equals sign that links the subject to the recipe; and the recipe itself, which when used, works out the value of the subject.

◁ **Area of a tennis court**
A tennis court is a rectangle. The area of the court depends on its length (L) and width (W).

area is the space occupied by the tennis court

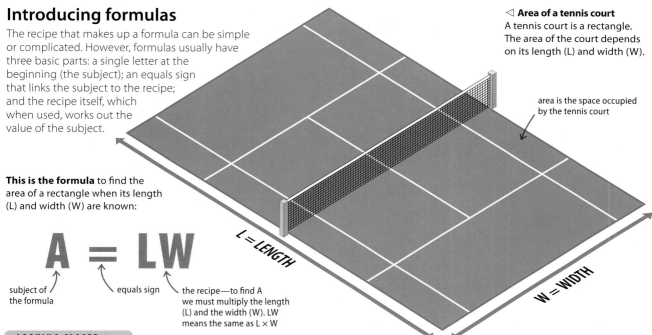

L = LENGTH

W = WIDTH

This is the formula to find the area of a rectangle when its length (L) and width (W) are known:

$$A = LW$$

subject of the formula

equals sign

the recipe—to find A we must multiply the length (L) and the width (W). LW means the same as L × W

LOOKING CLOSER

Formula triangles

Formulas can be rearranged to make different parts the subject of the formula. This is useful if the unknown value to be found is not the subject of the original formula—the formula can be rearranged so that the unknown becomes the subject, making solving the formula easier.

area (A) is the subject of the formula →

$$A = L \times W$$

area (A) = length (L) multiplied by width (W)

◁ **Simple rearrangement**
This triangle shows the different ways the formula for finding a rectangle can be rearranged.

A stands for area

L stands for length

W stands for width

length (L) = area (A) divided by width (W)

$$L = \frac{A}{W}$$

length (L) is the subject of the formula

width (W) = area (A) divided by length (L)

$$W = \frac{A}{L}$$

width (W) is the subject of the formula

CHANGING THE SUBJECT OF A FORMULA

Changing the subject of a formula involves moving letters or numbers (terms) from one side of the formula to the other, leaving a new term on its own. The way to do this depends on whether the term being moved is positive (+c), negative (-c), or whether it is part of a multiplication (bc) or division (b/c). When moving terms, whatever is done to one side of the formula needs to be done to the other.

Moving a positive term

$$A = b + c$$

To make b the subject, +c needs to be moved to the other side of the equals sign.

−c is brought in to the left of the equals sign   −c is brought in to the right of the equals sign

$$A - c = b + c - c$$

Add −c to both sides. To move +c, its opposite (−c) must first be added to both sides of the formula to keep it balanced.

+c−c cancels out because c − c = 0

$$A - c = b + \cancel{c} - \cancel{c}$$

Simplify the formula by canceling out −c and +c on the right, leaving b by itself as the subject of the formula.

a formula must have a single symbol on one side of the equals sign

$$A - c = b$$

The formula can now be rearranged so that it reads **b = A − c.**

Moving a negative term

$$A = b - c$$

To make b the subject, −c needs to be moved to the other side of the equals sign.

+c is brought in to the left of the equals sign   +c is brought in to the right of the equals sign

$$A + c = b - c + c$$

Add +c to both sides. To move −c, its opposite (+c) must first be added to both sides of the formula to keep it balanced.

−c+c cancels out because c − c = 0

$$A + c = b - \cancel{c} + \cancel{c}$$

Simplify the formula by canceling out −c and +c on the right, leaving b by itself as the subject of the formula.

a formula must have a single symbol on one side of the equals sign

$$A + c = b$$

The formula can now be rearranged so that it reads **b = A + c.**

Moving a term in a multiplication problem

bc means b × c

$$A = bc$$

In this example, b is multiplied by c. To make b the subject, c needs to move to the other side.

÷c (or /c) is brought in to the left of the equals sign   ÷c (or /c) is brought in to the right of the equals sign

$$\frac{A}{c} = \frac{bc}{c}$$

Divide both sides by c. To move the c to the other side, you must do the opposite of multiplying, which is dividing.

c/c cancels out because c/c equals 1

$$\frac{A}{c} = \frac{b\cancel{c}}{\cancel{c}}$$

Simplify the formula by canceling out c/c on the right, leaving b by itself as the subject of the formula.

a formula must have a single symbol on one side of the equals sign

$$\frac{A}{c} = b$$

The formula can now be rearranged so that it reads **b = A/c.**

Moving a term in a division problem

b/c means b ÷ c

$$A = \frac{b}{c}$$

In this example, b is divided by c. To make b the subject, c needs to move to the other side.

×c is brought in to the left of the equals sign   ×c is brought in to the right of the equals sign

$$A \times c = \frac{b \times c}{c}$$

Multiply both sides by c. To move the c to the other side, you must do the opposite of dividing, which is multiplying.

c/c cancels out because c/c equals 1

$$A \times c = \frac{b\cancel{c}}{\cancel{c}}$$

Simplify the formula by canceling out c/c on the right, leaving b by itself as the subject of the formula.

remember that A × c is written as Ac

a formula must have a single symbol on one side of the equals sign

$$Ac = b$$

The formula can now be rearranged so that it reads **b = Ac.**

FORMULAS IN ACTION

A formula can be used to calculate how much interest (the amount a bank pays someone in exchange for being able to borrow their money) is paid into a bank account over a particular period of time. The formula for this is principal (or amount of money) × rate of interest × time. This formula is shown here.

this stands for principal, which just means the amount

this stands for rate of interest

$$I = PRT$$

this stands for the time it will take to earn interest

this stands for interest

There is a bank account with $500 in it, earning simple interest (see pp.74–75) at 2% a year. To find out how much time (T) it will take to earn interest of $50, the formula above is used. First, the formula must be rearranged to make T the subject. Then the real values can be put in to work out T.

▷ **Move P**
The first step is to divide each side of the formula by P to move it to the left of the equals sign.

$$I = PRT \quad \Rightarrow \quad \frac{I}{P} = RT$$

remember that dividing the right side by **P** gives **P**RT/**P**, but the **P**s cancel out, leaving **RT**

to remove P from the right side, divide each side of the formula by P

▷ **Move R**
The next step is to divide each side of the formula by R to move it to the left of the equals sign.

to remove R from the right side, divide each side of the formula by R

$$\frac{I}{P} = RT \quad \Rightarrow \quad \frac{I}{PR} = T$$

remember that dividing the right side by **R** gives **R**T/**R**, but the **R**s cancel out, leaving **T**.

▷ **Put in real values**
Put in the real values for I ($50), P ($500), and R (2%) to find the value of T (the time it will take to earn interest of $50).

interest (I) is $50

length of time (T) to earn interest of $50 is 5 years

$$T = \frac{I}{PR} \quad \Rightarrow \quad \frac{50}{500 \times 0.02} = \textbf{5 years}$$

principal (P) is $500

rate of interest (R) is 2%, written as a decimal as 0.02

Solving equations

AN EQUATION IS A MATHEMATICAL STATEMENT THAT
CONTAINS AN EQUALS SIGN.

Equations can be rearranged to find the value of
an unknown variable, such as x or y.

Simple equations

Equations can be rearranged to find the value of an unknown
number, or variable. A variable is represented by a letter, such
as x or y. Whatever action is taken on one side of an equation
must also be made on the other side, so that both sides
remain equal.

Left-hand side   Right-hand side

$$a + b = c + d$$

◁ **Balancing**
The expressions on either
side of the equals sign in an
equation are always equal.

To find the value of x the equation must
be rearranged so that x is by itself on one
side of the equation.

to get rid of this
2, 2 must also be
taken from the
other side

variable

this expression has the same
value as the expression on the
other side of the equals sign

$$2 + x = 8$$

Changes made to one side of the equation
must also be made to the other side.
Subtract 2 from both sides to isolate x.

subtract 2 on this side

2 was subtracted from
the other side, so it must
also be subtracted from
this side

$$2 + x - 2 = 8 - 2$$

Simplify the equation by canceling out
the +2 and −2 on the left side. This leaves
x on its own on the left.

cancel out +2 and
−2, which gives 0

$$\cancel{2} + x \cancel{-2} = 8 - 2$$

Once x is the subject of the equation,
working out the right side of the
equation gives the value of x.

x is now the subject of
the equation

$$x = 6$$

working out the right side
of the equation (8 − 2)
gives the value of (6)

LOOKING CLOSER

Creating an equation

Equations can be created to explain day-to-day situations. For
example, a taxi firm charges $3 to pick up a customer, and $2
per mile traveled. This can be written as an equation.

If a customer pays $18 for a trip, the equation can be used to work
out how far the customer traveled.

pick-up cost

cost per mile
multiplied by
distance

$$c = 3 + 2d$$

total cost of the
trip

total cost of trip

cost per mile multiplied
by distance

$$18 = 3 + 2d$$

pick-up cost

Substitute the cost of the
trip into the equation.

3 has been
taken from
this side

$$15 = 2d$$

3 has been
taken from
this side

Rearrange the equation
– subtract 3 from both sides.

this side has been
divided by 2

$$7\tfrac{1}{2}\,\mathrm{mi} = d$$

to get rid of 2
in 2d, divide
both sides by 2

Find the distance traveled
by dividing both sides by 2.

MORE COMPLICATED EQUATIONS

More complicated equations are rearranged in the same way as simple equations—anything done to simplify one side of the equation must also be done to the other side so that both sides of the equation remain equal. The equation will give the same answer no matter where the rearranging is started.

Example 1

This equation has numerical and unknown terms on both sides, so it needs several rearrangements to solve.

First, rearrange the numerical terms. To remove the −9 from the right-hand side, add 9 to both sides of the equation.

Next, rearrange so that the a's are on the opposite side to the number. This is done by subtracting 2a from both sides.

Then rearrange again to make a the only subject of the equation. Since the equation contains 3a, divide the whole equation by 3.

The subject of the equation, a, is now on its own on the right side of the equation, and there is only a number on the other side.

Reverse the equation to show the unknown variable (a) first. This does not affect the meaning of the equation, because both sides are equal.

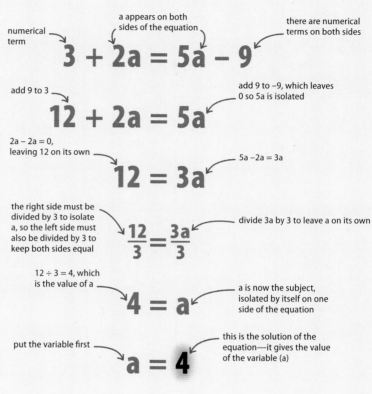

numerical term

a appears on both sides of the equation

there are numerical terms on both sides

$$3 + 2a = 5a - 9$$

add 9 to 3

add 9 to −9, which leaves 0 so 5a is isolated

$$12 + 2a = 5a$$

2a − 2a = 0, leaving 12 on its own

5a −2a = 3a

$$12 = 3a$$

the right side must be divided by 3 to isolate a, so the left side must also be divided by 3 to keep both sides equal

divide 3a by 3 to leave a on its own

$$\frac{12}{3} = \frac{3a}{3}$$

12 ÷ 3 = 4, which is the value of a

a is now the subject, isolated by itself on one side of the equation

$$4 = a$$

put the variable first

this is the solution of the equation—it gives the value of the variable (a)

$$a = 4$$

Example 2

This equation has unknown and numerical terms on both sides, so it will take several rearrangements to solve.

First rearrange the numerical terms. Subtract 4 from both sides of the equation so that there are numbers on only one side.

Then rearrange the equation so that the unknown variable is on the opposite side to the number, by adding 2a to both sides.

Finally, divide each side by 8 to make a the subject of the equation, and to find the solution of the equation.

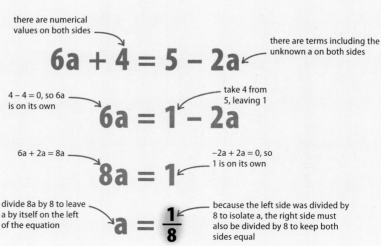

there are numerical values on both sides

there are terms including the unknown a on both sides

$$6a + 4 = 5 - 2a$$

4 − 4 = 0, so 6a is on its own

take 4 from 5, leaving 1

$$6a = 1 - 2a$$

6a + 2a = 8a

−2a + 2a = 0, so 1 is on its own

$$8a = 1$$

divide 8a by 8 to leave a by itself on the left of the equation

because the left side was divided by 8 to isolate a, the right side must also be divided by 8 to keep both sides equal

$$a = \frac{1}{8}$$

Linear graphs

GRAPHS ARE A WAY OF PICTURING AN EQUATION. A LINEAR
EQUATION ALWAYS HAS A STRAIGHT LINE.

Graphs of linear equations

A linear equation is an equation that does not contain a squared variable such as x^2, or a variable of a higher power, such as x^3. Linear equations can be represented by straight line graphs, where the line passes through coordinates that satisfy the equation. For example, one of the sets of coordinates for $y = x + 5$ is (1, 6), because $6 = 1 + 5$.

slope, or gradient   value of x

$$y = mx + b$$

value of y

value of y intercept—the point where the line crosses y axis

△ **The equation of a straight line**
All straight lines have an equation. The value of m is the slope (or slope) of the line and b is where it cuts the y axis.

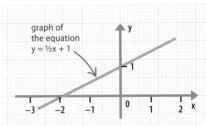

graph of the equation $y = \frac{1}{2}x + 1$

△ **A linear graph**
The graph of an equation is a set of points with coordinates that satisfy the equation.

Finding the equation of a line

To find the equation of a given line, use the graph to find its slope and y intercept. Then substitute them into the equation for a line, $y = mx + b$.

To find the slope of the line (m), draw lines out from a section of the line as shown. Then divide the vertical distance by horizontal distance—the result is the slope.

$$\text{slope} = \frac{\text{vertical distance}}{\text{horizontal distance}}$$

$$\frac{4}{4} = +1$$ ← slope

division sign

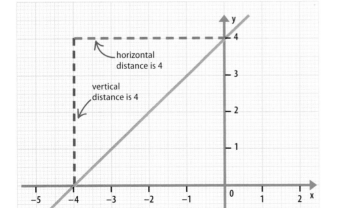

horizontal distance is 4

vertical distance is 4

▶ **Finally, substitute the values** that have been found from the graph into the equation for a line. This gives the equation for the line shown above.

To find the y intercept, look at the graph and find where the line crosses the y axis. This is the y intercept, and is b in the equation.

$$\text{y intercept} = (0,4)$$

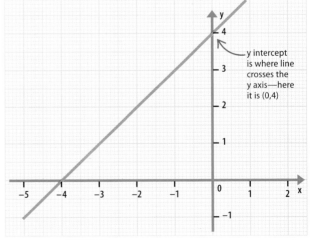

y intercept is where line crosses the y axis—here it is (0,4)

slope is +1

y intercept is 4

$$y = mx + b$$

1x simplifies to x

$$y = x + 4$$

Positive slopes

Lines that slope upward from left to right have positive slopes. The equation of a line with a positive slope can be worked out from its graph, as described below.

Find the slope of the line by choosing a section of it and drawing horizontal (green) and vertical (red) lines out from it so they meet. Count the units each new line covers, then divide the vertical by the horizontal distance.

$$slope = \frac{vertical\ distance}{horizontal\ distance} = \frac{6}{3} = +2$$

+ sign means line slopes upward from left to right

The y intercept can be easily read off the graph —it is the point where the line crosses the y axis.

$$y\ intercept = (0,1)$$

Substitute the values for the slope and y intercept into the equation of a line to find the equation for this given line.

slope is +2
y intercept is 1

$$y = mx + b \implies y = 2x + 1$$

slope
y intercept

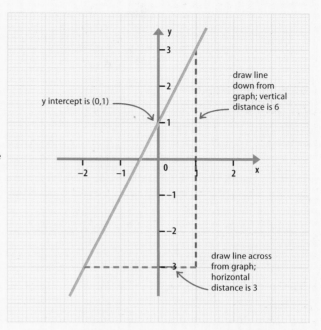

y intercept is (0,1)

draw line down from graph; vertical distance is 6

draw line across from graph; horizontal distance is 3

Negative slopes

Lines that slope downward from left to right have negative slopes. The equation of these lines can be worked out in the same way as for a line with a positive slope.

Find the slope of the line by choosing a section of it and drawing horizontal (green) and vertical (red) lines out from it so they meet. Count the units each new line covers, then divide the vertical by the horizontal distance.

$$slope = \frac{vertical\ distance}{horizontal\ distance} = \frac{4}{1} = 4 \implies -4$$

insert minus sign to show line slopes downward from left to right

The y intercept can be easily read off the graph —it is the point where the line crosses the y axis.

$$y\ intercept = (0,-4)$$

Substitute the values for the slope and y intercept into the equation of a line to find the equation for this given line.

y intercept is (0,−4)
slope is −4

$$y = mx + b \implies y = -4x - 4$$

slope
y intercept

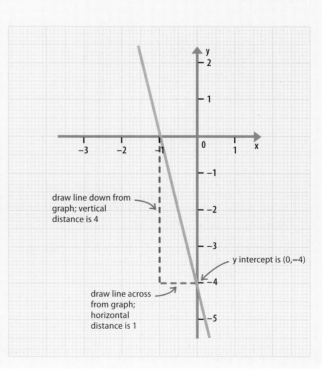

draw line down from graph; vertical distance is 4

y intercept is (0,−4)

draw line across from graph; horizontal distance is 1

How to plot a linear graph

The graph of a linear equation can be drawn by working out several different sets of values for x and y and then plotting these values on a pair of axes. The x values are measured along the x axis, and the y values along the y axis.

this means 2
multiplied by x

▷ **The equation**
This shows that each of the y values for this equation will be double the size of each of the x values.

$$y = 2x$$

first, choose some possible values of x

x	y =2x
1	2
2	4
3	6
4	8

then find corresponding values of y by doubling each x value

First, choose some possible values of x—numbers below 10 are easiest to work with. Find the corresponding values of y using a table. Put the x values in the first column, then multiply each number by 2 to find the corresponding values for y.

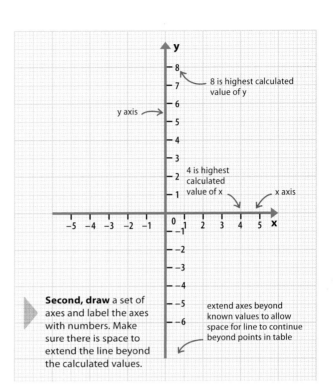

8 is highest calculated value of y

y axis

4 is highest calculated value of x

x axis

Second, draw a set of axes and label the axes with numbers. Make sure there is space to extend the line beyond the calculated values.

extend axes beyond known values to allow space for line to continue beyond points in table

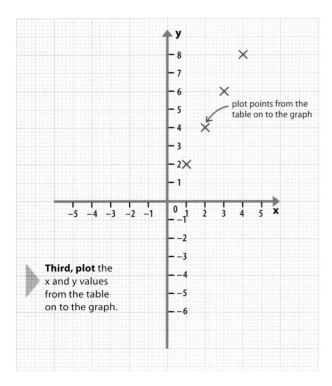

plot points from the table on to the graph

Third, plot the x and y values from the table on to the graph.

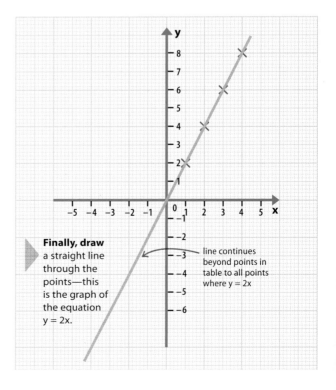

Finally, draw a straight line through the points—this is the graph of the equation y = 2x.

line continues beyond points in table to all points where y = 2x

Downward-sloping graph

Graphs of linear equations are read from left to right and slope down or up. Downward-sloping graphs have a negative gradient; upward-sloping ones have a positive gradient.

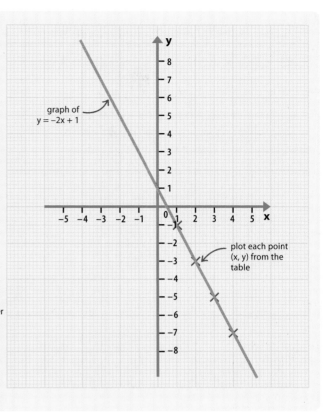

graph of
y = −2x + 1

The equation here contains the term −2x. Because x is multiplied by a negative number (−2), the graph will slope downward.

this means x multiplied by −2

$$y = -2x + 1$$

plot each point (x, y) from the table

Use a table to find some values for x and y. This equation is more complex than the last, so add more rows to the table: −2x and 1. Calculate each of these values, then add them to find y. It is important to keep track of negative signs in front of numbers.

write down some possible values of x

x	−2x	+1	y=−2x+1
1	−2	+1	−1
2	−4	+1	−3
3	−6	+1	−5
4	−8	+1	−7

work out corresponding values for y by adding together the parts of the equation

values of x multiplied by −2

+1 is constant

REAL WORLD

Temperature conversion graph

A linear graph can be used to show the conversion between the two main methods of measuring temperature—Fahrenheit and Celsius. To convert any temperature from Fahrenheit into Celsius, start at the position of the Fahrenheit temperature on the y axis, read horizontally across to the line, and then vertically down to the x axis to find the Celsius value.

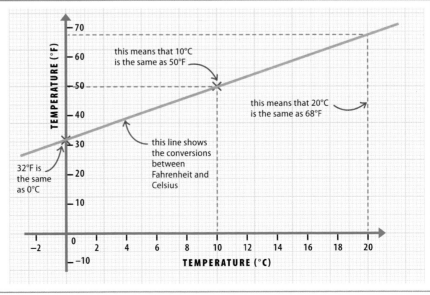

this means that 10°C is the same as 50°F

this means that 20°C is the same as 68°F

this line shows the conversions between Fahrenheit and Celsius

32°F is the same as 0°C

°F	°C
32.0	0
50.0	10

△ **Temperature conversion**
Two sets of values for Fahrenheit (F) and Celsius (C) give all the information that is needed to plot the conversion graph.

Simultaneous equations

SEE ALSO

⟨ 172–173 Working with expressions

⟨ 177–179 Formulas

SIMULTANEOUS EQUATIONS ARE PAIRS OF EQUATIONS WITH THE SAME UNKNOWN VARIABLES, THAT ARE SOLVED TOGETHER.

Solving simultaneous equations

Simultaneous equations are pairs of equations that contain the same variables and are solved together. There are three ways to solve a pair of simultaneous equations: elimination, substitution, and by graph; they all give the same answer.

both equations contain the variable x

both equations contain the variable y

$$3x - 5y = 4$$
$$4x + 5y = 17$$

◁ **A pair of equations** These simultaneous equations both contain the unknown variables x and y.

Solving by elimination

Make the x or y terms the same for both equations, then add or subtract them to eliminate that variable. The resulting equation finds the value of one variable, which is then used to find the other.

▷ **Equation pair** Solve this pair of simultaneous equations using the elimination method.

$$10x + 3y = 2$$
$$2x + 2y = 6$$

Multiply or divide one of the equations to make one variable the same as in the other equation. Here, the second equation is multiplied by 5 to make the x terms the same.

the second equation is multiplied by 5

$$10x + 3y = 2$$ — first equation stays as it is

$$2x + 2y = 6 \quad \times 5 \quad 10x + 10y = 30$$

this is the second equation

the x term is now the same as in the first equation

the second equation is multiplied by 5, so both equations now have the same value of x (10x)

Then add or subtract each set of terms in the second equation from or to each set in the first, to remove the matching terms. The new equation can then be solved. Here, the second equation is subtracted from the first, and the remaining variables are rearranged to isolate y.

this will cancel out the x terms

$$10x - 10x + 3y - 10y = 2 - 30$$

subtract the numerical terms from each other as well as the unknown terms

the x terms have been eliminated as 10x − 10x = 0

$$-7y = -28$$

this side is divided by −7 to isolate y

$$y = \frac{-28}{-7}$$

this side must also be divided by −7

$$y = 4$$ — this gives the value of y

Choose one of the two original equations—it does not matter which—and put in the value for y that has just been found. This eliminates the y variable from the equation, leaving only the x variable. Rearranging the equation means that it can be solved, and the value of the x can be found.

$$2x + 2y = 6$$ — the second equation has been chosen

$$2x + (2 \times 4) = 6$$ — it is already known that y = 4 so 2y = 8

$$2x + 8 = 6$$ — $2 \times 4 = 8$

subtracting 8 from this side to isolate 2x

$$2x = -2$$ — subtract 8 from this side: 6 − 8 = −2

divide this side by 2 to isolate x

$$x = \frac{-2}{2}$$ — this side must also be divided by 2

$$x = -1$$ — this is the value of x

Both unknown variables have now been found—these are the solutions to the original pair of equations.

$$x = -1 \qquad y = 4$$

Solving by substitution

To use this method, rearrange one of the two equations so that the two unknown values (variables) are on different sides of the equation, then substitute this rearranged equation into the other equation. The new, combined equation contains only one unknown value and can be solved. Substituting the new value into one of the equations means that the other variable can also be found. Equations that cannot be solved by elimination can usually be solved by substitution.

▷ **Equation pair**
Solve this pair of simultaneous equations using the substitution method.

$$x + 2y = 7$$
$$4x - 3y = 6$$

Choose one of the equations, and rearrange it so that one of the two unknown values is the subject. Here x is made the subject by subtracting 2y from both sides of the equation.

choose one of the equations; this is the first equation

$$x + 2y = 7$$

make x the subject by subtracting 2y from both sides of the equation

$$x = 7 - 2y$$

2y must be subtracted from both sides of the equation

Then substitute the expression that has been found for that variable ($x = 7 - 2y$) into the other equation. This gives only one unknown value in the newly compiled equation. Rearrange this new equation to isolate y and find its value.

substitute the expression for x which has been found in the previous step

$$4x - 3y = 6$$

take the other equation

$$4(7 - 2y) - 3y = 6$$

this equation now has only one unknown value so it can be solved

$$28 - 8y - 3y = 6$$

multiply out the parentheses above: $4 \times 7 = 28$ and $4 \times -2y = -8y$

$$28 - 11y = 6$$

simplify the two y terms: $-8y - 3y = -11y$

$$-11y = -22$$

28 must also be subtracted from this side: $6 - 28 = -22$

isolate the y term by subtracting 28 from this side

$$\frac{-11y}{-11} = \frac{-22}{-11}$$

this side must also be divided by −11

divide this side by −11 to isolate y ($-11y \div -11 = y$)

$$y = 2$$

this is the value of y

Substitute the value of y that has just been found into either of the original pair of equations. Rearrange this equation to isolate x and find its value.

choose one of the equations; this is the first one

$$x + 2y = 7$$

$$x + (2 \times 2) = 7$$

because y = 2, 2y is $2 \times 2 = 4$

$$x + 4 = 7$$

work out the terms in the parentheses: $2 \times 2 = 4$

$$x = 3$$

4 has been subtracted from the other side of the equation, so it must also be subtracted from this side: $7 - 4 = 3$

subtract 4 from this side to isolate x

Both unknown variables have now been found—these are the solutions to the original pair of equations.

$$x = 3 \qquad y = 2$$

Solving simultaneous equations with graphs

Simultaneous equations can be solved by rearranging each equation so that it is expressed in terms of y, using a table to find sets of x and y coordinates for each equation, then plotting the graphs. The solution is the coordinates of the point where the graphs intersect.

▷ **A pair of equations**
This pair of simultaneous equations can be solved using a graph. Each equation will be represented by a line on the graph.

there are y terms in both equations

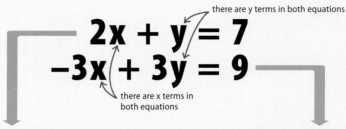

$$2x + y = 7$$
$$-3x + 3y = 9$$

there are x terms in both equations

To isolate y in the first equation, rearrange the equation so that y is left on its own on one side of the equals sign. Here, this is done by subtracting 2x from both sides of the equation.

2x + y = 7 is the first equation

$$2x + y = 7$$

−2x has also been added to this side

−2x has been added to this side to cancel out the 2x and isolate y

$$y = 7 - 2x$$

To isolate y in the second equation, rearrange so that y is left on its own on one side of the equals sign. Here, this is done by first adding 3x to both sides, then dividing both sides by 3.

−3x + 3y = 9 is the second equation

$$-3x + 3y = 9$$

3x must also be added to this side

3x has been added to this side to cancel out −3x; this isolates 3y

$$3y = 9 + 3x$$

divide both sides of equation by 3 to isolate y

$$y = 3 + x$$

3y ÷ 3 = y   9 ÷ 3 = 3   3x ÷ 3 = x

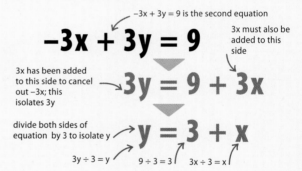

Find the corresponding x and y values for the rearranged first equation using a table. Choose a set of x values that are close to zero, then work out the y values using a table.

Find the corresponding x and y values for the rearranged second equation using a table. Choose the same set of x values as for the other table, then use the table to work out the y values.

the 7 does not depend on x

choose a set of values for x that are close to 0

x	1	2	3	4
7	7	7	7	7
−2x	−2	−4	−6	−8
y (7 − 2x)	5	3	1	−1

work out the value of −2x for each value of x

the y value is the sum of 7 and −2x   7 − 6 = 1

choose the same values of x as in the other table

the 3 does not depend on the value of x

the value of +x is the same as x

x	1	2	3	4
3	3	3	3	3
+x	1	2	3	4
y (3 + x)	4	5	6	7

the y value is the sum of 3 and x   3 + 3 = 6

Draw a set of axes, then plot the two sets of x and y values. Join each set of points with a straight line, continuing the line past where the points lie. If the pair of simultaneous equations has a solution, then the two lines will cross.

LOOKING CLOSER

Unsolvable simultaneous equations

Sometimes a pair of simultaneous equations does not have a solution. For example, the graphs of the two equations x + y = 1 and x + y = 2 are always equidistant from each other (parallel) and, because they do not intersect, there is no solution to this pair of equations.

x + y = 2

x + y = 1

y

value of y is read off y axis: 4.3

this is the graph of the equation y = 3 + x, which is the rearranged form of the second equation: −3x + 3y = 9

point of intersection represents solution to pair of simultaneous equations

this is the graph of the equation y = 7 − 2x, which is the rearranged form of the first equation: 2x + y = 7

the value of x is read off the x axis: 1.3

The solution to the pair of simultaneous equations is the coordinates of the point where the two lines cross. Read from this point down to the x axis and across to the y axis to find the values of the solution.

x = **1.3**   y = **4.3**

x^2 Factorizing quadratic equations

SOME QUADRATIC EQUATIONS (EQUATIONS IN THE FORM AX²+ BX + C = 0)
CAN BE SOLVED BY FACTORIZING.

SEE ALSO

❬ **176** Quadratic expressions

The quadratic formula   **192–193** ❭

Quadratic factorization

Factorization is the process of finding the terms that multiply together to form another term. A quadratic equation is factorized by rearranging it into two bracketed parts, each containing a variable and a number. To find the values in the parentheses, use the rules from multiplying parentheses (see p.176)—that the numbers add together to give b and multiply together to give c of the original quadratic equation.

parentheses set next to each other are multiplied together

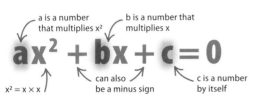

a is a number that multiplies x²

b is a number that multiplies x

$$ax^2 + bx + c = 0$$

$x^2 = x \times x$

can also be a minus sign

c is a number by itself

$$(x + \boxed{??})(x + \boxed{??}) = 0$$

these two unknown numbers add together to give b and multiply together to give c of the original equation

△ **A quadratic equation**

All quadratic equations have a squared term (x²), a term that is multiplied by x, and a numerical term. The letters a, b, and, c all stand for different numbers.

△ **Two parentheses**

A quadratic equation can be factorized as two parentheses, each with an x and a number. Multiplied out, they result in the equation.

Solving simple quadratic equations

To solve quadratic equations by factorization, first find the missing numerical terms in the parentheses. Then solve each one separately to find the answers to the original equation.

these two numbers add together to give 6 and multiply together to give 8

To solve a quadratic equation, first look at its b and c terms. The terms in the two parentheses will need to add together to give b (6 in this case) and multiply together to give c (8 in this case).

x² means 1x²   c term is 8

$$x^2 + 6x + 8 = 0$$

b term is 6   answer is always 0

$$(x + \boxed{??})(x + \boxed{??}) = 0$$

To find the unknown terms, draw a table. In the first column, list the possible combinations of numbers that multiply together to give the value of c = 8. In the second column, add these terms together to see if they add up to b = 6.

list possible factors of c=8

add factors to find their sum

Two numbers that multiply to give c=8	The sum of the two numbers
8 and 1	8 + 1 = 9
4 and 2	4 + 2 = 6

all sets of numbers in this column multiply to give c=8

✗ not all the factors add up to produce the needed sum (b), which is 6

✓ 4 and 2 are the factors needed, as 4 + 2 = 6, which is b

Insert the factors into the parentheses after the x terms. Because the two parentheses multiplied together equal the original quadratic expression, they can also be set to equal 0.

insert first value here

$$(x + \boxed{??})(x + \boxed{??}) = 0$$

$$(x + 4)(x + 2) = 0$$

insert second value here

solve for first value

subtract 4 from both sides to isolate x

$$x + 4 = 0$$

$$x = -4$$

one possible solution is –4

For the two parentheses to multiply to equal 0, the value of either one needs to be 0. Set each one equal to 0 and solve. The resulting values are the two solutions of the original equation.

solve for second value

subtract 2 from both sides to isolate x

$$x + 2 = 0$$

$$x = -2$$

another possible solution is –2

Solving more complex quadratic equations

Quadratic equations do not always appear in the standard form of $ax^2 + bx + c = 0$. Instead, several x^2 terms, x terms, and numbers may appear on both sides of the equals sign. However, if all terms appear at least once, the equation can be rearranged in the standard form, and solved using the same methods as for simple equations.

This equation is not written in standard quadratic form, but contains an x^2 term and a term multiplied by x so it is known to be one. In order to solve it needs to be rearranged to equal 0.

these terms need to be moved to other side of equation for it to equal 0

$$x^2 + 11x + 13 = 2x - 7$$

Start by moving the numerical term from the right-hand side of the equals sign to the left by adding its opposite to both sides of the equation. In this case, −7 is moved by adding 7 to both sides.

7 has been added to this side (13 + 7 = 20)

7 has been added to this side, which cancels out −7, leaving 2x on its own

$$x^2 + 11x + 20 = 2x$$

Next, move the term multiplied by x to the left of the equals sign by adding its opposite to both sides of the equation. In this case, 2x is moved by subtracting 2x from both sides.

adding −2x to 11x gives 9x

subtracting 2x from this side cancels out 2x

$$x^2 + 9x + 20 = 0$$

It is now possible to solve the equation by factorizing. Draw a table for the possible numerical values of x. In one column, list all values that multiply together to give the c term, 20; in the other, add them together to see if they give the b term (9).

list possible factors of c = 20

add the factors to find their sum

Factors of +20	Sum of factors	
20, 1	21	✗
2, 10	12	✗
5, 4	9	✓

stop when the factors add to the b term, 9

all sets of numbers in this column multiply to give 20

Write the correct pair of factors into parentheses and set them equal to 0. The two factors of the quadratic (x + 5) and (x + 4) multiply together to give 0, therefore one of the factors must be equal to 0.

parentheses set next to each other are multiplied together

entire equation equals 0

$$(x + 5)(x + 4) = 0$$

Solve the quadratic equation by solving each of the bracketed expressions separately. Make each bracketed expression equal to 0, then find its solution. The two resulting values are the two solutions to the quadratic equation: −5 and −4.

solve for first value

subtract 5 from both sides to isolate x

$$x + 5 = 0 \quad \Rightarrow \quad x = -5$$

one possible solution is −5

solve for second value

subtract 4 from both sides to isolate x

$$x + 4 = 0 \quad \Rightarrow \quad x = -4$$

another possible solution is −4

LOOKING CLOSER

Not all quadratic equations can be factorized

Some quadratic equations cannot be factorized, as the sum of the factors of the purely numerical component (c term) does not equal the term multiplied by x (b term). These equations must be solved by formula (see pp.192–193).

b term (3)

c term (1)

$$x^2 + 3x + 1 = 0$$

both sets of numbers multiply together to give c (1)

Factors of +1	Sum of factors	
1, 1	2	✗
−1, −1	−2	✗

a sum of +3 is needed as the b term is 3

The equation above is a typical quadratic equation, but cannot be solved by factorizing.

Listing all the possible factors and their sums in a table shows that there is no set of factors that add to b (3), and multiply to give c (1).

SEE ALSO

⟨ 177–179 Formulas
⟨ 190–191 Factorizing
quadratic equations
Quadratic
graphs   194–197 ⟩

x^2 The quadratic formula

QUADRATIC EQUATIONS CAN BE SOLVED USING A FORMULA.

The quadratic formula

The quadratic formula can be used to solve any quadratic equation. Quadratic equations take the form $ax^2 + bx + c = 0$, where a, b, and c are numbers and x is the unknown.

△ **A quadratic equation**
Quadratic equations include a number multiplied by x^2, a number multiplied by x, and a number by itself.

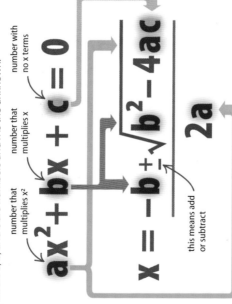

number that multiplies x^2

number that multiplies x

number with no x terms

$$ax^2 + bx + c = 0$$

△ **The quadratic formula**
The quadratic formula allows any quadratic equation to be solved. Substitute the different values in the equation into the quadratic formula to solve the equation.

$$x = \frac{-b \pm \sqrt{b^2 - 4ac}}{2a}$$

this means add or subtract

LOOK CLOSER

Quadratic variations

Quadratic equations are not always the same. They can include negative terms or terms with no numbers in front of them ("x" is the same as "1x"), and do not always equal 0.

the values in the equation can be negative as well as positive

quadratic equations are not always equal to 0

$$-4x^2 + x - 3 = 8$$

when an x appears without a number in front of it, x=1

Using the quadratic formula

To use the quadratic formula, substitute the values for a, b, and c in a given equation into the formula, then work through the formula to find the answers. Take great care with the signs (+, –) of a, b, and c.

Given a quadratic equation, work out the values of a, b, and c. Once these values are known, substitute them into the quadratic formula, making sure that their positive and negative signs do not change. In this example, a is 1, b is 3, and c is –2.

the value of a is 1

the value of b is 3

the value of c is –2

$$x^2 + 3x - 2 = 0$$

$$x = \frac{-3 \pm \sqrt{3^2 - 4 \times 1 \times (-2)}}{2 \times 1}$$

substitute values from equation into the formula, keeping their signs the same

Work through the formula step-by-step to find the answer to the equation. First simplify the values under the square root sign. Work out the square of 3 (which equals 9), then work out the value of $4 \times 1 \times -2$ (which equals –8).

$3 \times 3 = 9$

$4 \times 1 \times (-2) = -8$

$$x = \frac{-3 \pm \sqrt{9 - (-8)}}{2}$$

two minus signs cancel out, so $9 - (-8) = 9 + 8$

Work out the numbers under the square root sign: $9 - (-8)$ equals $9 + 8$, which equals 17. Then, use a calculator to find the square root of 17.

$9 + 8 = 17$

$$x = \frac{-3 \pm \sqrt{17}}{2}$$

$$x = \frac{-3 \pm 4.12}{2}$$

4.12 is the square root of 17 rounded to 2 decimal places.

Once the sum is simplified, it must be split to find the two answers—one when the second value is subtracted from the first, and the other where they are added.

–

+

Subtract the second value on the top part of the fraction; here the values are –3 and –4.12.

$$x = \frac{-3 - 4.12}{2}$$

$-3 - 4.12 = -7.12$

Divide the top part of the fraction by the bottom part to find an answer.

$$x = \frac{-7.12}{2}$$

$$x = -3.56$$

quadratic equations always have two solutions

Add the two values on the top part of the fraction; here the values are –3 and 4.12.

$$x = \frac{-3 + 4.12}{2}$$

$-3 + 4.12 = 1.12$

Divide the top part of the fraction by the bottom part to find an answer.

$$x = \frac{1.12}{2}$$

$$x = 0.56$$

Give both answers, because quadratic equations always have two solutions.

Quadratic graphs

THE GRAPH OF A QUADRATIC EQUATION IS A SMOOTH CURVE.

The exact shape of the curve of a quadratic graph varies, depending on the values of the numbers a, b, and c in the quadratic equation $y = ax^2 + bx + c$.

Quadratic equations all have the same general form: $y = ax^2 + bx + c$. With a particular quadratic equation, the values of a, b, and c are known, and corresponding sets of values for x and y can be worked out and put in a table. These values of x and y are then plotted as points (x,y) on a graph. The points are then joined by a smooth line to create the graph of the equation.

A quadratic equation can be shown as a graph. Pairs of x and y values are needed to plot the graph. In quadratic equations, the y values are given in terms of x—in this example each y value is equal to the value of x squared (x multiplied by itself), added to 3 times x, added to 2.

this group of terms is used to find the y value for each value of x

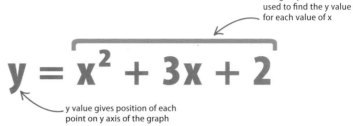

$$y = x^2 + 3x + 2$$

y value gives position of each point on y axis of the graph

Find sets of values for x and y in order to plot the graph. First, choose a set of x values. Then, for each x value, work out the different values (x^2, 3x, 2) for each value at each stage of the equation. Finally, add the stages to find the corresponding y value for each x value.

choose some values of x around 0

$y = x^2 + 3x + 2$, so it is difficult to work out the y values right away

work out x^2 in this column

work out 3x in this column

+2 is the same for each x value

add values in each purple row to find y values

x	y
−3	
−2	
−1	
0	
1	
2	
3	

x	x^2	3x	+2	y
−3	9	−9	2	
−2	4	−6	2	
−1	1	−3	2	
0	0	0	2	
1	1	3	2	
2	4	6	2	
3	9	9	2	

x	x^2	3x	+2	y
−3	9	−9	2	2
−2	4	−6	2	0
−1	1	−3	2	0
0	0	0	2	2
1	1	3	2	6
2	4	6	2	12
3	9	9	2	20

y is the sum of numbers in each purple row

+   +   =

△ **Values of x**
The value of y depends on the value of x, so choose a set of x values and then find the corresponding values of y. Choose x values either side of 0 as they are easiest to work with.

△ **Different parts of the equation**
Each quadratic equation has 3 different parts—a squared x value, a multiplied x value, and an ordinary number. Work out the different values of each part of the equation for each value of x, being careful to pay attention to when the numbers are positive or negative.

△ **Corresponding values of y**
Add the three parts of the equation together to find the corresponding values of y for each x value, making sure to pay attention to when the different parts of the equation are positive or negative.

Draw the graph of the equation. Use the values of x and y that have been found in the table as the coordinates of points on the graph. For example, x = 1 has the corresponding value y = 6. This becomes the point on the graph with the coordinates (1, 6).

▷ **Draw the axes and plot the points**
Draw the axes of the graph so that they cover the values found in the tables. It is often useful to make the axes a bit longer than needed, in case extra values are added later. Then plot the corresponding values of x and y as points on the graph.

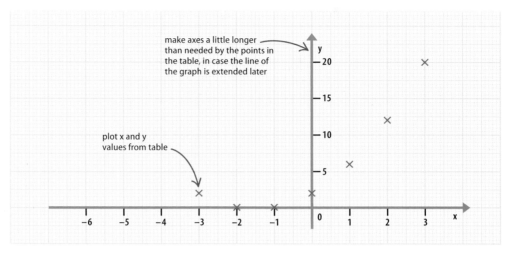

make axes a little longer than needed by the points in the table, in case the line of the graph is extended later

plot x and y values from table

▷ **Join the points**
Draw a smooth line to join the points plotted on the graph. This line is the graph of the equation y = x² + 3x + 2. Bigger and smaller values of x could have been chosen, so the line continues past the values that have been plotted.

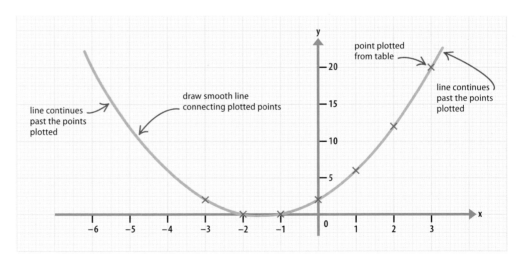

point plotted from table

line continues past the points plotted

draw smooth line connecting plotted points

line continues past the points plotted

LOOKING CLOSER

The shape of a quadratic graph

The shape of a quadratic graph depends on whether the number that multiplies x² is positive or negative. If it is positive, the graph is a smile; if it is negative, the graph is a frown.

◁ **y = ax² + bx + c**
If the value of the a term is positive, then the graph of the equation is shaped like this.

◁ **y = −ax² + bx + c**
If the value of the a term is negative, then the graph of the equation is shaped like this.

Using graphs to solve quadratic equations

A quadratic equation can be solved by drawing a graph. If a quadratic equation has a y value that is not 0, it can be solved by drawing both a quadratic and a linear graph (the linear graph is of the y value that is not 0) and finding where the two graphs cross. The solutions to the equation are the x values where the two graphs cross.

This equation has two parts: a quadratic equation on the left and a linear equation on the right. To find the solutions to this equation, draw the quadratic and linear graphs on the same axes. To draw the graphs, it is necessary to find sets of x and y values for both sides of the equation.

linear part of equation

$$-x^2 - 2x + 3 = -5$$

quadratic part of equation

y values for quadratic part of equation are dependent on value of x

y values for linear part of equation are all −5

$$y = -5$$

$$y = -x^2 - 2x + 3$$

Find values of x and y for the quadratic part of the equation using a table. Choose x values either side of 0 and split the equation into parts (−x², −2x, and +3). Work out the value of each part for each value of x, then add the values of all three parts to find the y value for each x value.

◁ **y = −5**
This graph is very simple: whatever value x takes, y is always −5. This means that the graph is a straight horizontal line that passes through the y axis at −5.

choose some values of x around 0

y = −x² − 2x + 3, so it is difficult to work out the y values right away

work out x² first then put a minus sign in front to give values

work out −2x in this column

+3 is the same for each x value

add values in each purple row to find y values

x	y
−4	
−3	
−2	
−1	
0	
1	
2	

x	−x²	−2x	3	y
−4	−16	+8	+3	
−3	−9	+6	+3	
−2	−4	+4	+3	
−1	−1	+2	+3	
0	0	0	+3	
1	−1	−2	+3	
2	−4	−4	+3	

x	−x²	−2x	3	y
−4	−16	+8	+3	−5
−3	−9	+6	+3	0
−2	−4	+4	+3	3
−1	−1	+2	+3	4
0	0	0	+3	3
1	−1	−2	+3	0
2	−4	−4	+3	−5

y is the sum of numbers in each purple row

+ + =

△ **Values of x**
Each value of y depends on the value of x. Choose a number of values for x, and work out the corresponding values of y. It is easiest to include 0 and values of x that are on either side of 0.

△ **Different parts of the equation**
The equation has 3 different parts: −x², −2x, and +3. Work out the values of each part of the equation for each value of x, being careful to pay attention to whether the values are positive or negative. The last part of the equation, +3, is the same for each x value.

△ **Corresponding values of y**
Finally, add the three parts of the equation together to find the corresponding values of y for each x value. Make sure to pay attention to whether the different parts of the equation are positive or negative.

Plot the quadratic graph. First draw a set of axes, then plot the points of the graph, using the values of x and y from the table as the coordinates of each point. For example, when x = −4, y has the value y = −5. This gives the coordinates of the point (−4, −5) on the graph. After plotting the points, draw a smooth line to join them.

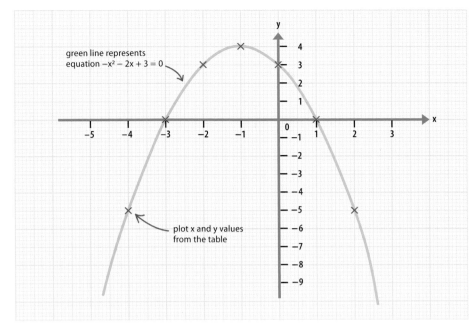

green line represents equation $-x^2 - 2x + 3 = 0$

plot x and y values from the table

Then plot the linear graph. The linear graph (y = −5) is a horizontal straight line that passes through the y axis at −5. The points at which the two lines cross are the solutions to the equation $-x^2 - 2x + 3 = -5$.

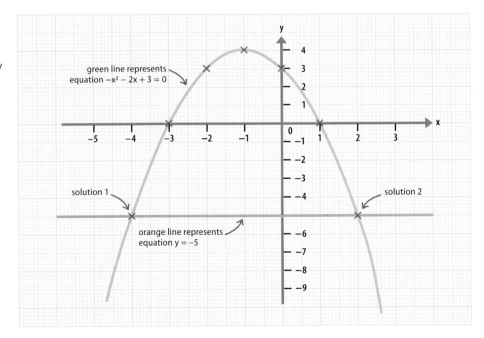

green line represents equation $-x^2 - 2x + 3 = 0$

solution 1

solution 2

orange line represents equation y = −5

The solutions are read off the graph—they are the two x values of the points where the lines cross: −4 and 2.

coordinates of first solution

coordinates of second solution

first solution to the equation

second solution to the equation

$(-4, -5)$ and $(2, -5)$ ➡ $x = -4$ $x = 2$

Inequalities

AN INEQUALITY IS USED TO SHOW THAT ONE
QUANTITY IS NOT EQUAL TO ANOTHER.

SEE ALSO

❮ 34–35 Positive and
negative numbers
❮ 172–173 Working with
expressions
❮ 180–181 Solving
equations

Inequality symbols

An inequality symbol shows that the numbers on either side of
it are different in size and how they are different. There are five
main inequality symbols. One simply shows that two numbers
are not equal, the others show in what way they are not equal.

◁ **Not equal to**
This sign shows that x
is not equal to y; for
example, $3 \neq 4$.

$$x > y$$

△ **Greater than**
This sign shows that x is greater
than y; for example, $7 > 5$.

$$x \geq y$$

△ **Greater than or equal to**
This sign shows that x is greater
than or equal to y.

$$x < y$$

△ **Less than**
This sign shows that x is less
than y. For example, $-2 < 1$.

$$x \leq y$$

△ **Less than or equal to**
This sign shows that x is less
than or equal to y.

▽ **Inequality number line**
Inequalities can be shown on a number line. The empty circles represent
greater than (>) or less than (<), and the filled circles represent greater
than or equal to (≥) or less than or equal to (≤).

$x < 2$ (x is less
than 2)

$5 \leq x < 8$ (x lies
between 5 and 8)

$x \geq 9$ (x is greater
or equal to 9)

LOOKING CLOSER

Rules for inequalities

Inequalities can be rearranged,
as long as any changes are made
to both sides of the inequality. If
an inequality is multiplied or
divided by a negative number,
then its sign is reversed.

▷ **Multiplying or dividing
by a positive number**
When an inequality is multiplied
or divided by a positive number,
its sign does not change.

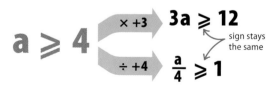

$a \geq 4$ $\times +3$ → $3a \geq 12$ sign stays the same

$\div +4$ → $\dfrac{a}{4} \geq 1$

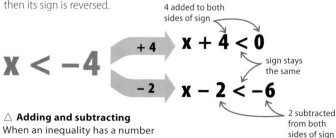

4 added to both
sides of sign

$x < -4$ $+4$ → $x + 4 < 0$ sign stays the same

-2 → $x - 2 < -6$ 2 subtracted from both sides of sign

△ **Adding and subtracting**
When an inequality has a number
added to or subtracted from it, its
sign does not change.

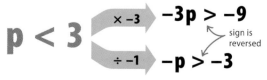

$p < 3$ $\times -3$ → $-3p > -9$ sign is reversed

$\div -1$ → $-p > -3$

△ **Multiplying or dividing by a negative number**
When an inequality is multiplied or divided by a
negative number, its sign is reversed. In this example,
a less than sign becomes a greater than sign.

Solving inequalities

Inequalities can be solved by rearranging them, but anything that is done to one side of the inequality must also be done to the other. For example, any number added to cancel a numerical term from one side must be added to the numerical term on the other side.

To solve this inequality, add 2 to both sides then divide by 3.

$$3b - 2 \geqslant 10$$

adding 2 to 3b − 2 leaves 3b on its own ⟶   10 + 2 = 12

To isolate 3b, −2 needs to be removed, which means adding +2 to both sides.

$$3b \geqslant 12$$

Solve the inequality by dividing both sides by 3 to isolate b.

3b divided by 3 leaves b on its own

$$b \geqslant 4$$ 12 ÷ 3 = 4

To solve this inequality, subtract 3 from both sides then divide by 3.

$$3a + 3 < 12$$

subtracting 3 leaves 3a on its own   12 − 3 = 9

Rearrange the inequality by subtracting 3 from each side to isolate the a term on the left.

$$3a < 9$$

3a divided by 3 leaves a on its own   9 ÷ 3 = 3

Solve the inequality by dividing both sides by 3 to isolate a. This is the solution to the inequality.

$$a < 3$$

Solving double inequalities

To solve a double inequality, deal with each side separately to simplify it, then combine the two sides back together again in a single answer.

This is a double inequality that needs to be split into two smaller inequalities for the solution to be found.

$$-1 \leqslant 3x + 5 < 11$$

$$-1 \leqslant 3x + 5$$

These are the two parts the double inequality is split into; each one needs to be solved separately.

$$3x + 5 < 11$$

subtracting 5 from −1 gives −6

$$-6 \leqslant 3x$$ subtracting 5 from 3x + 5 leaves 3x on its own

Isolate the x terms by subtracting 5 from both sides of the smaller parts.

subtracting 5 from 3x + 5 leaves 3x on its own

$$3x < 6$$ subtracting 5 from 11 gives 6

−6 ÷ 3 = −2

$$-2 \leqslant x$$ 3x ÷ 3 = x

Solve the part inequalities by dividing both of them by 3.

3x ÷ 3 = x

   6 ÷ 3 = 2

$$x < 2$$

$$-2 \leqslant x < 2$$

Finally, combine the two small inequalities back into a single double inequality, with each in the same position as it was in the original double inequality.

Statistics

What is statistics?

STATISTICS IS THE COLLECTION, ORGANIZATION, AND PROCESSING OF DATA.

Organizing and analyzing data helps make large quantities of information easier to understand. Graphs and other visual charts present information in a way that is instantly understandable.

Working with data

Data is information, and it is everywhere, in enormous quantities. When data is collected, for example from a questionnaire, it often forms long lists that are hard to understand. It can be made easier to understand if the data is reorganized into tables, and even more accessible by taking the table and plotting its information as a graph or circle graph. Graphs show trends clearly, making the data much easier to analyze. Circle graphs present data in an instantly accessible way, allowing the relative sizes of groups to be seen immediately.

group	number
Female teachers	10
Male teachers	5
Female students	66
Male students	19
Total people	100

△ **Collecting data**
Once data has been collected, it must be organized into groups before it can be effectively analyzed. A table is the usual way to do this. This table shows the different groups of people in a school.

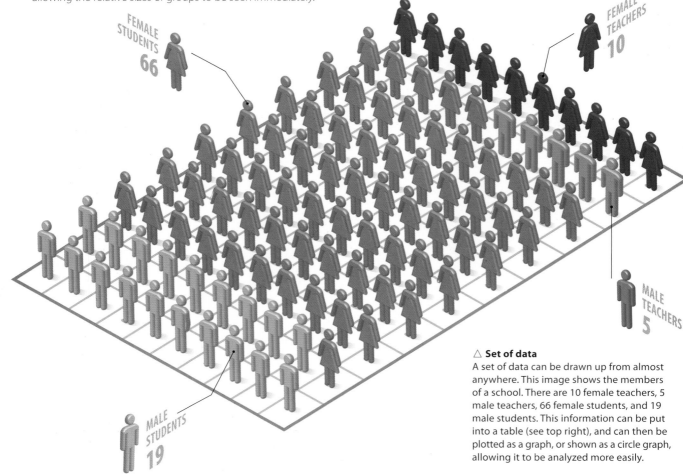

△ **Set of data**
A set of data can be drawn up from almost anywhere. This image shows the members of a school. There are 10 female teachers, 5 male teachers, 66 female students, and 19 male students. This information can be put into a table (see top right), and can then be plotted as a graph, or shown as a circle graph, allowing it to be analyzed more easily.

FEMALE STUDENTS 66

FEMALE TEACHERS 10

MALE TEACHERS 5

MALE STUDENTS 19

Presenting data

There are many ways of presenting statistical data. It can be presented simply as a table, or in visual form, as a graph or diagram. Bar graphs, pictograms, line graphs, circle graphs, and histograms are among the most common ways of showing data visually.

number of times a value appears

Group of data	Frequency
Group 1	4
Group 2	8
Group 3	6
Group 4	4
Group 5	5

△ **Table of data**
Information is put into tables to organize it into categories, to give a better idea of what trends the data shows. The table can then be used to draw a graph or pictogram.

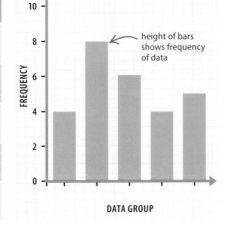

△ **Bar graph**
Bar graphs show groups of data on the x axis, and frequency on the y axis. The height of each "bar" shows what frequency of data there is in each group.

height of bars shows frequency of data

△ **Pictogram**
Pictograms are a very basic type of bar graph. Each image on a pictogram represents a number of pieces of information, for example, it could represent four musicians.

number of images shows frequency of data

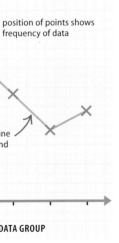

△ **Line graph**
Line graphs show data groups on the x axis, and frequency on the y axis. Points are plotted to show the frequency for each group, and lines between the points show trends.

position of points shows frequency of data

shape of line shows trend

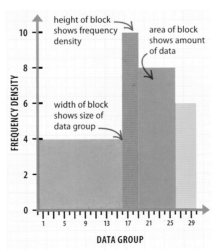

△ **Histogram**
Histograms use the area of rectangular blocks to show the different sizes of groups of data. They are useful for showing data from groups of different sizes.

height of block shows frequency density

area of block shows amount of data

width of block shows size of data group

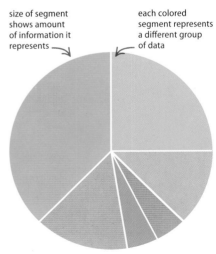

△ **Circle graph**
Circle graphs show groups of information as sections of a circle. The bigger the section of the circle, the larger the amount of data it represents.

size of segment shows amount of information it represents

each colored segment represents a different group of data

Collecting and organizing data

BEFORE INFORMATION CAN BE PRESENTED AND ANALYZED, THE DATA
MUST BE CAREFULLY COLLECTED AND ORGANIZED.

What is data?

In statistics, the information that is collected, usually in the form of lists of numbers, is known as data. To make sense of these lists, the data needs to be sorted into groups and presented in an easy-to-read form, for example as tables or diagrams. Before it is organized, it is sometimes called raw data.

choice of drinks

COLA, ORANGE JUICE,

PINEAPPLE JUICE, MILK,

APPLE JUICE, WATER

◁ **Questions**
Before designing a questionnaire, start with an idea of a question to collect data, for example, which drinks do children prefer?

Collecting data

A common way of collecting information is in a survey. A selection of people are asked about their preferences, habits, or opinions, often in the form of a questionnaire. The answers they give, which is the raw data, can then be organized into tables and diagrams.

Beverage questionnaire

This questionnaire is being used to find out what children's favorite soft drinks are. Put a cross in the box that relates to you.

1) Are you a boy or a girl?

X boy   ☐ girl

2) What is your favorite drink?

☐ pineapple juice   ☐ orange juice   X apple juice

☐ milk   ☐ cola   ☐ other

information from these answers is collected as lists of data

3) How often do you drink it?

☐ once a week or less   X 2–3 times a week   ☐ 3–5 times a week

☐ over 5 times a week

▷ **Questionnaire**
Questionnaires often take the form of a series of multiple choice questions. The replies to each question are then easy to sort into groups of data. In this example, the data would be grouped by the drinks chosen.

4) Where is you favorite drink usually bought from?

☐ supermarket   X deli   ☐ other

Tallying

Results from a survey can be organized into a chart. The left-hand column shows the groups of data from the questionnaire. A simple way to record the results is by making a tally mark in the chart for each answer. To tally, mark a line for each unit and cross through the lines when 5 is reached.

making tally marks in groups of five makes chart easier to read; the line that goes across is the 5th

Soft drink	Tally
Cola	ЖНГ I
Orange juice	ЖНГ ЖНГ I
Apple juice	II
Pineapple juice	I
Milk	II
Other	I

△ **Tally chart**
This tally chart shows the results of the survey with tally marks.

Soft drink	Tally	Frequency
Cola	ЖНГ I	6
Orange juice	ЖНГ ЖНГ I	11
Apple juice	II	2
Pineapple juice	I	1
Milk	II	2
Other	I	1

△ **Frequency table**
Counting the tally marks for each group, the results (frequency) can be entered in a separate column to make a frequency table.

Tables

Tables showing the frequency of results for each group are a useful way of presenting data. Values from the frequency column can be analyzed and used to make charts or graphs of the data. Frequency tables can have more columns to show more detailed information.

Drink	Frequency
Cola	6
Orange juice	11
Apple juice	2
Pineapple juice	1
Milk	2
Other	1

△ **Frequency table**
Data can be presented in a table. In this example, the number of children that chose each type of drink is shown.

Drink	Boy	Girl	Total
Cola	4	2	6
Orange juice	5	6	11
Apple juice	0	2	2
Pineapple juice	1	0	1
Milk	1	1	2
Other	1	0	1

△ **Two-way table**
This table has extra columns that break down the information further. It also shows the numbers of boys and girls and their preferences.

Bias

In surveys it is important to question a wide selection of people, so that the answers provide an accurate picture. If the survey is too narrow, it may be unrepresentative and show a bias toward a particular answer.

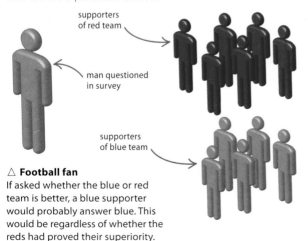

supporters of red team

man questioned in survey

supporters of blue team

△ **Football fan**
If asked whether the blue or red team is better, a blue supporter would probably answer blue. This would be regardless of whether the reds had proved their superiority.

LOOKING CLOSER

Data logging

A lot of data is recorded by machines—information about the weather, traffic, or internet usage for instance. The data can then be organized and presented in charts, tables, and graphs that make it easier to understand and analyze.

◁ **Seismometer**
A seismometer records movements of the ground that are associated with earthquakes. The collected data is analyzed to find patterns that may predict future earthquakes.

Bar graphs

BAR GRAPHS ARE A WAY OF PRESENTING DATA AS A DIAGRAM.

A bar graph displays a set of data graphically. Bars of different lengths are drawn to show the size (frequency) of each group of data in the set.

SEE ALSO

❮ **204–205** Collecting and organizing data

Pie charts	**210–211 ❯**
Line graphs	**212–213 ❯**
Histograms	**224–225 ❯**

Using bar graphs

Presenting data in the form of a diagram makes it easier to read than a list or table. A bar graph shows a set of data as a series of bars, with each bar representing a group within the set. The height of each bar represents the size of each group—a value known as the group's "frequency." Information can be seen clearly and quickly from the height of the bars, and accurate values for the data can be read from the vertical axis of the chart. A bar graph can be drawn with a pencil, a ruler, and graph paper, using information from a frequency table.

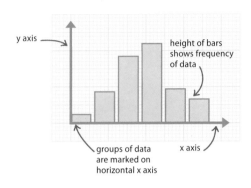

y axis

height of bars shows frequency of data

groups of data are marked on horizontal x axis

x axis

◁ **A bar graph**
In a bar graph, each bar represents a group of data from a particular data set. The size (frequency) of each data group is shown by the height of the corresponding bar.

This frequency table shows the groups of data and the size (frequency) of each group in a data set.

To draw a bar graph, first choose a suitable scale for your data. Then draw a vertical line for the y axis and a horizontal line for the x axis. Label each axis according to the columns of the table, and mark with the data from the table.

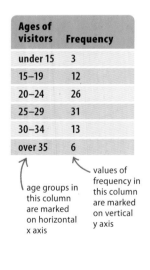

Ages of visitors	Frequency
under 15	3
15–19	12
20–24	26
25–29	31
30–34	13
over 35	6

age groups in this column are marked on horizontal x axis

values of frequency in this column are marked on vertical y axis

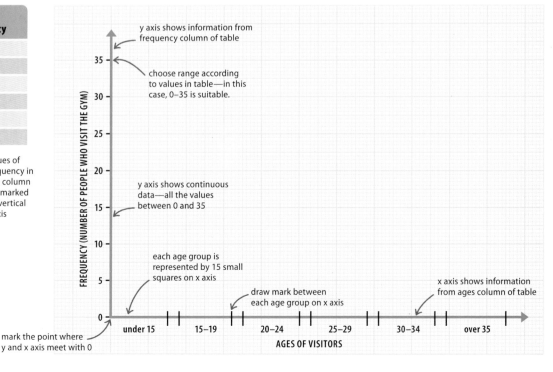

y axis shows information from frequency column of table

choose range according to values in table—in this case, 0–35 is suitable.

FREQUENCY (NUMBER OF PEOPLE WHO VISIT THE GYM)

y axis shows continuous data—all the values between 0 and 35

each age group is represented by 15 small squares on x axis

draw mark between each age group on x axis

x axis shows information from ages column of table

mark the point where y and x axis meet with 0

under 15   15–19   20–24   25–29   30–34   over 35

AGES OF VISITORS

From the table, take the number (frequency) for the first group of data (3 in this case) and find this value on the vertical y axis. Draw a horizontal line between the value on the y axis and the end of the first age range, marked on the x axis. Next, draw a line for the second frequency (in this case, 12) above the second age group marked on the x axis, and similar lines for all the remaining data.

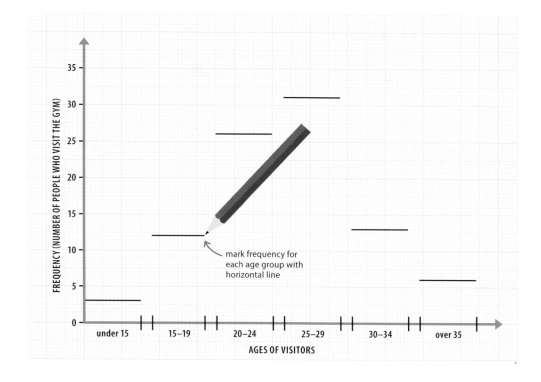

mark frequency for each age group with horizontal line

To complete the bar graph, draw vertical lines up from the dividing marks on the x axis. These will meet the ends of the lines you have drawn from the frequency table, making the bars. Coloring in the bars makes the graph easier to read.

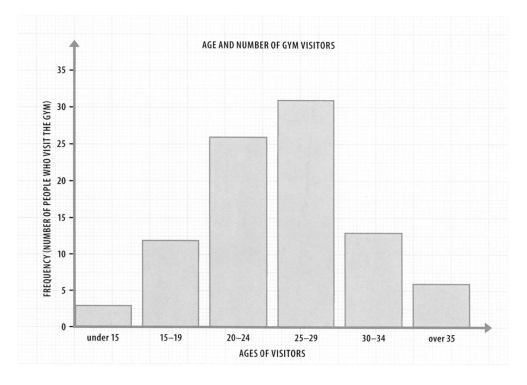

Different types of bar graph

There are several different ways of presenting information in a bar graph. The bars may be drawn horizontally, as three-dimensional blocks, or in groups of two. In every type, the size of the bar shows the size (frequency) of each group of data.

Hobby	Frequency (number of children)
Reading	25
Sports	45
Computer games	30
Music	19
Collecting	15

◁ **Table of data**
This data table shows the results of a survey in which a number of children were asked about their hobbies.

▷ **Horizontal bar graph**
In a horizontal bar graph, the bars are drawn horizontally rather than vertically. Values for the number of children in each group, the frequency, can be read on the horizontal x axis.

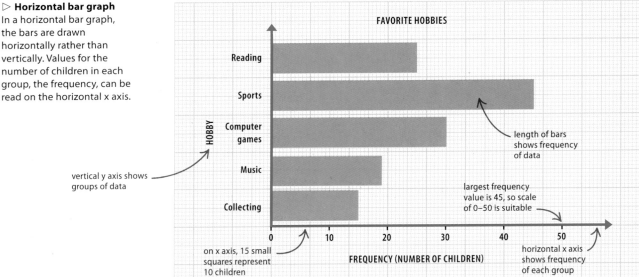

vertical y axis shows groups of data

length of bars shows frequency of data

largest frequency value is 45, so scale of 0–50 is suitable

on x axis, 15 small squares represent 10 children

horizontal x axis shows frequency of each group

▷ **Three-dimensional bar graph**
The three-dimensional blocks in this type of bar graph give it more visual impact, but can make it misleading. Because of the perspective, the tops of the blocks appear to show two values for frequency—the true value is read from the front edge of the block.

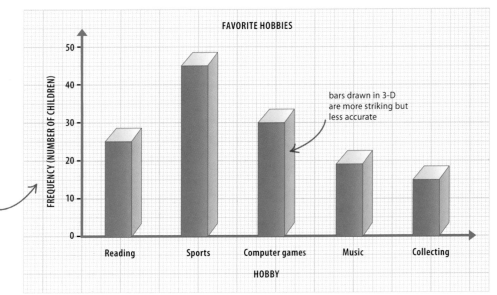

number of children in each group is difficult to find quickly

bars drawn in 3-D are more striking but less accurate

Compound and composite bar graphs

For data divided into sub-groups, compound or composite bar graphs can be used. In a compound bar graph, bars for each sub-group of data are drawn side by side. In a composite bar graph, two sub-groups are combined into one bar.

Hobby	Boys	Girls	Total frequency
Reading	10	15	25
Sports	25	20	45
Computer games	20	10	30
Music	10	9	19
Collecting	5	10	15

◁ **Table of data**
This data table shows the results of the survey on children's hobbies divided into separate figures for boys and girls.

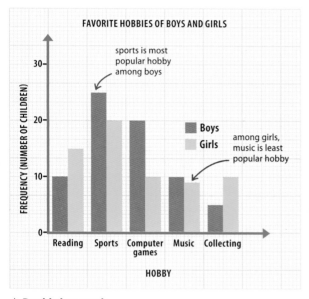

△ **Double bar graph**
In a double bar graph, each data group has two or more bars of different colors, each of which representing a subgroup of that data. A key shows which color represents which groups.

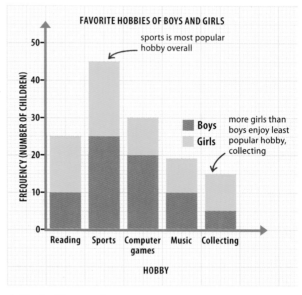

△ **Stacked bar graph**
In a stacked bar graph, two or more subgroups of data are shown as one bar, one subgroup on top of the other. This has the advantage of also showing the total value of the group of data.

Frequency polygons

Another way of presenting the same information as a bar graph is in a frequency polygon. Instead of bars, the data is shown as a line on the chart. The line connects the midpoints of each group of data.

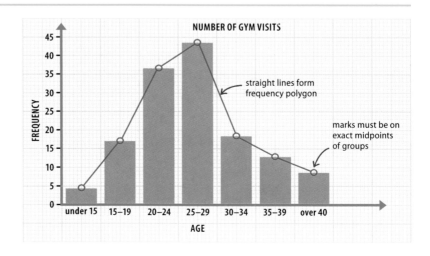

▷ **Drawing a frequency polygon**
Mark the frequency value at the midpoint of each group of data, in this case, the middle of each age range. Join the marks with straight lines.

Pie charts

PIE CHARTS ARE A USEFUL VISUAL WAY TO PRESENT DATA.

A pie chart shows data as a circle divided into segments, or slices, with each slice representing a different part of the data.

SEE ALSO
❮ 84–85 Angles
❮ 150–151 Arcs and Sectors
❮ 204–205 Collecting and organizing data
❮ 206–209 Bar graphs

Why use a pie chart?

Pie charts are often used to present data because they have an immediate visual impact. The size of each slice of the pie clearly shows the relative sizes of different groups of data, which makes the comparison of data quick and easy.

◁ **Reading a pie chart**
When a pie chart is divided into slices, it is easy to understand the information. It is clear in this example that the red section represents the largest group of data.

Identifying data

To get the information necessary to calculate the size, or angle, of each slice of a pie chart, a table of data known as a frequency table is created. This identifies the different groups of data, and shows both their size (frequency of data) and the size of all of the groups of data together (total frequency).

Country of origin	Frequency of data
United Kingdom	375
United States	250
Australia	125
Canada	50
China	50
Unknown	150
TOTAL FREQUENCY	1,000

◁ **Frequency table**
The table shows the number of hits on a website, split into the countries where they occurred.

"frequency of data" is broken down country by country

data from each country is used to calculate size of each slice

"total frequency" is total number of website hits from all countries

▽ **Calculating the angles**
To find the angle for each slice of the pie chart, take the information in the frequency table and use it in this formula.

$$\text{angle} = \frac{\text{frequency of data}}{\text{total frequency}} \times 360°$$

For example:

number of website hits

divide both numbers

angle for pie chart

$$\text{angle for United Kingdom} = \frac{375}{1,000} \times 360° = 135°$$

total number of website hits

United Kingdom 135°

The angles for the remaining slices are calculated in the same way, taking the data for each country from the frequency table and using the formula. The angles of all the slices of the pie should add up to 360°—the total number of degrees in a circle.

$$\text{United States} = \frac{250}{1,000} \times 360 = 90°$$

$$\text{Australia} = \frac{125}{1,000} \times 360 = 45°$$

$$\text{Canada} = \frac{50}{1,000} \times 360 = 18°$$

$$\text{China} = \frac{50}{1,000} \times 360 = 18°$$

$$\text{Unknown} = \frac{150}{1,000} \times 360 = 54°$$

Drawing a pie chart

Drawing a pie chart requires a compass to draw the circle, a protractor to measure the angles accurately, and a ruler to draw the slices of the pie.

center point

First, draw a circle using a compass (see pp.82–83).

circumference of circle

Draw a straight line from the center point of the circle to the circumference (edge of the circle).

90°

Measure the angle of a slice from the center and straight line. Mark it on the edge of the circle. Draw a line from the center to this mark.

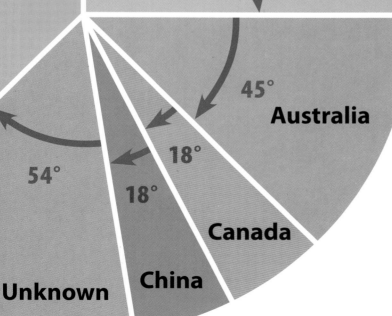

United States
90°

45°
Australia

18°
18°
Canada

54°

Unknown
China

◁ **Finished pie chart**
After drawing each slice on the circle, the pie chart can be labeled and color coded, as necessary. The angles add up to 360°, so all of the slices fit into the circle exactly.

LOOKING CLOSER

Labeling pie charts

There are three different ways to label the different slices of a pie chart: with annotation (a,b), with labels (c,d), or with a key (e,f). Annotation and keys can be useful tools when slices are too small to label the required data.

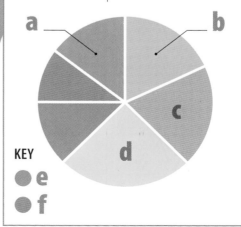

a

b

c

d

KEY

● e
● f

Line graphs

LINE GRAPHS SHOW DATA AS LINES ON A SET OF AXES.

SEE ALSO

❰ 182–185 Linear graphs
❰ 204–205 Collecting and organizing data

Line graphs are a way of accurately presenting information in an easy-to-read form. They are particularly useful for showing data over a period of time.

Drawing a line graph

A pencil, a ruler, and graph paper are all that is needed to draw a line graph. Data from a table is plotted on the graph, and these points are joined to create a line.

Day	Sunshine (hours)
Monday	12
Tuesday	9
Wednesday	10
Thursday	4
Friday	5
Saturday	8
Sunday	11

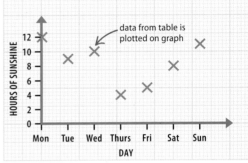

The columns of the table provide the information for the horizontal and vertical lines—the x and y axes.

▷ **Draw a set of axes.** Label the x axis with data from the first column of the table (days). Label the y axis with data from the second (hours of sunshine).

▷ **Read up the y axis** from Monday on the x axis and mark the first value. Do this for each day, reading up from the x axis and across from the y axis.

▷ **Use a ruler** and a pen or pencil to connect the points and complete the line graph once all the data has been marked (or plotted). The resulting line clearly shows the relationship between the two sets of data.

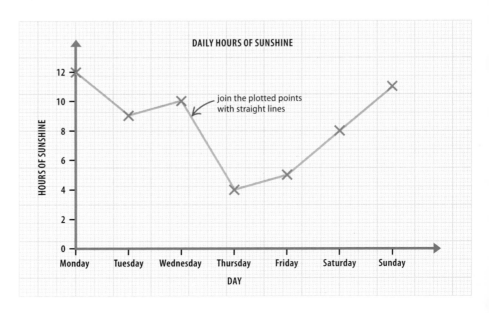

Interpreting line graphs

This graph shows temperature changes over a 24-hour period. The temperature at any time of the day can be found by locating that time on the x axis, reading up to the line, and then across to the y axis.

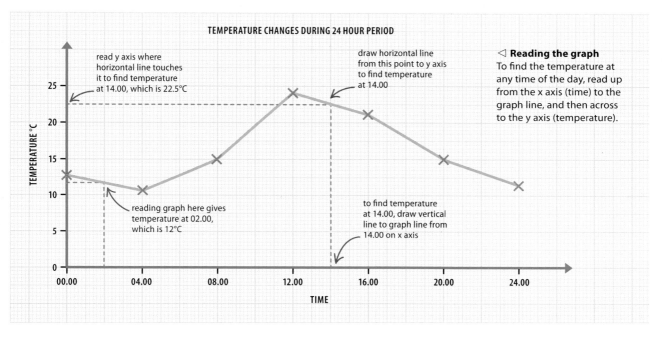

TEMPERATURE CHANGES DURING 24 HOUR PERIOD

read y axis where horizontal line touches it to find temperature at 14.00, which is 22.5°C

draw horizontal line from this point to y axis to find temperature at 14.00

◁ **Reading the graph**
To find the temperature at any time of the day, read up from the x axis (time) to the graph line, and then across to the y axis (temperature).

reading graph here gives temperature at 02.00, which is 12°C

to find temperature at 14.00, draw vertical line to graph line from 14.00 on x axis

TEMPERATURE °C

TIME

Cumulative frequency graphs

A cumulative frequency diagram is a type of line graph that shows how often each value occurs in a group of data. Joining the points of a cumulative frequency graph with straight lines usually creates an "S" shape, and the curve of the S shows which values occur most frequently within the set of data.

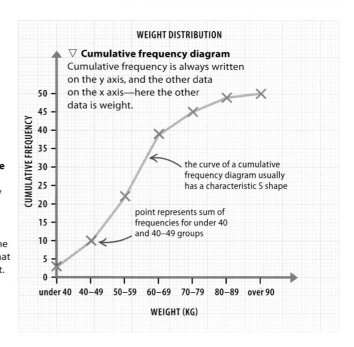

WEIGHT DISTRIBUTION

▽ **Cumulative frequency diagram**
Cumulative frequency is always written on the y axis, and the other data on the x axis—here the other data is weight.

the curve of a cumulative frequency diagram usually has a characteristic S shape

point represents sum of frequencies for under 40 and 40–49 groups

CUMULATIVE FREQUENCY

WEIGHT (KG)

weight is shown in grouped data

frequency, in this case number of people, is shown for each group

cumulative frequency is sum of all frequencies

Weight (kg)	Frequency	Cumulative frequency
under 40	3	3
40–49	7	10 (3+7)
50–59	12	22 (3+7+12)
60–69	17	39 (3+7+10+17)
70–79	6	45 (3+7+10+17+6)
80–89	4	49 (3+7+10+17+6+4)
over 90	1	50 (3+7+10+17+6+4+1)

cumulative frequency is plotted on graph

◁ **Cumulative frequency**
The frequency is cumulative because each frequency is added to all the frequencies that come before it.

Averages

AN AVERAGE IS A "MIDDLE" VALUE OF A SET OF DATA. IT IS A TYPICAL VALUE THAT REPRESENTS THE ENTIRE SET OF DATA.

SEE ALSO
⟨ **204–205** Collecting and organizing data
Moving averages **218–219** ⟩
Measuring spread **220–223** ⟩

Different types of averages

There are several different types of average. The main ones are called the mean, the median, and the mode. Each one gives slightly different information about the data. In everyday life, the term "average" usually refers to the mean.

The mode

The mode is the value that appears most frequently in a set of data. It is easier to find the mode if you put the data list into an ascending order of values (from lowest to highest). If different values appear the same number of times, there may be more than one mode.

150, 160, 170, 180, 180

working out averages often requires listing a set of data arranged in ascending order

this color represents mode because it appears most often

◁ **The mode color**
The set of data in this example is a series of colored figures. The pink people appear the most often, so pink is the mode value.

150, 160, 170, 180, 180

180 occurs twice in this list, more often than any other value, so it is the mode, or most frequent, value

▷ **Average heights**
The heights of this group of people can be arranged as a list of data. From this list, the different types of average can be found—mean, median, and mode.

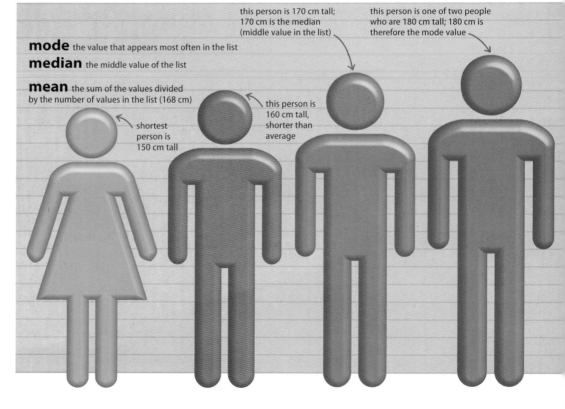

this person is 170 cm tall; 170 cm is the median (middle value in the list)

this person is one of two people who are 180 cm tall; 180 cm is therefore the mode value

mode the value that appears most often in the list
median the middle value of the list
mean the sum of the values divided by the number of values in the list (168 cm)

this person is 160 cm tall, shorter than average

shortest person is 150 cm tall

The mean

The mean is the sum of all the values in a set of data divided by the number of values in the list. It is what most people understand by the word "average." To find the mean, a simple formula is used.

$$\text{Mean} = \frac{\text{Sum total of values}}{\text{Number of values}}$$

formula to find mean

First, take the list of data and put it in order. Count the number of values in the list. In this example, there are five values.

$$150, 160, 170, 180, 180$$

there are five numbers in list

Add all of the values in the list together to find the sum total of the values. In this example the sum total is 840.

add numbers together

sum total of values

$$150 + 160 + 170 + 180 + 180 = 840$$

Divide the sum total of the values, in this case 840, by the number of values, which is 5. The answer, 168, is the mean value of the list.

sum total of values

number of values

168 is the mean

$$\frac{840}{5} = 168$$

this person is also 180 cm tall

HEIGHT (CM)

210 200 190 **180** **170** **160** **150** 140 130 120 110 100 90 80 70 60 50 40 30 20 10 0

The median

The median is the middle value in a set of data. In a list of five values, it is the third value. In a list of seven values, it would be the fourth value.

median is middle value, in this case the orange figure

Firstly, put the data in ascending order (from lowest to highest)

$$170, 180, 180, 160, 150$$

The median is the middle value in a list with an odd number of values.

in this list of five values, third value is the median

$$150, 160, \mathbf{170}, 180, 180$$

LOOKING CLOSER

Median of an even number of values

In a list with an even number of values, the median is worked out using the two middle values. In a list of six values, these are the third and fourth values.

3rd value — 4th value

$$150, 160, \mathbf{170}, \mathbf{180}, 180, 190$$

middle values

▷ **Calculating the median**
Add the two middle values and divide by two to find the median.

median value

$$\frac{170 + 180}{2} = \frac{350}{2} = 175$$

WORKING WITH FREQUENCY TABLES

Data that deals with averages is often presented in what is known as a frequency table. Frequency tables show the frequency with which certain values appear in a set of data.

Finding the median using a frequency table

The process for finding the median (middle) value from a frequency table depends on whether the total frequency is an odd or an even number.

The following marks were scored in a test and entered in a frequency table:

20, 20, 18, 20, 18, 19, 20, 20, 20

Mark	Frequency
18	2
19	1 (2 + 1 = 3)
20	6 (3 + 6 = 9)
	9

number of times each mark appears

median frequency (entry contains 5th value in list)

median mark

total frequency

Because the total frequency of 9 is odd, to find the median first add 1 to it and then divide it by 2. This makes 5, meaning that the 5th value is the median. Count down the frequency column adding the values until reaching the row containing the 5th value. The median mark is 20.

The following marks were scored in a test and entered in a frequency table:

18, 17, 20 19, 19, 18, 19, 18

frequency contains 4th value

frequency contains 5th value

Mark	Frequency
17	1
18	3 (1 + 3 = 4)
19	3 (4 + 3 = 7)
20	1 (7 + 1 = 8)
	8

total frequency

The total frequency of 8 is even (8), so there are two middle values (4th and 5th). Count down the frequency column adding values to find them.

▽ **An even total frequency**
If the total frequency is even, the median is calculated from the two middle values.

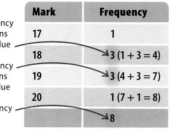

$$\text{Median} = \frac{\text{1st middle value} + \text{2nd middle value}}{2}$$

1st middle value

2nd middle value

$$\frac{18 + 19}{2} = \mathbf{18.5}$$

median

The two middle values (4th and 5th) represent the marks 18 and 19 respectively. The median is the mean of these two marks, so add them together and divide by 2. The median mark is 18.5.

Finding the mean from a frequency table

To find the mean from a frequency table, calculate the total of all the data as well as the total frequency. Here, the following marks were scored in a test and entered into a table:

16, 18, 20, 19, 17, 19, 18, 17, 18, 19, 16, 19

Mark	Frequency
16	2
17	2
18	3
19	4
20	1

range of values

frequency shows number of times each mark was scored

Mark	Frequency	Total marks (mark × frequency)
16	2	16×2=32
17	2	17×2=34
18	3	18×3=54
19	4	19×4=76
20	1	20×1=20
	12	216

add frequencies together to get total frequency

total marks

$$\text{Mean} = \frac{\textbf{Sum of values}}{\textbf{Number of values}}$$

total marks

total frequency

total marks

$$216 \div 12 = \mathbf{18}$$

total frequency

mean mark

Enter the given data into a frequency table.

Find the total marks scored by multiplying each mark by its frequency. The total sum of each part of the data is the sum of values.

To find the mean, divide the sum of values, in this example, the total marks, by the number of values, which is the total frequency.

Finding the mean of grouped data

Grouped data is data that has been collected into groups of values, rather than appearing as specific or individual values. If a frequency table shows grouped data, there is not enough information to calculate the sum of values, so only an estimated value for the mean can be found.

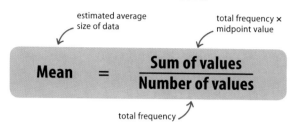

$$\text{Mean} = \frac{\text{Sum of values}}{\text{Number of values}}$$

estimated average size of data → (arrow to Sum of values)
total frequency × midpoint value → (arrow to Sum of values)
total frequency → (arrow to Number of values)

In grouped data the sum of the values can be calculated by finding the midpoint of each group and multiplying it by the frequency. Then add the results for each group together to find the total frequency × midpoint value. This is divided by the total number of values to find the mean. The example below shows a group of marks scored in a test.

LOOKING CLOSER

Weighted mean

If some individual values within grouped data contribute more to the mean than other individual values in the group, a "weighted" mean results.

Students in group	15	20	22
Mean exam mark	18	17	13

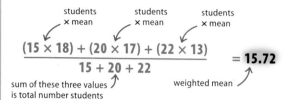

$$\frac{(15 \times 18) + (20 \times 17) + (22 \times 13)}{15 + 20 + 22} = 15.72$$

students × mean (×3)
sum of these three values is total number students
weighted mean

△ **Finding the weighted mean**
Multiply the number of students in each group by the mean mark and add the results. Divide by the total students to give the weighted mean.

Mark	Frequency
under 50	2
50–59	1
60–69	8
70–79	5
80–89	3
90–99	1

Mark	Frequency	Midpoint	Frequency × midpoint
under 50	2	25	2 × 25 = 50
50–59	1	54.5	1 × 54.5 = 54.5
60–69	8	64.5	8 × 64.5 = 516
70–79	5	74.5	5 × 74.5 = 372.5
80–89	3	84.5	3 × 84.5 = 253.5
90–99	1	94.5	1 × 94.5 = 94.5
	20		1,341

total frequency (under 20)
total frequency × midpoint (under 1,341)

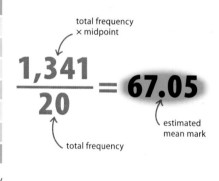

$$\frac{1{,}341}{20} = 67.05$$

total frequency × midpoint
total frequency
estimated mean mark

To find the midpoint of a set of data, add the upper and lower values and divide the answer by 2. For example, the midpoint in the 90–99 mark group is 94.5.

Multiply the midpoint by the frequency for each group and enter this in a new column. Add the results to find the total frequency multiplied by the midpoint.

Dividing the total frequency × midpoint by the total frequency gives the estimated mean mark. It is an estimated value as the exact marks scored are not known – only a range has been given in each group.

LOOKING CLOSER

The modal class

In a frequency table with grouped data, it is not possible to find the mode (the value that occurs most often in a group). But it is easy to see the group with the highest frequency in it. This group is known as the modal class.

▷ **More than one modal class**
When the highest frequency in the table is in more than one group, there is more than one modal class.

Mark	0–25	26–50	51–75	76–100
Frequency	2	6	8	8

modal class

Moving averages

MOVING AVERAGES SHOW GENERAL TRENDS IN DATA OVER A CERTAIN PERIOD OF TIME.

What is a moving average?

When data is collected over a period of time, the values sometimes change, or fluctuate, noticeably. Moving averages, or averages over specific periods of time, smooth out the highs and lows of fluctuating data and instead show its general trend.

Showing moving averages on a line graph

Taking data from a table, a line graph of individual values over time can be plotted. The moving averages can also be calculated from the table data, and a line of moving averages plotted on the same graph.

The table below shows sales of ice cream over a two-year period, with each year divided into four quarters. The figures for each quarter show how many thousands of ice cream cones were sold.

	YEAR ONE				YEAR TWO			
Quarter	1st	2nd	3rd	4th	5th	6th	7th	8th
Sales (in thousands)	1.25	3.75	4.25	2.5	1.5	4.75	5.0	2.75

△ **Table of data**
These figures can be presented as a line graph, with sales shown on the y axis and time (measured in quarters of a year) shown on the x axis.

▷ **Sales graph**
The sales graph shows quarterly highs and lows (pink line), while a moving average (green line) shows the trend over the two-year period.

REAL WORLD

Seasonality

Seasonality is the name given to regular changes in a data series that follow a seasonal pattern. These seasonal fluctuations may be caused by the weather, or by annual holiday periods such as Christmas or Easter. For example, retail sales experience a predictable peak around the Christmas period and low during the summer vacation period.

▷ **Ice cream sales**
Sales of ice cream tend to follow a predictable seasonal pattern.

Calculating moving averages

From the figures in the table, an average for each period of four quarters can be calculated and a moving average on the graph plotted.

Average for quarters 1–4
Calculate the mean of the four figures for year one. Mark the answer on the graph at the midpoint of the quarters.

$$1.25 + 3.75 + 4.25 + 2.5 = 11.75$$

sum of sales figures for quarters 1–4

mean value (rounded to 2 decimal places)

$$\frac{11.75}{4} = 2.94$$

number of values

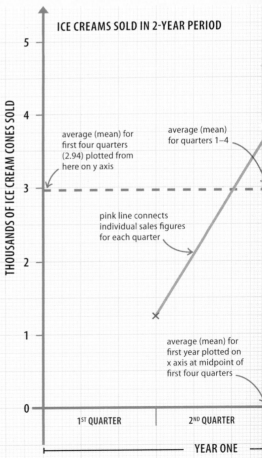

ICE CREAMS SOLD IN 2-YEAR PERIOD

THOUSANDS OF ICE CREAM CONES SOLD

average (mean) for first four quarters (2.94) plotted from here on y axis

average (mean) for quarters 1–4

pink line connects individual sales figures for each quarter

average (mean) for first year plotted on x axis at midpoint of first four quarters

1ST QUARTER

2ND QUARTER

YEAR ONE

$$\text{Average (mean)} = \frac{\text{Sum total of values}}{\text{Number of values}}$$

◁ **Calculating the mean**
Use this formula to find the average (or mean) for each period of four quarters.

Average for quarters 2–5
Calculate the mean of the figures for quarters 2–5 and mark it at the quarters' midpoint.

$$3.75 + 4.25 + 2.5 + 1.5 = 12$$

sum of sales figures for quarters 2–5

mean value

$$\frac{12}{4} = \mathbf{3}$$

number of values

Average for quarters 3–6
Calculate the mean of the figures for quarters 3–6 and mark it at the quarters' midpoint.

$$4.25 + 2.5 + 1.5 + 4.75 = 13$$

sum of sales figures for quarters 3–6

mean value

$$\frac{13}{4} = \mathbf{3.25}$$

number of values

Average for quarters 4–7
Calculate the mean of the figures for quarters 4–7 and mark it at the quarters' midpoint.

$$2.5 + 1.5 + 4.75 + 5 = 13.75$$

sum of sales figures for quarters 4–7

$$\frac{13.75}{4} = \mathbf{3.44}$$

number of values

mean value (rounded to 2 decimal places)

Average for quarters 5–8
Find the mean for quarters 5–8, mark it on the graph, and join all of the marks.

$$1.5 + 4.75 + 5 + 2.75 = 14$$

sum of sales figures for quarters 5–8

mean value

$$\frac{14}{4} = \mathbf{3.5}$$

number of values

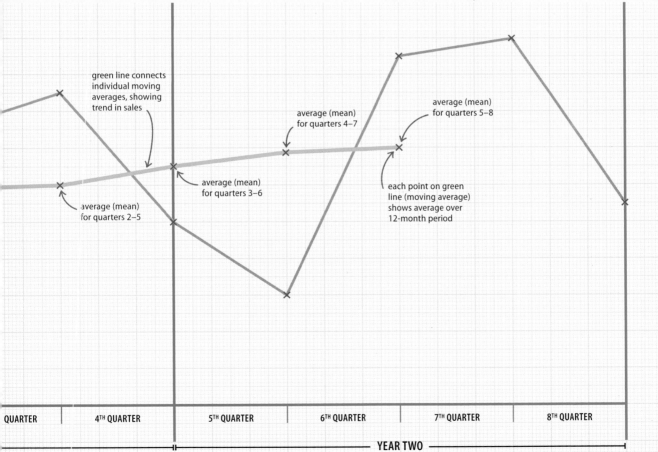

green line connects individual moving averages, showing trend in sales

average (mean) for quarters 4–7

average (mean) for quarters 5–8

average (mean) for quarters 3–6

average (mean) for quarters 2–5

each point on green line (moving average) shows average over 12-month period

QUARTER | 4TH QUARTER | 5TH QUARTER | 6TH QUARTER | 7TH QUARTER | 8TH QUARTER

— YEAR TWO —

Measuring spread

SEE ALSO

❮ **204–205** Collecting and organizing data

Histograms **224–225** ❯

MEASURES OF SPREAD SHOW THE RANGE OF DATA, AND ALSO GIVE MORE INFORMATION ABOUT THE DATA THAN AVERAGES ALONE.

Diagrams showing the measure of spread give the highest and lowest figures (the range) of the data and give information about how it is distributed.

Range and distribution

From tables or lists of data, diagrams can be created that show the ranges of different sets of data. This shows the distribution of the data, whether it is spread over a wide or narrow range.

Subject	Ed's results	Bella's results
Math	47	64
English	95	68
French	10	72
Geography	65	61
History	90	70
Physics	60	65
Chemistry	81	60
Biology	77	65

This table shows the marks of two students. Although their average (see pp.214–215) marks are the same (65.625), the ranges of their marks are very different.

REAL WORLD

Broadband bandwidth

Internet service providers often give a maximum speed for their broadband connections, for example 20Mb per second. However, this information can be misleading. An average speed gives a better idea of what to expect, but the range and distribution of the data is the information really needed to get the full picture.

lowest mark

highest mark

Ed: **10**, 47, 60, 65, 77, 81, 90, **95**

Bella: **60**, 61, 64, 65, 65, 68, 70, **72**

◁ **Finding the range**
To calculate the range of each student's marks, subtract the lowest figure from the highest in each set. Ed's lowest mark is 10, and highest 95, so his range is 85. Bella's lowest mark is 60, and highest 72, giving a range of 12.

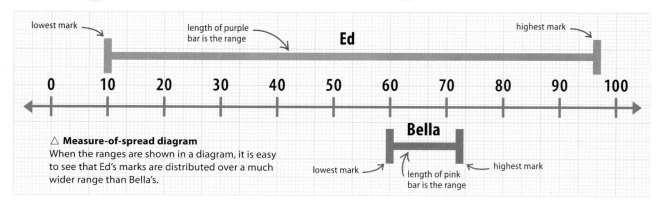

lowest mark

length of purple bar is the range

Ed

highest mark

0 10 20 30 40 50 60 70 80 90 100

Bella

lowest mark

length of pink bar is the range

highest mark

△ **Measure-of-spread diagram**
When the ranges are shown in a diagram, it is easy to see that Ed's marks are distributed over a much wider range than Bella's.

Stem-and-leaf diagrams

Another way of showing data is in stem-and-leaf diagrams. These give a clearer picture of the way the data is distributed within the range than a simple measure-of-spread diagram.

This is how the data appears before it has been organized.

34, 48, 7, 15, 27, 18, 21, 14, 24, 57, 25, 12, 30, 37, 42, 35, 3, 43, 22, 34, 5, 43, 45, 22, 49, 50, 34, 12, 33, 39, 55

Sort the list of data into numerical order, with the smallest number first. Add a zero in front of any number smaller than 10.

03, 05, 07, 12, 12, 14, 15, 18, 21, 22, 22, 24, 25, 27, 30, 33, 34, 34, 34, 35, 37, 39, 42, 43, 43, 45, 48, 49, 50, 55, 57

To draw a stem-and-leaf diagram, draw a cross with more space to the right of it than the left. Write the data into the cross, with the tens in the "stem" column to the left of the cross, and the ones for each number as the "leaves" on the right hand side. Once each value of tens has been entered into the stem, do not repeat it, but continue to repeat the values entered into the leaves.

this is the stem. 1 stands for 10, 2 for 20, and so on

this is the leaf, which is joined to the stem to form a complete number

KEY **1 5 = 15**

STEM	LEAVES
0	3 5 7
1	2 2 4 5 8
2	1 2 2 4 5 7
3	0 3 4 4 4 5 7 9
4	2 3 3 5 8 9
5	0 5 7

this stands for any number in the list of data that has 1 as its first digit

there is no data of 60 or more

18 appears once

34 appears 3 times

there is most data in the middle of the range

fewer figures are distributed toward ends of range than in the middle

QUARTILES

Quartiles are dividing points in the range of a set of data that give a clear picture of distribution. The median marks the center point, the upper quartile marks the midpoint between the median and the top of the distribution, and the lower quartile the midpoint between the median and the bottom. Estimates of quartiles can be found from a graph, or calculated precisely using formulas.

Estimating quartiles

Quartiles can be estimated by reading values from a cumulative frequency graph (see p.213).

Make a table with the data given for range and frequency, and add up the cumulative frequency. Use this data to make a cumulative frequency graph, with cumulative frequency on the y axis, and range on the x axis.

Range	Frequency	Cumulative frequency
30–39	2	2
40–49	3	5 (= 2+3)
50–59	4	9 (= 2+3+4)
60–69	6	15 (= 2+3+4+6)
70–79	5	20 (= 2+3+4+6+5)
80–89	4	24 (= 2+3+4+6+5+4)
>90	3	27 (= 2+3+4+6+5+4+3)

this sign means greater than

add each number to those before it to find cumulative frequency

▷ **Divide the total cumulative frequency** by 4 (this will be the cumulative frequency of the last entry in the table), and use the result to divide the y axis into 4 parts.

total cumulative frequency

divide the y axis into sections of this length

$$\frac{27}{4} = 6.75$$

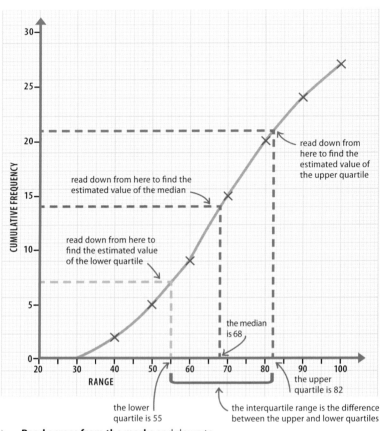

read down from here to find the estimated value of the upper quartile

read down from here to find the estimated value of the median

read down from here to find the estimated value of the lower quartile

the median is 68

the lower quartile is 55

the upper quartile is 82

the interquartile range is the difference between the upper and lower quartiles

▷ **Read across from the marks** and down to the x axis to find estimated values for the quartiles. These are only approximate values.

Calculating quartiles

Exact values of quartiles can be found from a list of data. These formulas give the position of the quartiles and median in a list of data in ascending order, using the total number of data items in the list, n.

n is the total number of values in the list

$$\frac{(n + 1)}{4}$$

△ **Lower quartile**
This shows the position of the lower quartile in a list of data.

$$\frac{(n + 1)}{2}$$

△ **Median**
This shows the position of the median in a list of data.

$$\frac{3(n + 1)}{4}$$

△ **Upper quartile**
This shows the position of the upper quartile in a list of data.

How to calculate quartiles

To find the values of the quartiles in a list of data, first arrange the list of numbers in ascending order from lowest to highest.

37,38,45,47,48,51,54,54,58,60,62,63,63,65,69,71,74,75,78,78,80,84,86,89,92,94,96

▷ **Using the formulas,** calculate where to find the quartiles and the median in this list. The answers give the position of each value in the list.

n is the total number of values in the list

position of lower quartile (7th value)

position of median (14th value)

position of upper quartile (21st value)

$$\frac{(n+1)}{4} = \frac{(27+1)}{4} = 7$$

formula to find lower quartile

$$\frac{(n+1)}{2} = \frac{(27+1)}{2} = 14$$

formula to find median

$$\frac{3(n+1)}{4} = \frac{3(27+1)}{4} = 21$$

formula to find upper quartile

△ **Lower quartile**
This calculation gives the answer 7, so the lower quartile is the 7th value in the list.

△ **Median**
The answer to this calculation is 14, so the median is the 14th value in the list.

△ **Upper quartile**
The answer to this calculation is 21, so the upper quartile is the 21st value in the list.

▷ **To find the values** of the quartiles and the median, count along the list to the positions that have just been calculated.

lower quartile

median

upper quartile

| 1 | 2 | 3 | 4 | 5 | 6 | 7 | 8 | 9 | 10 | 11 | 12 | 13 | 14 | 15 | 16 | 17 | 18 | 19 | 20 | 21 | 22 | 23 | 24 | 25 | 26 | 27 |

37,38,45,47,48,51,**54**,54,58,60,62,63,63,**65**,69,71,74,75,78,78,**80**,84,86,89,92,94,96

LOOKING CLOSER

Box-and-whisker diagram

Box-and-whisker diagrams are a way of showing the spread and distribution of a range of data in an graphic way. The range is plotted on a number line, with the interquartile range between the upper and lower quartiles shown as a box.

▽ **Using the diagram**
This box-and-whisker diagram shows a range with a lower limit of 1 and an upper limit of 9. The median is 4, the lower quartile 3, and the upper quartile 6.

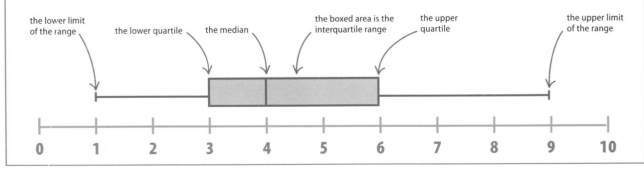

the lower limit of the range

the lower quartile

the median

the boxed area is the interquartile range

the upper quartile

the upper limit of the range

Histograms

A HISTOGRAM IS A TYPE OF BAR GRAPH. IN A HISTOGRAM, THE AREA OF
THE BARS, NOT THEIR LENGTH, REPRESENTS THE SIZE OF THE DATA.

SEE ALSO
❰ **204–205** Collecting and organizing data
❰ **206–209** Bar graphs
❰ **220–223** Measuring spread

What is a histogram?

A histogram is a diagram made up of blocks on a graph. Histograms are useful for showing data when it is grouped into groups of different sizes. This example looks at the number of downloads of a music file in a month (frequency) by different age groups. Each age group (class) is a different size because each covers a different age range. The width of each block represents the age range, known as class width. The height of each block represents frequency density, which is calculated by dividing the number of downloads (frequency) in each age group (class) by the class width (age range).

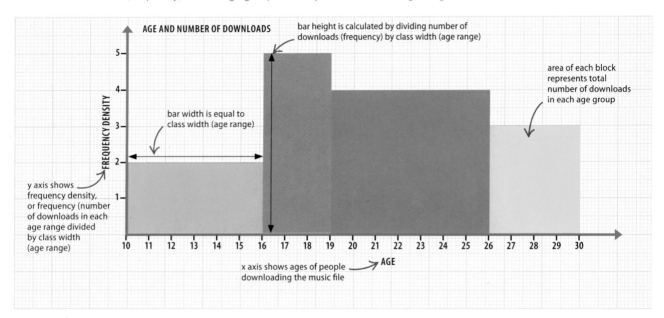

LOOKING CLOSER

Histograms and bar graphs

Bar graphs look like histograms, but show data in a different way. In a bar graph, the bars are all the same width. The height of each bar represents the total (frequency) for each group, while in a histogram, totals are represented by the area of the blocks.

▷ **Bar graph**
This bar graph shows the same data as shown above. Although class widths are different, the bar widths are the same.

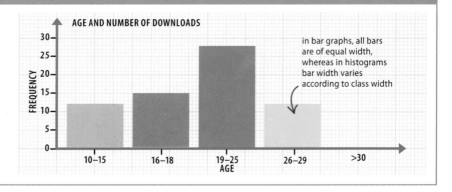

How to draw a histogram

To draw a histogram, begin by making a frequency table for the data. Next, using the class boundaries, find the width of each class of data. Then calculate frequency density for each by dividing frequency by class width.

upper class boundary for any group is lower boundary of next group

class boundaries for this data are 10, 16, 19, 26, and 30

find class width by subtracting lower class boundary from the upper class boundary, for example 16 − 10 = 6

number of downloads per month

divide frequency by class width to find frequency density

Age (year)	Frequency (downloads in a month)
10–15	12
16–18	15
19–25	28
26–29	12
>30	0

Age	Class width	Frequency	Frequency density
10–15	6	12	2
16–18	3	15	5
19–25	7	28	4
26–29	4	12	3
>30	–	0	–

there is no data to enter for this group

▷ **The information needed** to draw a histogram is the range of each class of data and frequency data. From this information, the class width and frequency density can be calculated.

▷ **To find class width**, begin by finding the class boundaries of each group of data. These are the two numbers that all the values in a group fall in between—for example, for the 10–15 group they are 10 and 16. Next, find class width by subtracting the lower boundary from the upper for each group.

▷ **To find frequency density**, divide the frequency by the class width of each group. Frequency density shows the frequency of each group in proportion to its class width.

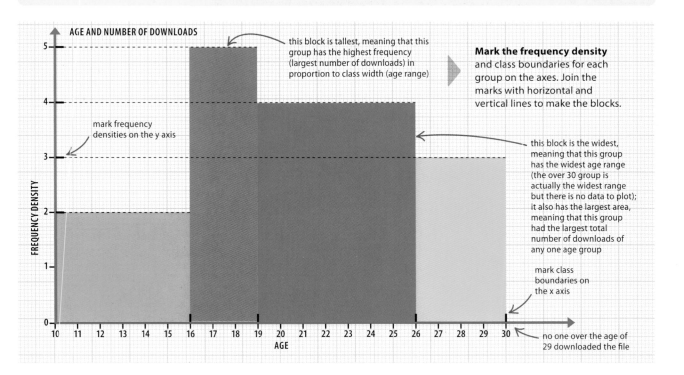

AGE AND NUMBER OF DOWNLOADS

this block is tallest, meaning that this group has the highest frequency (largest number of downloads) in proportion to class width (age range)

▷ **Mark the frequency density** and class boundaries for each group on the axes. Join the marks with horizontal and vertical lines to make the blocks.

mark frequency densities on the y axis

this block is the widest, meaning that this group has the widest age range (the over 30 group is actually the widest range but there is no data to plot); it also has the largest area, meaning that this group had the largest total number of downloads of any one age group

mark class boundaries on the x axis

FREQUENCY DENSITY

AGE

no one over the age of 29 downloaded the file

Scatter diagrams

SCATTER DIAGRAMS PRESENT INFORMATION FROM TWO SETS OF
DATA AND REVEAL THE RELATIONSHIP BETWEEN THEM.

SEE ALSO

❰ **204–205** Collecting and organizing data

❰ **212–213** Line graphs

What is a scatter diagram?

A scatter diagram is a graph made from two sets of data. Each set of data is measured on an axis of the graph. The data always appears in pairs—one value will need to be read up from the x axis, the other read across from the y axis. A point is marked where each pair meet. The pattern made by the points shows whether there is any connection, or correlation, between the two sets of data.

▽ **Table of data**
This table shows two sets of data—the height and weight of 13 people. With each person's height the corresponding weight measurement is given.

Height (cm)	173	171	189	167	183	181	179	160	177	180	188	186	176
Weight (kg)	69	68	90	65	77	76	74	55	70	75	86	81	68

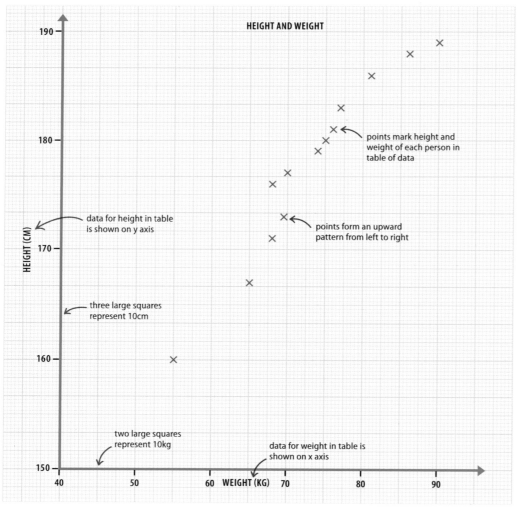

◁ **Plotting the points**
Draw a vertical axis (y) and a horizontal axis (x) on graph paper. Mark out measurements for each set of data in the table along the axes. Read each corresponding height and weight in from its axis and mark where they meet. Do not join the points marked.

◁ **Positive correlation**
The pattern of points marked between the two axes shows an upward trend from left to right. An upward trend is known as positive correlation. The correlation between the two sets of data in this example is that as height increases, so does weight.

Negative and zero correlations

The points in a scatter diagram can form many different patterns, which reveal different types of correlation between the sets of data. This can be positive, negative, or nonexistent. The pattern can also reveal how strong or how weak the correlation is between the two sets of data.

Energy used (kwh)	1,000	1,200	1,300	1,400	1,450	1,550	1,650	1,700
Temperature (°C)	55	50	45	40	35	30	25	20

IQ	141	127	117	150	143	111	106	135
Shoe size	8	10	11	6	11	10	9	7

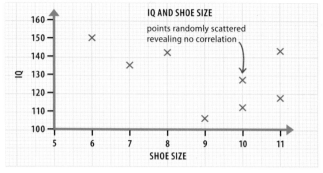

△ **Negative correlation**
In this graph, the points form a downward pattern from left to right. This reveals a connection between the two sets of data—as the temperature increases, energy consumption goes down. This relationship is called negative correlation.

△ **No correlation**
In this graph, the points form no pattern at all—they are widely spaced and do not reveal any trend. This shows there is no connection between a person's shoe size and their IQ, which means there is zero correlation between the two sets of data.

Line of best fit

To make a scatter diagram clearer and easier to read, a straight line can be drawn that follows the general pattern of the points, with an equal number of points on both sides of the line. This line is called the line of best fit.

◁ **Finding approximate values**
When the line of best fit is drawn, approximate values of any weight and height can be found by reading across from the y axis, or up from the x axis.

△ **Weak correlation**
Here the points are farther away from the line of best fit. This shows that the correlation between height and shoe size is weak. The farther the points are from the line, the weaker the correlation.

Probability

? What is probability?

PROBABILITY IS THE LIKELIHOOD OF SOMETHING HAPPENING.

Math can be used to calculate the likelihood or chance that something will happen.

How is probability shown?

Probabilities are given a value between 0, which is impossible, and 1, which is certain. To calculate these values, fractions are used. Follow the steps to find out how to calculate the probability of an event happening and then how to show it as a fraction.

total of specific events that can happen

$$\frac{1}{8}$$

total of all possible events that can happen

◁ **Writing a probability**
The top number shows the chances of a specific event, while the bottom number shows the total chances of all of the possible events happening.

▷ **Total chances**
Decide what the total number of possibly outcomes is. In this example, with 5 candies to pick 1 candy from, the total is 5—any one of 5 candies may be picked.

there are 5 candies, 4 are red and 1 is yellow

▷ **Chance of red candy**
Of the 5 candies, 4 are red. This means that there are 4 chances out of 5 that the candy chosen is red. This probability can be written as the fraction ⁴/₅.

total number of red candies that can be chosen

total of 5 candies to choose from

▷ **Chance of yellow candy**
Because 1 candy is yellow there is 1 chance in 5 of the candy picked being yellow. This probability can be written as the fraction ¹/₅.

1 yellow candy can be chosen

total of 5 candies to choose from

▷ **A hole in one**
A hole in one during a game of golf is highly unlikely, so it has a probability close to 0 on the scale. However, it can still happen!

△ **Identical snowflakes**
Every snowflake is unique and the chance that there can be two identical snowflakes is 0 on the scale, or impossible.

0

IMPOSSIBLE

UNLIKELY

▷ **Probability scale**
All probabilities can be shown on a line known as a probability scale. The more likely something is to occur the further to the right, or towards 1, it is placed.

LESS LIKELY

Calculating probabilities

This example shows how to work out the probability of randomly picking a red candy from a group of 10 candies. The number of ways this event could happen is put at the top of the fraction and the total number of possible events is put at the bottom.

number of red candies that can be chosen

$$\frac{3 \text{ red}}{10 \text{ candies}}$$

total that can be chosen

chance of red candy being chosen, as fraction

$$\frac{3}{10} \text{ or } 0.3$$

chance of red candy being chosen, as decimal

△ **Pick a candy**
There are 10 candies to choose from. Of these, 3 are colored red. If one of the candies is picked, what is the chance of it being red?

△ **Red randomly chosen**
One candy is chosen at random from the 10 colored candies. The candy chosen is one of the 3 red candies available.

△ **Write as a fraction**
There are three reds that can be chosen, so 3 is put at the top of the fraction. As there are ten candies in total, 10 is at the bottom.

△ **What is the chance?**
The probability of a red candy being picked is 3 out of 10, written as the fraction ³⁄₁₀, the decimal 0.3, or the percentage 30%.

◁ **Heads or tails**
If a coin is tossed there is a 1 in 2, or even, chance of throwing either a head or a tail. This is shown as 0.5 on the scale, which is the same as half, or 50%.

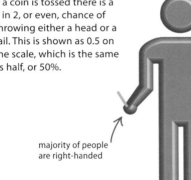

majority of people are right-handed

▷ **Earth turning**
It is a certainty that each day the Earth will continue to turn on its axis, making it a 1 on the scale.

◁ **Being right-handed**
The chances of picking at random a right-handed person are very high—almost 1 on the scale. Most people are right-handed.

0.5
EVEN CHANCE

LIKELY

1
CERTAIN

MORE LIKELY

Expectation and reality

EXPECTATION IS AN OUTCOME THAT IS ANTICIPATED TO OCCUR;
REALITY IS THE OUTCOME THAT ACTUALLY OCCURS.

SEE ALSO

❮ 48–55 Fractions

❮ 230–231 What is probability?

Combined probabilities 234–235 ❯

The difference between what is expected to occur and what actually occurs can often be considerable.

What is expectation?

There is an equal chance of a 6-sided dice landing on any number. It is expected that each of the 6 numbers on it will be rolled once in every 6 throws ($\frac{1}{6}$ of the time). Similarly, if a coin is tossed twice, it is expected that it will land on heads once and tails once. However, this does not always happen in real life.

WHAT ARE THE CHANCES?	
Two random phone numbers ending in same digit	1 chance in 10
Randomly selected person being left-handed	1 chance in 12
Pregnant woman giving birth to twins	1 chance in 33
An adult living to 100	1 chance in 50
A random clover having four leaves	1 chance in 10,000
Being struck by lightning in a year	1 chance in 2.5 million
A specific house being hit by a meteor	1 chance in 182 trillion

chance of rolling each number is 1 in 6

△ **Roll a dice**
Roll a dice 6 times and it seems likely that each of the 6 numbers on the dice will be seen once.

Expectation versus reality

Mathematical probability expects that when a dice is rolled 6 times, the numbers 1, 2, 3, 4, 5, and 6 will appear once each, but it is unlikely this outcome would actually occur. However, over a longer series of events, for example, throwing a dice a thousand times, the total numbers of 1s, 2s, 3s, 4s, 5s, and 6s thrown would be more even.

reasonable to expect 4 in first 6 throws

▷ **Expectation**
Mathematical probability expects that, when a dice is rolled 6 times, a 4 will be thrown once.

unexpected third 5 in 6 throws

unexpected third 6 in 6 throws

▷ **Reality**
Throwing a dice 6 times may create any combination of the numbers on a dice.

Calculating expectation

Expectation can be calculated. This is done by expressing the likelihood of something happening as a fraction, and then multiplying the fraction by the number of times the occurrence has the chance to happen. This example shows how expectation can be calculated in a game where balls are pulled from a bucket, with numbers ending in 0 or 5 winning a prize.

◁ **Numbered balls**
There are 30 balls in the game and 5 are removed at random. The balls are then checked for winning numbers—numbers that end in 0 or 5.

6 winning balls

There are 6 winning balls that can be picked out of the total of 30 balls.

number of winning balls in game

6

30 numbered balls to pick from

The total number of balls that can be picked in the game is 30.

total number of balls in game

30

there are 6 winning balls

both parts of the fraction can divide by 6, so it can be reduced

chances of winning ball being picked
$6 \div 6 = 1$

The probability of a winning ball being picked is 6 (balls) out of 30 (balls). This can be written as the fraction $^6/_{30}$, and is then reduced to $^1/_5$. The chance of picking a winning ball is 1 in 5, so the chance of winning a prize is 1 in 5.

$$\frac{6}{30} = \frac{1}{5}$$

$30 \div 6 = 5$

ball picked

20

1 prize "probably" won

It is expected that a prize will be won exactly 1 out of 5 times. The probability of winning a prize is therefore $^1/_5$ of 5, which is 1.

$$\frac{1}{5} \times 5 = 1$$

probability of picking a winning ball is 1 in 5

opportunities to pick a ball

"expect" 1 prize

20 = **PRIZE**

winning ball

Expectation suggests that 1 prize will be won if 5 balls are picked. However, in reality no prize or even 5 prizes may be won.

1 prize won?

Combined probabilities

SEE ALSO

❮ 230–231 What is probability?

❮ 232–233 Expectation and reality

THE PROBABILITY OF ONE OUTCOME FROM TWO OR MORE EVENTS HAPPENING AT THE SAME TIME, OR ONE AFTER THE OTHER.

Calculating the chance of one outcome from two things happening at the same time is not as complex as it might appear.

What are combined probabilities?

To find out the probability of one possible outcome happening from more than one event, all of the possible outcomes need to be worked out first. For example, if a coin is tossed and a dice is rolled at the same time, what is the probability of the coin landing on tails and the dice rolling a 4?

coin has 2 sides

dice has 6 sides

COIN

DICE

Coin and dice
A coin has 2 sides (heads and tails) while a dice has 6 sides—numbers 1 through to 6, represented by numbers of dots on each side.

▷ **Tossing a coin**
There are 2 sides to a coin, and each is equally likely to show if the coin is tossed. This means that the chance of the coin landing on tails is exactly 1 in 2, shown as the fraction ½.

chance of heads is 1 in 2

HEADS

chance of tails is 1 in 2

TAILS

$$\frac{1}{2}$$

represents chance of single event, for example chance of coin landing on tails

represents total possible outcomes if coin is tossed

▷ **Rolling a dice**
Because there are 6 sides to a dice, and each side is equally likely to show when the dice is rolled, the chance of rolling a 4 is exactly 1 in 6, shown as the fraction ⅙.

chance of rolling 1 is 1 in 6

chance of rolling 2 is 1 in 6

chance of rolling 3 is 1 in 6

chance of rolling 4 is 1 in 6

chance of rolling 5 is 1 in 6

chance of rolling 6 is 1 in 6

$$\frac{1}{6}$$

represents chance of single event, for example chance of rolling a 4

represents total possible outcomes if dice is thrown

▷ **Both events**
To find out the chances of both a coin landing on tails and a dice simultaneously rolling a 4, multiply the individual probabilities together. The answer shows that there is a ¹⁄₁₂ chance of this outcome.

coin lands on tails

multiply the 2 probabilities together

chance of dice rolling a 4 is 1 in 6

$$\frac{1}{2} \times \frac{1}{6} = \frac{1}{12}$$

TAILS

chance of coin landing on tails is 1 in 2

chance of specific outcome

chance of coin landing on tails and rolling a 4 is 1 in 12

total possible outcomes

Figuring out possible outcomes

A table can be used to work out all the possible outcomes of two combined events. For example, if two dice are rolled, their scores will have a combined total of between 2 and 12. There are 36 possible outcomes, which are shown in the table below. Read down from each red dice and across from each blue dice for each of their combined results.

blue dice throws

red dice throws

Red / Blue	⚀	⚁	⚂	⚃	⚄	⚅	
⚀	2	3	4	5	6	7	6 ways out of 36 to throw 7, for example blue dice rolling 1 and red dice rolling 6
⚁	3	4	5	6	7	8	5 ways out of 36 to throw 8, for example blue dice rolling 2 and red dice rolling 6
⚂	4	5	6	7	8	9	4 ways out of 36 to throw 9, for example blue dice rolling 3 and red dice rolling 6
⚃	5	6	7	8	9	10	3 ways out of 36 to throw 10, for example blue dice rolling 4 and red dice rolling 6
⚄	6	7	8	9	10	11	2 ways out of 36 to throw 11, for example blue dice rolling 5 and red dice rolling 6
⚅	7	8	9	10	11	12	1 way out of 36 to throw 12

KEY

 Least likely
The least likely outcome of throwing 2 dice is either 2 (each dice is 1) or 12 (each is 6). There is a $1/36$ chance of either result.

 Most likely
The most likely outcome of throwing 2 dice is a 7. With 6 ways to throw a 7, there is a $6/36$, or $1/6$, chance of this result.

Dependent events

THE CHANCES OF SOMETHING HAPPENING CAN CHANGE ACCORDING
TO THE EVENTS THAT PRECEDED IT. THIS IS A DEPENDENT EVENT.

SEE ALSO
❰ 232–233 Expectation
and reality

Dependent events

In this example, the probability of picking any one of four
green cards from a pack of 40 is 4 out of 40 (4/40). It is an
independent event. However, the probability of the second
card picked being green depends on the color of the card
picked first. This is known as a dependent event.

▷ **Color-coded**
This pack of cards
contains 10
groups, each with
its own color.
There are 4 cards
in each group.

there are 4 cards of each color

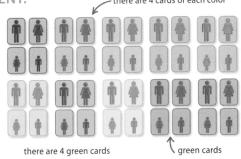

there are 4 green cards   green cards

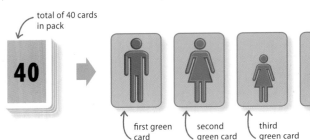

total of 40 cards
in pack

first green card / second green card / third green card / fourth green card

4/40

◁ **What are the chances?**
The chances of the first card picked
being green is 4 in 40 (4/40). This is
independent of other events because
it is the first event.

there are 40 cards in total

Dependent events and decreasing probability

If the first card chosen from a pack of 40 is one of the 4 green cards, then the chances that the next card is green are
reduced to 3 in 39 (3/39). This example shows how the chances of a green card being picked next gradually shrink to zero.

The first card is chosen and is green. The next card picked will be chosen from the remaining 39 cards.

1 green card chosen

39 — 39 cards remain

chances of next card being green

3/39 — cards left

◁ **The chances of the** next card picked being green are 3 in 39 (3/39). With 1 of the 4 green cards picked there are 3 left in the pack.

The first 3 cards have been chosen and were all green. The next card to be picked will be chosen from the remaining 37 cards.

3 green cards chosen

37 — 37 cards remain

chances of next card being green

1/37 — cards left

◁ **The chances of the** next card being green are 1 in 37 (1/37). With 3 of the 4 green cards picked there is 1 green card left in the pack.

The first 4 cards have been chosen and were all green. The next card to be chosen will be picked from the remaining 36 cards.

4 green cards chosen

36 — 36 cards remain

chances of next card being green as all green cards are picked

0/36 = 0 — cards left

◁ **The chances of the** next card being green are 0 in 36, or zero. With all 4 green cards picked there are no green cards left in the pack.

Dependent events and increasing probability

If the first card chosen from a pack of 40 is not one of the 4 pink cards, then the probability of the next card being pink grow to 4 out of the remaining 39 cards (4/39). In this example, the probability of a pink card being the next to be picked grows to a certainty with each non-pink card picked.

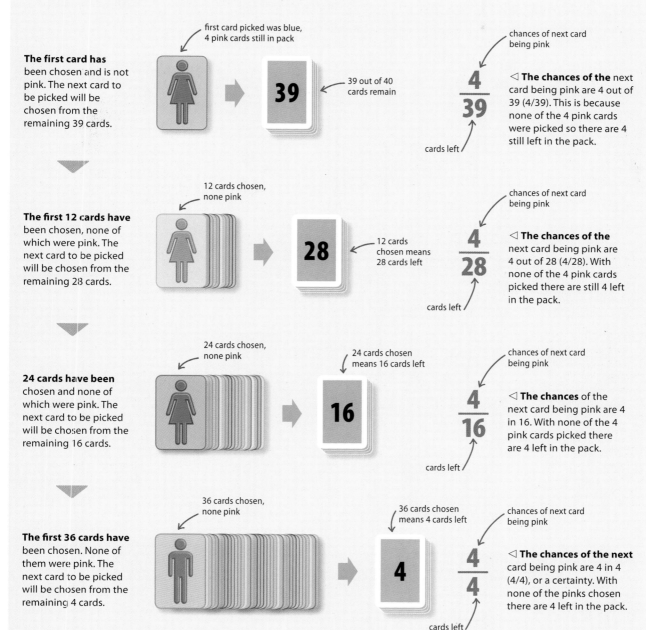

first card picked was blue, 4 pink cards still in pack

The first card has been chosen and is not pink. The next card to be picked will be chosen from the remaining 39 cards.

39 out of 40 cards remain

chances of next card being pink

$$\frac{4}{39}$$

cards left

◁ **The chances of the** next card being pink are 4 out of 39 (4/39). This is because none of the 4 pink cards were picked so there are 4 still left in the pack.

12 cards chosen, none pink

The first 12 cards have been chosen, none of which were pink. The next card to be picked will be chosen from the remaining 28 cards.

12 cards chosen means 28 cards left

chances of next card being pink

$$\frac{4}{28}$$

cards left

◁ **The chances of the** next card being pink are 4 out of 28 (4/28). With none of the 4 pink cards picked there are still 4 left in the pack.

24 cards chosen, none pink

24 cards have been chosen and none of which were pink. The next card to be picked will be chosen from the remaining 16 cards.

24 cards chosen means 16 cards left

chances of next card being pink

$$\frac{4}{16}$$

cards left

◁ **The chances** of the next card being pink are 4 in 16. With none of the 4 pink cards picked there are 4 left in the pack.

36 cards chosen, none pink

The first 36 cards have been chosen. None of them were pink. The next card to be picked will be chosen from the remaining 4 cards.

36 cards chosen means 4 cards left

chances of next card being pink

$$\frac{4}{4}$$

cards left

◁ **The chances of the next** card being pink are 4 in 4 (4/4), or a certainty. With none of the pinks chosen there are 4 left in the pack.

Tree diagrams

TREE DIAGRAMS CAN BE CONSTRUCTED TO HELP CALCULATE THE
PROBABILITY OF MULTIPLE EVENTS OCCURRING.

SEE ALSO

❮ **230–231** What is probability?

❮ **234–235** Combined probabilities

❮ **236–237** Dependent events

A range of probable outcomes of future events can be shown using
arrows, or the "branches" of a "tree," flowing from left to right.

Building a tree diagram

The first stage of building a tree diagram is
to draw an arrow from the start position to
each of the possible outcomes. Here, the
start is a cell phone, and the outcomes are
5 messages sent to 2 other phones, with
each of these other phones at the end of
1 of 2 arrows. Because no event came
before, they are single events.

▷ **Single events**
Of 5 messages, 2 are
sent to the first
phone, shown by the
fraction ²/₅, and 3 out
of 5 are sent to the
second phone, shown
by the fraction ³/₅.

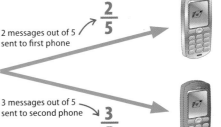

2 messages out of 5 sent to first phone $\frac{2}{5}$

3 messages out of 5 sent to second phone $\frac{3}{5}$

Tree diagrams showing multiple events

To draw a tree diagram that shows multiple events, begin with a start position,
with arrows leading to the right to each of the possible outcomes. This is stage 1.
Each of the outcomes of stage 1 then becomes a new start position, with further
arrows each leading to a new stage of possible outcomes. This is stage 2. More
stages can then follow on from the outcomes of previous stages. Because one
stage of events comes before another, these are multiple events.

vacation flight to France

2 out of 3 fly to France $\frac{2}{3}$

vacation flight to Italy

1 out of 3 flies to Italy $\frac{1}{3}$

STAGE 1: FRANCE OR ITALY?

$\frac{2}{5}$ arriving in France, 2 out of 5 stay in Paris

$\frac{3}{5}$ arriving in France, 3 out of 5 stay in the Alps

$\frac{1}{2}$ arriving in Italy, 1 out of 2 stays in Rome

$\frac{1}{2}$ arriving in Italy, 1 out of 2 stays in Naples

Find the probability

To work out the chance of a randomly
selected person flying to Italy, staying
in Naples, and visiting Vesuvius,
multiply the chances of each stage of
this trip together for the answer.

staying in Naples

visiting Vesuvius

$$\frac{1}{3} \times \frac{1}{2} \times \frac{1}{4} = \frac{1}{24}$$

1 out of 3 flies to Italy

chance of person visiting Italy, then Naples, then Vesuvius

△ **Multiple events in 3 stages**
The tree diagram above shows 3
stages of a vacation. In stage 1,
people fly to France or Italy.

When multiple events are dependent

Tree diagrams show how the chances of one event can depend on the previous event. In this example, each event is someone picking a fruit from a bag and not replacing it.

△ **Dependent events**
The first person picks from a bag of 10 fruits (3 oranges, 7 apples). The next picks from 9 fruits, when the chances of what is picked are out of 9.

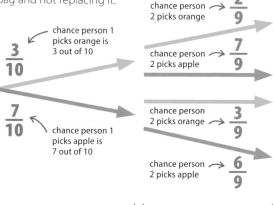

chance person 1 picks orange is 3 out of 10
$\frac{3}{10}$

chance person 1 picks apple is 7 out of 10
$\frac{7}{10}$

chance person 2 picks orange $\rightarrow$ $\frac{2}{9}$

chance person 2 picks apple $\frac{7}{9}$

chance person 2 picks orange $\rightarrow$ $\frac{3}{9}$

chance person 2 picks apple $\frac{6}{9}$

person 1 chooses from 10 fruits

person 2 chooses from 9 fruits

Find the probability

What are the chances that the first and second person will each choose an orange? Multiply the chances of both events together.

chance person 2 picks orange

$$\frac{3}{10} \times \frac{2}{9} = \frac{6}{90}$$

chance person 1 picks orange

chance both pick orange

or

$\frac{1}{15}$ ← fraction $\frac{6}{90}$ reduced down to $\frac{1}{15}$ by dividing 6 and 90 by 6

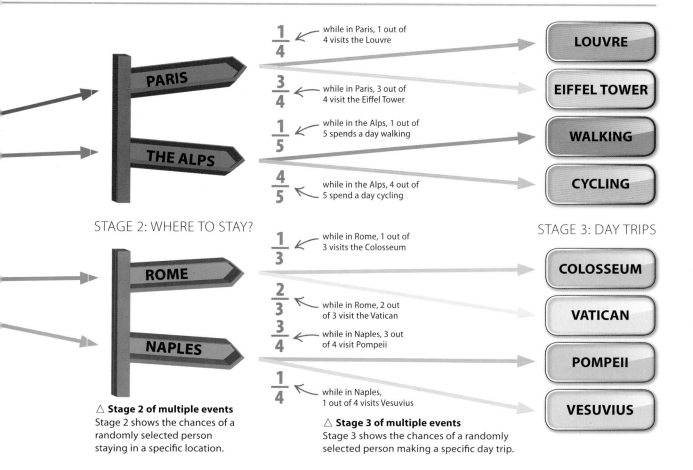

$\frac{1}{4}$ ← while in Paris, 1 out of 4 visits the Louvre

PARIS

$\frac{3}{4}$ ← while in Paris, 3 out of 4 visit the Eiffel Tower

$\frac{1}{5}$ ← while in the Alps, 1 out of 5 spends a day walking

THE ALPS

$\frac{4}{5}$ ← while in the Alps, 4 out of 5 spend a day cycling

LOUVRE

EIFFEL TOWER

WALKING

CYCLING

STAGE 2: WHERE TO STAY?

STAGE 3: DAY TRIPS

$\frac{1}{3}$ ← while in Rome, 1 out of 3 visits the Colosseum

ROME

$\frac{2}{3}$ ← while in Rome, 2 out of 3 visit the Vatican

$\frac{3}{4}$ ← while in Naples, 3 out of 4 visit Pompeii

NAPLES

$\frac{1}{4}$ ← while in Naples, 1 out of 4 visits Vesuvius

COLOSSEUM

VATICAN

POMPEII

VESUVIUS

△ **Stage 2 of multiple events**
Stage 2 shows the chances of a randomly selected person staying in a specific location.

△ **Stage 3 of multiple events**
Stage 3 shows the chances of a randomly selected person making a specific day trip.

Reference section

Mathematical signs and symbols

This table shows a selection of signs and symbols commonly used in mathematics. Using signs and symbols, mathematicians can express complex equations and formulas in a standardized way that is universally understood.

Symbol	Definition	Symbol	Definition	Symbol	Definition
$+$	plus; positive	$:$	ratio of (6:4)	∞	infinity
$-$	minus; negative	$::$	proportionately equal (1:2::2:4)	n^2	squared number
$\pm$	plus or minus; positive or negative; degree of accuracy	$\approx, \doteqdot, \triangleq$	approximately equal to; equivalent to; similar to	n^3	cubed number
$\mp$	minus or plus; negative or positive			n^4, n^5, etc	power, exponent
$\times$	multiplied by (6 × 4)	$\cong$	congruent to; identical with	$\sqrt[2]{\ }$	square root
$\cdot$	multiplied by (6·4); scalar product of two vectors (A·B)	$>$	greater than	$\sqrt[3]{\ }, \sqrt[4]{\ }$	cube root, fourth root, etc.
$\div$	divided by (6 ÷ 4)	$\gg$	much greater than	$\%$	percent
$/$	divided by; ratio of ($^6/_4$)	$\ngtr$	not greater than	$°$	degrees (°F); degree of arc, for example 90°
$-$	divided by; ratio of ($\frac{6}{4}$)	$<$	less than	$\angle, \angle^s$	angle(s)
$\bigcirc$	circle	$\ll$	much less than	$\stackrel{\vee}{=}$	equiangular
$\blacktriangle$	triangle	$\nless$	not less than	π	(pi) the ratio of the circumference to the diameter of a circle ≈ 3.14
$\square$	square	$\geqslant, \geqq, \gtreqless$	greater than or equal to		
$\square$	rectangle	$\leqslant, \leqq, \lesseqgtr$	less than or equal to	α	alpha (unknown angle)
$\square$	parallelogram	$\propto$	directly proportional to	θ	theta (unknown angle)
$=$	equals	$(\ )$	parentheses, can mean multiply	$\perp$	perpendicular
$\neq$	not equal to			$\llcorner$	right angle
$\equiv$	identical with; congruent to	$-$	vinculum: division (a-b); chord of circle or length of line (AB);	$\parallel, =$	parallel
$\not\equiv$	not identical with	$\overrightarrow{AB}$	vector	$\therefore$	therefore
$\triangleq$	corresponds to	$\overline{AB}$	line segment	$\because$	because
		$\overleftrightarrow{AB}$	line	$\stackrel{m}{=}$	measured by

Prime numbers

A prime number is any number that can only be exactly divided by 1 and itself without leaving a remainder. By definition, 1 is not a prime. There is no one formula for yielding every prime. Shown here are the first 250 prime numbers.

2	3	5	7	11	13	17	19	23	29
31	37	41	43	47	53	59	61	67	71
73	79	83	89	97	101	103	107	109	113
127	131	137	139	149	151	157	163	167	173
179	181	191	193	197	199	211	223	227	229
233	239	241	251	257	263	269	271	277	281
283	293	307	311	313	317	331	337	347	349
353	359	367	373	379	383	389	397	401	409
419	421	431	433	439	443	449	457	461	463
467	479	487	491	499	503	509	521	523	541
547	557	563	569	571	577	587	593	599	601
607	613	617	619	631	641	643	647	653	659
661	673	677	683	691	701	709	719	727	733
739	743	751	757	761	769	773	787	797	809
811	821	823	827	829	839	853	857	859	863
877	881	883	887	907	911	919	929	937	941
947	953	967	971	977	983	991	997	1,009	1,013
1,019	1,021	1,031	1,033	1,039	1,049	1,051	1,061	1,063	1,069
1,087	1,091	1,093	1,097	1,103	1,109	1,117	1,123	1,129	1,151
1,153	1,163	1,171	1,181	1,187	1,193	1,201	1,213	1,217	1,223
1,229	1,231	1,237	1,249	1,259	1,277	1,279	1,283	1,289	1,291
1,297	1,301	1,303	1,307	1,319	1,321	1,327	1,361	1,367	1,373
1,381	1,399	1,409	1,423	1,427	1,429	1,433	1,439	1,447	1,451
1,453	1,459	1,471	1,481	1,483	1,487	1,489	1,493	1,499	1,511
1,523	1,531	1,543	1,549	1,553	1,559	1,567	1,571	1,579	1,583

Squares, cubes, and roots

The table below shows the square, cube, square root, and cube root of whole numbers, to 3 decimal places.

No.	Square	Cube	Square root	Cube root
1	1	1	1.000	1.000
2	4	8	1.414	1.260
3	9	27	1.732	1.442
4	16	64	2.000	1.587
5	25	125	2.236	1.710
6	36	216	2.449	1.817
7	49	343	2.646	1.913
8	64	512	2.828	2.000
9	81	729	3.000	2.080
10	100	1,000	3.162	2.154
11	121	1,331	3.317	2.224
12	144	1,728	3.464	2.289
13	169	2,197	3.606	2.351
14	196	2,744	3.742	2.410
15	225	3,375	3.873	2.466
16	256	4,096	4.000	2.520
17	289	4,913	4.123	2.571
18	324	5,832	4.243	2.621
19	361	6,859	4.359	2.668
20	400	8,000	4.472	2.714
25	625	15,625	5.000	2.924
30	900	27,000	5.477	3.107
50	2,500	125,000	7.071	3.684

Multiplication table

This multiplication table shows the products of each whole number from 1 to 12, multiplied by each whole number from 1 to 12.

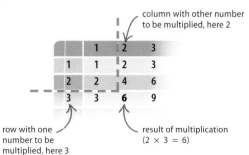

column with other number to be multiplied, here 2

row with one number to be multiplied, here 3

result of multiplication (2 × 3 = 6)

	1	2	3	4	5	6	7	8	9	10	11	12
1	1	2	3	4	5	6	7	8	9	10	11	12
2	2	4	6	8	10	12	14	16	18	20	22	24
3	3	6	9	12	15	18	21	24	27	30	33	36
4	4	8	12	16	20	24	28	32	36	40	44	48
5	5	10	15	20	25	30	35	40	45	50	55	60
6	6	12	18	24	30	36	42	48	54	60	66	72
7	7	14	21	28	35	42	49	56	63	70	77	84
8	8	16	24	32	40	48	56	64	72	80	88	96
9	9	18	27	36	45	54	63	72	81	90	99	108
10	10	20	30	40	50	60	70	80	90	100	110	120
11	11	22	33	44	55	66	77	88	99	110	121	132
12	12	24	36	48	60	72	84	96	108	120	132	144

Units of measurement

A unit of measurement is a quantity used as a standard, allowing values of things to be compared. These include seconds (time), meters (length), and kilograms (mass). Two widely used systems of measurement are the metric system and the imperial system.

AREA		
metric		
100 square millimeters (mm^2)	=	1 square centimeter (cm^2)
10,000 square centimeters (cm^2)	=	1 square meter (m^2)
10,000 square meters (m^2)	=	1 hectare (ha)
100 hectares (ha)	=	1 square kilometer (km^2)
1 square kilometer (km^2)	=	1,000,000 square meters (m^2)
imperial		
144 square inches (sq in)	=	1 square foot (sq ft)
9 square feet (sq ft)	=	1 square yard (sq yd)
1,296 square inches (sq in)	=	1 square yard (sq yd)
43,560 square feet (sq ft)	=	1 acre
640 acres	=	1 square mile (sq mile)

LIQUID VOLUME		
metric		
1,000 milliliters (ml)	=	1 liter (l)
100 liters (l)	=	1 hectoliter (hl)
10 hectoliters (hl)	=	1 kiloliter (kl)
1,000 liters (l)	=	1 kiloliter (kl)
imperial		
8 fluid ounces (fl oz)	=	1 cup
20 fluid ounces (fl oz)	=	1 pint (pt)
4 gills (gi)	=	1 pint (pt)
2 pints (pt)	=	1 quart (qt)
4 quarts (qt)	=	1 gallon (gal)
8 pints (pt)	=	1 gallon (gal)

MASS		
metric		
1,000 milligrams (mg)	=	1 gram (g)
1,000 grams (g)	=	1 kilogram (kg)
1,000 kilograms (kg)	=	1 tonne (t)
imperial		
16 ounces (oz)	=	1 pound (lb)
14 pounds (lb)	=	1 stone
112 pounds (lb)	=	1 hundredweight
20 hundredweight	=	1 ton

LENGTH		
metric		
10 millimeters (mm)	=	1 centimeter (cm)
100 centimeters (cm)	=	1 meter (m)
1,000 millimeters (mm)	=	1 meter (m)
1,000 meters (m)	=	1 kilometer (km)
imperial		
12 inches (in)	=	1 foot (ft)
3 feet (ft)	=	1 yard (yd)
1,760 yards (yd)	=	1 mile
5,280 feet (ft)	=	1 mile
8 furlongs	=	1 mile

TIME		
metric and imperial		
60 seconds	=	1 minute
60 minutes	=	1 hour
24 hours	=	1 day
7 days	=	1 week
52 weeks	=	1 year
1 year	=	12 months

TEMPERATURE		Fahrenheit	Celsius	Kelvin
Boiling point of water	=	212°	100°	373°
Freezing point of water	=	32°	0°	273°
Absolute zero	=	−459°	−273°	0°

Conversion tables

The tables below show metric and imperial equivalents for common measurements for length, area, mass, and volume. Conversions between Celcius, Fahrenheit, and Kelvin temperature require formulas, which are also given below.

LENGTH

metric		imperial
1 millimeter (mm)	=	0.03937 inch (in)
1 centimeter (cm)	=	0.3937 inch (in)
1 meter (m)	=	1.0936 yards (yd)
1 kilometer (km)	=	0.6214 mile
imperial		**metric**
1 inch (in)	=	2.54 centimeters (cm)
1 foot (ft)	=	0.3048 meter (m)
1 yard (yd)	=	0.9144 meter (m)
1 mile	=	1.6093 kilometers (km)
1 nautical mile	=	1.853 kilometers (km)

AREA

metric		imperial
1 square centimeter (cm^2)	=	0.155 square inch (sq in)
1 square meter (m^2)	=	1.196 square yard (sq yd)
1 hectare (ha)	=	2.4711 acres
1 square kilometer (km^2)	=	0.3861 square miles
imperial		**metric**
1 square inch (sq in)	=	6.4516 square centimeters (cm^2)
1 square foot (sq ft)	=	0.0929 square meter (m^2)
1 square yard (sq yd)	=	0.8361 square meter (m^2)
1 acre	=	0.4047 hectare (ha)
1 square mile	=	2.59 square kilometers (km^2)

MASS

metric		imperial
1 milligram (mg)	=	0.0154 grain
1 gram (g)	=	0.0353 ounce (oz)
1 kilogram (kg)	=	2.2046 pounds (lb)
1 tonne/metric ton (t)	=	0.9842 imperial ton
imperial		**metric**
1 ounce (oz)	=	28.35 grams (g)
1 pound (lb)	=	0.4536 kilogram (kg)
1 stone	=	6.3503 kilogram (kg)
1 hundredweight (cwt)	=	50.802 kilogram (kg)
1 imperial ton	=	1.016 tonnes/metric tons

VOLUME

metric		imperial
1 cubic centimeter (cm^3)	=	0.061 cubic inch (in^3)
1 cubic decimeter (dm^3)	=	0.0353 cubic foot (ft^3)
1 cubic meter (m^3)	=	1.308 cubic yard (yd^3)
1 liter (l)/1 dm^3	=	1.76 pints (pt)
1 hectoliter (hl)/100 l	=	21.997 gallons (gal)
imperial		**metric**
1 cubic inch (in^3)	=	16.387 cubic centimeters (cm^3)
1 cubic foot (ft^3)	=	0.0283 cubic meters (m^3)
1 fluid ounce (fl oz)	=	28.413 milliliters (ml)
1 pint (pt)/20 fl oz	=	0.5683 liter (l)
1 gallon/8 pt	=	4.5461 liters (l)

TEMPERATURE

To convert from Fahrenheit (°F) to Celsius (°C)	=	$C = (F - 32) \times 5 \div 9$
To convert from Celsius (°C) Fahrenheit (°F)	=	$F = (C \times 9 \div 5) + 32$
To convert from Celsius (°C) to Kelvin (K)	=	$K = C + 273$
To convert from Kelvin (K) to Celsius (°C)	=	$C = K - 273$

Fahrenheit °F	−4	14	32	50	68	86	104	122	140	158	176	194	212
Celsius °C	−20	−10	0	10	20	30	40	50	60	70	80	90	100
Kelvin	253	263	273	283	293	303	313	325	333	343	353	363	373

How to convert

The table below shows how to convert between metric and imperial units of measurement. The left table shows how to convert from one unit to its metric or imperial equivalent. The right table shows how to do the reverse conversion.

HOW TO CONVERT METRIC and IMPERIAL MEASURES		
to change	**to**	**multiply by**
acres	hectares	0.4047
centimeters	feet	0.03281
centimeters	inches	0.3937
cubic centimeters	cubic inches	0.061
cubic feet	cubic meters	0.0283
cubic inches	cubic centimeters	16.3871
cubic meters	cubic feet	35.315
feet	centimeters	30.48
feet	meters	0.3048
gallons	liters	4.546
grams	ounces	0.0353
hectares	acres	2.471
inches	centimeters	2.54
kilograms	pounds	2.2046
kilometers	miles	0.6214
kilometers per hour	miles per hour	0.6214
liters	gallons	0.2199
liters	pints	1.7598
meters	feet	3.2808
meters	yards	1.0936
meters per minute	centimeters per second	1.6667
meters per minute	feet per second	0.0547
miles	kilometers	1.6093
miles per hour	kilometers per hour	1.6093
miles per hour	meters per second	0.447
millimeters	inches	0.0394
ounces	grams	28.3495
pints	liters	0.5682
pounds	kilograms	0.4536
square centimeters	square inches	0.155
square inches	square centimeters	6.4516
square feet	square meters	0.0929
square kilometers	square miles	0.386
square meters	square feet	10.764
square meters	square yards	1.196
square miles	square kilometers	2.5899
square yards	square meters	0.8361
tonnes (metric)	tons (imperial)	0.9842
tons (imperial)	tonnes (metric)	1.0216
yards	meters	0.9144

HOW TO CONVERT METRIC and IMPERIAL MEASURES		
to change	**to**	**divide by**
hectares	acres	0.4047
feet	centimeters	0.03281
inches	centimeters	0.3937
cubic inches	cubic centimeters	0.061
cubic meters	cubic feet	0.0283
cubic centimeters	cubic inches	16.3871
cubic feet	cubic meters	35.315
centimeters	feet	30.48
meters	feet	0.3048
liters	gallons	4.546
ounces	grams	0.0353
acres	hectares	2.471
centimeters	inches	2.54
pounds	kilograms	2.2046
miles	kilometers	0.6214
miles per hour	kilometers per hour	0.6214
gallons	liters	0.2199
pints	liters	1.7598
feet	meters	3.2808
yards	meters	1.0936
centimeters per second	meters per minute	1.6667
feet per second	meters per minute	0.0547
kilometers	miles	1.6093
kilometers per hour	miles per hour	1.6093
meters per second	miles per hour	0.447
inches	millimeters	0.0394
grams	ounces	28.3495
liters	pints	0.5682
kilograms	pounds	0.4536
square inches	square centimeters	0.155
square centimeters	square inches	6.4516
square meters	square feet	0.0929
square miles	square kilometers	0.386
square feet	square meters	10.764
square yards	square meters	1.196
square kilometers	square miles	2.5899
square meters	square yards	0.8361
tons (imperial)	tonnes (metric)	0.9842
tonnes (metric)	tons (imperial)	1.0216
meters	yards	0.9144

Numerical equivalents

Percentages, decimals, and fractions are different ways of presenting a numerical value as a proportion of a given amount. For example, 10 percent (10%) has the equivalent value of the decimal 0.1 and the fraction 1/10.

%	Decimal	Fraction	%	Decimal	Fraction	%	Decimal	Fraction	%	Decimal	Fraction	%	Decimal	Fraction
1	0.01	1/100	12.5	0.125	1/8	24	0.24	6/25	36	0.36	9/25	49	0.49	49/100
2	0.02	1/50	13	0.13	13/100	25	0.25	1/4	37	0.37	37/100	50	0.5	1/2
3	0.03	3/100	14	0.14	7/50	26	0.26	13/50	38	0.38	19/50	55	0.55	11/20
4	0.04	1/25	15	0.15	3/20	27	0.27	27/100	39	0.39	39/100	60	0.6	3/5
5	0.05	1/20	16	0.16	4/25	28	0.28	7/25	40	0.4	2/5	65	0.65	13/20
6	0.06	3/50	16.66	0.166	1/6	29	0.29	29/100	41	0.41	41/100	66.66	0.666	2/3
7	0.07	7/100	17	0.17	17/100	30	0.3	3/10	42	0.42	21/50	70	0.7	7/10
8	0.08	2/25	18	0.18	9/50	31	0.31	31/100	43	0.43	43/100	75	0.75	3/4
8.33	0.083	1/12	19	0.19	19/100	32	0.32	8/25	44	0.44	11/25	80	0.8	4/5
9	0.09	9/100	20	0.2	1/5	33	0.33	33/100	45	0.45	9/20	85	0.85	17/20
10	0.1	1/10	21	0.21	21/100	33.33	0.333	1/3	46	0.46	23/50	90	0.9	9/10
11	0.11	11/100	22	0.22	11/50	34	0.34	17/50	47	0.47	47/100	95	0.95	19/20
12	0.12	3/25	23	0.23	23/100	35	0.35	7/20	48	0.48	12/25	100	1.00	1

Angles

An angle shows the amount that a line "turns" as it extends in a direction away from a fixed point.

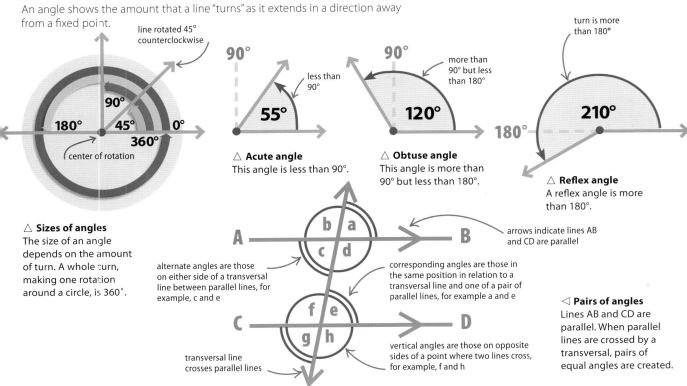

line rotated 45° counterclockwise

90°

180° — 45° — 0°

360°

center of rotation

△ **Sizes of angles**
The size of an angle depends on the amount of turn. A whole turn, making one rotation around a circle, is 360°.

90°

less than 90°

55°

△ **Acute angle**
This angle is less than 90°.

90°

more than 90° but less than 180°

120°

180°

△ **Obtuse angle**
This angle is more than 90° but less than 180°.

turn is more than 180°

210°

180°

△ **Reflex angle**
A reflex angle is more than 180°.

A — b a / c d — B

C — f e / g h — D

arrows indicate lines AB and CD are parallel

alternate angles are those on either side of a transversal line between parallel lines, for example, c and e

corresponding angles are those in the same position in relation to a transversal line and one of a pair of parallel lines, for example a and e

transversal line crosses parallel lines

vertical angles are those on opposite sides of a point where two lines cross, for example, f and h

◁ **Pairs of angles**
Lines AB and CD are parallel. When parallel lines are crossed by a transversal, pairs of equal angles are created.

Shapes

Two-dimensional shapes with straight lines are called polygons. They are named according to the number of sides they have. The number of sides is also equal to the number of interior angles. A circle has no straight lines, so it is not a polygon although it is a two-dimensional shape.

△ **Circle**
A shape formed by a curved line that is always the same distance from a central point.

△ **Triangle**
A polygon with three sides and three interior angles.

△ **Quadrilateral**
A polygon with four sides and four interior angles.

△ **Square**
A quadrilateral with four equal sides and four equal interior angles of 90˚ (right angles).

△ **Rectangle**
A quadrilateral with four equal interior angles and opposite sides of equal length.

△ **Parallelogram**
A quadrilateral with two pairs of parallel sides and opposite sides of equal length.

△ **Pentagon**
A polygon with five sides and five interior angles.

△ **Hexagon**
A polygon with six sides and six interior angles.

△ **Heptagon**
A polygon with seven sides and seven interior angles.

△ **Nonagon**
A polygon with nine sides and nine interior angles.

△ **Decagon**
A polygon with ten sides and ten interior angles.

△ **Hendecagon**
A polygon with eleven sides and eleven interior angles.

Sequences

A sequence is a series of numbers written as an ordered list where there is a particular pattern or "rule" that relates each number in the list to the numbers before and after it. Examples of important mathematical sequences are shown below.

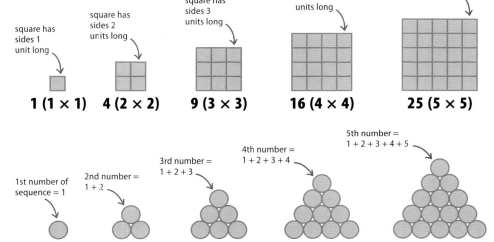

square has sides 1 unit long

square has sides 2 units long

square has sides 3 units long

square has sides 4 units long

square has sides 5 units long

1 (1 × 1) 4 (2 × 2) 9 (3 × 3) 16 (4 × 4) 25 (5 × 5)

◁ **Square numbers**
In a sequence of square numbers, each number is made by squaring its position in the sequence, for example the third number is 3^2 ($3 \times 3 = 9$) and the fourth number is 4^2 ($4 \times 4 = 16$).

1st number of sequence = 1

2nd number = 1 + 2

3rd number = 1 + 2 + 3

4th number = 1 + 2 + 3 + 4

5th number = 1 + 2 + 3 + 4 + 5

1   3   6   10   15

◁ **Triangular numbers**
In this sequence, each number is made by adding another row of dots to the triangular pattern. The numbers are also related mathematically, for example, the fifth number in the sequence is the sum of all numbers up to 5 ($1 + 2 + 3 + 4 + 5$).

Fibonacci sequence

Named after the Italian mathematician Leonardo Fibonacci (c.1175–c.1250), the Fibonacci sequence starts with 1. The second number is also 1. After that, each number in the sequence is the sum of the two numbers before it, for example, the sixth number, 8, is the sum of the fourth and fifth numbers, 3 and 5 ($3 + 5 = 8$).

sequence starts with 1

each number in sequence is sum of two numbers before it

1+1   1+2   2+3   3+5   5+8

1, 1, 2, 3, 5, 8, 13, ...

sequence continues in same way indefinitely

Pascal's Triangle

Pascal's triangle is a triangular arrangement of numbers. The number at the top of the triangle is 1, and every number down each side is also 1. Each of the other numbers is the sum of the two numbers diagonally above it; for example, in the third row, the 2 is made by adding the two 1s in the row above.

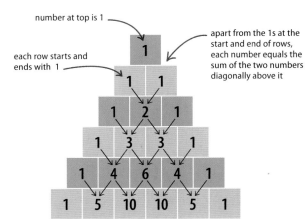

number at top is 1

each row starts and ends with 1

apart from the 1s at the start and end of rows, each number equals the sum of the two numbers diagonally above it

```
          1
        1   1
      1   2   1
    1   3   3   1
  1   4   6   4   1
1   5   10  10  5   1
```

FORMULAS

Formulas are mathematical "recipes" that relate various quantities or terms, so that if the value of one is unknown, it can be worked out if the values of the other terms in the formula are known.

Interest

There are two types of interest – simple and compound. In simple interest, the interest is paid only on the capital. In compound interest, the interest itself earns interest.

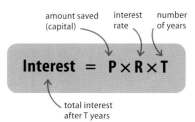

amount saved (capital)   interest rate   number of years

$$\text{Interest} = P \times R \times T$$

total interest after T years

◁ **Simple interest formula**
To find the simple interest made after a given number of years, substitute real values into this formula.

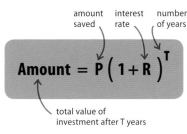

amount saved   interest rate   number of years

$$\text{Amount} = P \left(1 + R \right)^{T}$$

total value of investment after T years

◁ **Compound interest formula**
To find the total value of an investment (capital + interest) after a given number of years, substitute values into this formula.

Formulas in algebra

Algebra is the branch of mathematics that uses symbols to represent numbers and the relationship between them. Useful formulas are the standard formula of a quadratic equation and the formula for solving it.

squared value of x multiplied by a number   constant number with no x terms

$$ax^2 + bx + c = 0$$

x multiplied by a number

△ **Quadratic equation**
Quadratic equations take the form shown above. They can be solved by using the quadratic formula.

this means add or subtract

$$x = \frac{-b \pm \sqrt{b^2 - 4ac}}{2a}$$

△ **The quadratic formula**
This formula can be used to solve any quadratic equation. There are always two solutions.

symbol for pi

value to 2 decimal places

$$\pi = 3.14$$

value to 20 decimal places

$$3.14159265358979323846$$

◁ **The value of pi**
Pi occurs in many formulas, such as the formula used for working out the area of a circle. The numbers after the decimal point in pi go on for ever and do not follow any pattern.

Formulas in trigonometry

Three of the most useful formulas in trigonometry are those to find out the unknown angles of a right triangle when two of its sides are known.

$$\sin A = \frac{\text{opposite}}{\text{hypotenuse}}$$

△ **The sine formula**
This formula is used to find the size of angle A when the side opposite the angle and the hypotenuse are known.

$$\cos A = \frac{\text{adjacent}}{\text{hypotenuse}}$$

△ **The cosine formula**
This formula is used to find the size of angle A when the side adjacent to the angle and the hypotenuse are known.

$$\tan A = \frac{\text{opposite}}{\text{adjacent}}$$

△ **The tangent formula**
This formula is used to find the size of angle A when the sides opposite and adjacent to the angle are known.

Area

The area of a shape is the amount of space inside it. Formulas for working out the areas of common shapes are given below.

$$area = \pi r^2$$

$$area = \frac{1}{2}bh$$

$$area = bh$$

△ **Circle**
The area of a circle equals pi ($\pi = 3.14$) multiplied by the square of its radius.

△ **Triangle**
The area of a triangle equals half multiplied by its base multiplied by its vertical height.

△ **Rectangle**
The area of a rectangle equals its base multiplied by its height.

$$area = bh$$

$$area = \frac{1}{2}h(b_1+b_2)$$

$$area = bh$$

△ **Parallelogram**
The area of a parallelogram equals its base multiplied by its vertical height.

△ **Trapezoid**
The area of a trapezoid equals the sum of the two parallel sides, multiplied by the vertical height, then multiplied by $\frac{1}{2}$.

△ **Rhombus**
The area of a rhombus equals its base multiplied by its vertical height.

Pythagorean Theorem

This theorem relates the lengths of all the sides of a right triangle, so that if any two sides are known, the length of the third side can be worked out.

side a   side c (hypotenuse)

$$a^2 + b^2 = c^2$$

side b

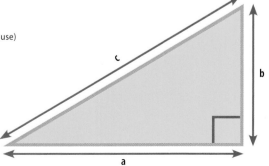

◁ **The theorem**
In a right triangle the square of the hypotenuse (the largest side, c) is the sum of the squares of the other two sides (a and b).

Surface and volume area

The illustrations below show three-dimensional shapes and the formulas for calculating their surface areas and their volumes. In the formulas, two letters together means that they are multiplied together, for example "2r" means "2" multiplied by "r". Pi (Π) is 3.14 (to 2 decimal places).

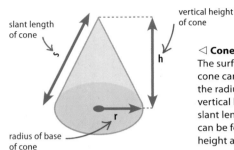

slant length of cone
vertical height of cone
radius of base of cone

◁ **Cone**
The surface area of a cone can be found from the radius of its base, its vertical height, and its slant length. The volume can be found from the height and radius.

$$\text{surface area} = \pi rs + \pi r^2$$
$$\text{volume} = \frac{1}{3}\pi r^2 h$$

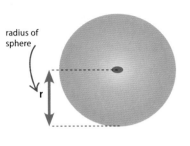

radius of sphere

◁ **Sphere**
The surface area and volume of a sphere can be found when only its radius is known, because pi is a constant number (equal to 3.14, to 2 decimal places).

$$\text{surface area} = 4\pi r^2$$
$$\text{volume} = \frac{4}{3}\pi r^3$$

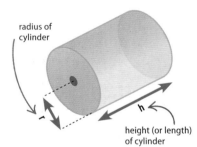

radius of cylinder
height (or length) of cylinder

◁ **Cylinder**
The surface area and volume of a cylinder can be found from its radius and height (or length).

$$\text{surface area} = 2\pi r^2 + 2\pi rh$$
$$\text{volume} = \pi r^2 h$$

length of side

◁ **Cube**
The surface area and volume of a cube can be found when only the length of its sides is known.

$$\text{surface area} = 6l^2$$
$$\text{volume} = l^3$$

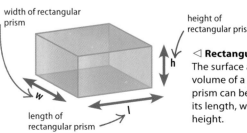

width of rectangular prism
height of rectangular prism
length of rectangular prism

◁ **Rectangular prism**
The surface area and volume of a rectangular prism can be found from its length, width, and height.

$$\text{surface area} = 2(lh+lw+hw)$$
$$\text{volume} = lwh$$

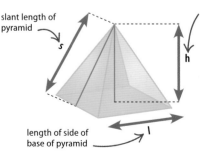

slant length of pyramid
vertical height of pyramid
length of side of base of pyramid

◁ **Square pyramid**
The surface area of a square pyramid can be found from the slant length and the side of its base. Its volume can be found from its height and the side of its base.

$$\text{surface area} = 2ls+l^2$$
$$\text{volume} = \frac{1}{3}l^2 h$$

Parts of a circle

Various properties of a circle can be measured using certain characteristics, such as the radius, circumference, or length of an arc, with the formulas given below. Pi (Π) is the ratio of the circumference to the diameter of a circle; pi is equal to 3.14 (to 2 decimal places).

◁ **Diameter and radius**
The diameter of a circle is a straight line running right across the circle and through its center. It is twice the length of the radius (the line from the center to the circumference).

$$\text{diameter} = 2r$$

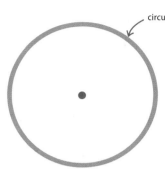

◁ **Diameter and circumference**
The diameter of a circle can be found when only its circumference (the distance around the edge) is known.

$$\text{diameter} = \frac{c}{\pi}$$

◁ **Circumference and diameter**
The circumference of a circle (distance around its edge) can be found when only its diameter is known.

$$\text{circumference} = \pi d$$

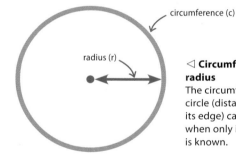

◁ **Circumference and radius**
The circumference of a circle (distance around its edge) can be found when only its radius is known.

$$\text{circumference} = 2\pi r$$

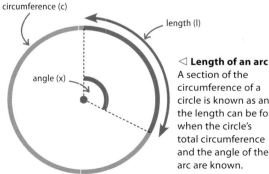

◁ **Length of an arc**
A section of the circumference of a circle is known as an arc, the length can be found when the circle's total circumference and the angle of the arc are known.

$$\text{length of an arc} = \frac{x}{360} \times c$$

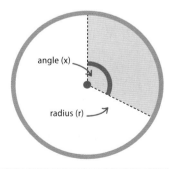

◁ **Area of a sector**
The area of a sector (or "slice") of a circle can be found when the circle's area and the angle of the sector are known.

$$\text{area of a sector} = \frac{x}{360} \times \pi r^2$$

Glossary

Acute
An acute angle is an angle that is smaller than 90º.

Addition
Working out the sum of a group of numbers. Addition is represented by the + symbol, e.g. 2 + 3 = 5. The order the numbers are added in does not affect the answer: 2 + 3 = 3 + 2.

Adjacent
A term meaning "next to". In two-dimensional shapes two sides are adjacent if they are next to each other and meet at the same point (vertex). Two angles are adjacent if they share a vertex and a side.

Algebra
The use of letters or symbols in place of unknown numbers to generalize the relationship between them.

Alternate angle
Alternate angles are formed when two parallel lines are crossed by another straight line. They are the angles on the opposite sides of each of the lines. Alternate angles are equal.

Angle
The amount of turn between two lines that meet at a common point (the vertex). Angles are measured in degrees, for example, 45°.

Apex
The tip of something e.g. the vertex of a cone.

Arc
A curve that is part of the circumference of a circle.

Area
The amount of space within a two-dimensional outline. Area

is measured in units squared, e.g. cm².

Arithmetic
Calculations involving addition, subtraction, multiplication, division, or combinations of these.

Average
The typical value of a group of numbers. There are three types of average: median, mode, and mean.

Axis (plural: axes)
Reference lines used in graphs to define coordinates and measure distances. The horizontal axis is the x-axis, the vertical axis is the y-axis.

Balance
Equality on every side, so that there is no unequal weighting, e.g. in an equation, the left-hand side of the equals sign must balance with the right-hand side.

Bar graph
A graph where quantities are represented by rectangles (bars), which are the same width but varying heights. A greater height means a greater amount.

Base
The base of a shape is its bottom edge. The base of a three-dimensional object is its bottom face.

Bearing
A compass reading. The angle measured clockwise from the North direction to the target direction, and given as 3 figures.

Bisect
To divide into two equal halves, e.g. to bisect an angle or a line.

Box-and-whisker diagram
A way to represent statistical data. The box is constructed from lines indicating where the lower quartile, median, and upper quartile measurements fall on a graph, and the whiskers mark the upper and lower limits of the range.

Brackets
1. Brackets indicate the order in which calculations must be done—calculations in brackets must be done first e.g. 2 x (4 +1) = 10.
2. Brackets mark a pair of numbers that are coordinates, e.g. (1, 1).
3. When a number appears before a bracketed calculation it means that the result of that calculation must be multiplied by that number.

Break even
In order to break even a business must earn as much money as its spends. At this point revenue and costs are equal.

Calculator
An electronic tool used to solve arithmetic.

Chart
An easy-to-read visual representation of data, such as a graph, table, or map.

Chord
A line that connects two different points on a curve, often on the circumference of a circle.

Circle
A round shape with only one edge, which is a constant distance from the centre point.

Circle graph
A circular graph in which segments represent different quantities.

Circumference
The edge of a circle.

Clockwise
A direction the same as that of a clock's hand.

Coefficient
The number in front of a letter in algebra. In the equation x² + 5x + 6 = 0 the coefficient of 5x is 5.

Common factor
A common factor of two or more numbers divides exactly into each of those numbers, e.g. 3 is a common factor of 6 and 18.

Compass
1. A magnetic instrument that shows the position of North and allows bearings to be found.
2. A tool that holds a pencil in a fixed position, allowing circles and arcs to be drawn.

Composite number
A number with more than two factors. A number is composite if it is not a prime number e.g. 4 is a composite factor as it has 1, 2, and 4 as factors.

Concave
Something curving inwards. A polygon is concave if one of its interior angles is greater than 180°.

Cone
A three-dimensional object with a circular base and a single point at its top.

Congruent/congruence
Two shapes are congruent if they are both the same shape and size.

Constant
A quantity that does not change and so has a fixed value, e.g. in the equation y = x + 2, the number 2 is a constant.

Construction
The drawing of shapes in geometry accurately, often with the aid of a compass and ruler.

Conversion
The change from one set of units to another e.g. the conversion from miles into kilometers.

Convex
Something curving outwards. A polygon is convex if all its interior angles are less than 180°.

Coordinate
Coordinates show the position of points on a graph or map, and are written in the form (x,y), where x is the horizontal position and y is the vertical position.

Correlate/correlation
There is a correlation between two things if a change in one causes a change in the other.

Corresponding angles
Corresponding angles are formed when two parallel lines are crossed by another straight side. They are the angles in the same position i.e. on the same side of each of the lines. Corresponding angles are equal.

Cosine
In trigonometry, cosine is the ratio of the side adjacent to a given angle with the hypotenuse of a right triangle.

Counter clockwise
Movement in the opposite direction to that of a clock's hand.

Cross section
A two-dimensional slice of a three-dimensional object.

Cube
A three-dimensional object made up of 6 identical square faces, 8 vertices, and 12 edges.

Cube root
A number's cube root is the number which, multiplied by itself three times, equals the given number. A cube root is indicated by this sign $\sqrt[3]{}$.

Cubed number
Cubing a number means multiplying it by itself three times e.g. 8 is a cubed number because 2 x 2 x 2 = 8, or 2^3.

Currency
A system of money within a country e.g. the currency in the US is $.

Curve
A line that bends smoothly. A quadratic equation represented on a graph is also a curve.

Cyclic quadrilateral
A shape with 4 vertices and 4 edges, and where every vertex is on the circumference of a circle.

Cylinder
A three-dimensional object with two parallel, congruent circles at opposite ends.

Data
A set of information, e.g. a collection of numbers or measurements.

Debit
An amount of money spent and removed from an account.

Debt
An amount of money that has been borrowed, and is therefore owed.

Decimal
1. A number system based on 10 (using the digits 0, 1, 2, 3, 4, 5, 6, 7, 8, and 9).
2. A number containing a decimal place.

Decimal point
The dot between the whole part of a number and the fractional part e.g. 2.5.

Decimal place
The position of the digit after the decimal point.

Degrees
The unit of measurement of an angle, represented by the symbol °.

Denominator
The number on the bottom of a fraction e.g. 3 is the denominator of $^2/_3$.

Density
The amount of mass per unit of volume, i.e. density = mass ÷ volume.

Diagonal
A line that joins two vertices of a shape or object that are not adjacent to each other.

Diameter
A straight line touching two points on the edge of a circle and passing through the center.

Difference
The amount by which one quantity is bigger or smaller than another quantity.

Digit
A single number, e.g. 34 is made up of the digits 3 and 4.

Dimension
The directions in which measurements can be made e.g. a solid object has three dimensions: its length, height, and width.

Direct proportion
Two numbers are in direct proportion if they increase or decrease proportionately, e.g. doubling one of them means the other also doubles.

Distribution
In probability and statistics, the distribution gives the range of values unidentified random variables can take and their probabilities.

Division/divide
The splitting of a number into equal parts. Division is shown by the symbol ÷ e.g. 12 ÷ 3 = 4 or by / as used in fractions, e.g. $^2/_3$.

Double negative
Two negative signs together create a double negative, which then becomes equal to a positive e.g. 5 − (−2) = 5 + 2.

Enlargement
The process of making something bigger, such as a transformation, where everything is multiplied by the same amount.

Equal
Things of the same value are equal, shown by the equals sign, =.

Equation
A mathematical statement that things are equal.

Equiangular
A shape is equiangular if all its angles are equal.

Equidistant
A point is equidistant to two or more points if it is the same distance from them.

Equilateral triangle
A triangle that has three 60° angles and sides of equal length.

Equiprobable events
Two events are equiprobable if they are equally likely to happen.

Equivalent fractions
Fractions that are equal but have different numerators and denominators e.g. $^1/_2$, $^2/_4$, and $^5/_{10}$ are equivalent fractions.

Estimation
An approximated amount or an approximation the answer to a calculation, often made by rounding up or down.

Even number
A number that is divisible by 2 e.g. -18, -6, 0, 2.

Exchange rate
The exchange rate describes what an amount of one currency is valued at in another currency.

Exponent
See power

Expression
A combination of numbers, symbols, and unknown variables that does not contain an equal sign.

Exterior angle
1. An angle formed on the outside of a polygon, when one side is extended outwards.
2. The angles formed in the region outside two lines intersected by another line.

Faces
The flat surfaces of a three-dimensional object, bordered by edges.

Factor
A number that divides exactly into another, larger number, e.g. 2 and 5 are both factors of 10.

Factorisation/factorize
1. Rewriting a number as the multiplication of its factors, e.g. $12 = 2 \times 2 \times 3$.
2. Rewriting an expression as the multiplication of smaller expressions e.g. $x^2 + 5x + 6 = (x + 2)(x + 3)$.

Fibonacci sequence
A sequence formed by adding the previous two numbers in the sequence together, which begins with 1, 1. The first ten numbers in the sequence are 1, 1, 2, 3, 5, 8, 13, 21, 34, and 55.

Formula
A rule that describes the relationship between variables, and is usually written as symbols, e.g. the formula for calculating the area of a circle is $A = 2\pi r$, in which A represents the area and r is the radius.

Fraction
A part of an amount, represented by one number (the numerator) on top of another number (the denominator) e.g. $^2/_3$.

Frequency
1. The number of times something occurs during a fixed period of time.
2. In statistics, the number of individuals in a class.

Geometry
The mathematics of shapes. Looks at the relationships between points, lines, and angles.

Gradient
The steepness of a line.

Graph
A diagram used to represent information, including the relationship between two sets of variables.

Greater than
An amount larger than another quantity. It is represented by the symbol >.

Greater than or equal to
An amount either larger or the same as another quantity. It is represented by the symbol ≥.

Greatest common factor
The largest number that divides exactly into a set of other numbers. It is often written as GCF, e.g. the GCF of 12 and 18 is 6.

Height
The upwards length, measuring between the lowest and highest points.

Hexagon
A two-dimensional shape with 6 sides.

Histogram
A bar graph that represents frequency distribution.

Horizontal
Parallel to the horizon. A horizontal line goes between left and right.

Hypotenuse
The side opposite the right-angle in a right triangle. It is the longest side of a right triangle.

Impossibility
Something that could never happen. The probability of an impossibility is written as 0.

Improper fraction
Fraction in which the numerator is greater than the denominator.

Included angle
An angle formed between two sides with a common vertex.

Income
An amount of money earned.

Independent events
Occurrences that have no influence on each other.

Indices (singular: index)
See power.

Indirect proportion
Two variables x and y are in indirect proportion if e.g. when one variable doubles, the other halves, or vice versa.

Inequalities
Inequalities show that two statements are not equal.

Infinite
Without a limit or end. Infinity is represented by the symbol ∞.

Integers
Whole numbers that can be positive, negative, or zero, e.g. -3, -1, 0, 2, 6.

Interest
An amount of money charged when money is borrowed, or the amount earned when it is invested. It is usually written as a percentage.

Interior angle
1. An included angle in a polygon.
2. An angle formed when two lines are intersected by another line.

Intercept
The point on a graph at which a line crosses an axis.

Interquartile range
A measure of the spread of a set of data. It is the difference between the lower and upper quartiles.

Intersection/intersect
A point where two or more lines or figures meet.

Inverse
The opposite of something, e.g. division is the inverse of multiplication and vice versa.

Investment/invest
An amount of money spent in an attempt to make a profit.

Isosceles triangle
A triangle with two equal sides and two equal angles.

Least common multiple
The smallest number that can be divided exactly into a set of values. It is often written LCM, e.g. the LCM of 4 and 6 is 12.

Length
The measurement of the distance between two points e.g. how long a line segment is between its two ends.

Less than
An amount smaller than another quantity. It is represented by the symbol <.

Less than or equal to
An amount smaller or the same as another quantity. It is represented by the symbol ≤.

Like terms
An expression in algebra that contains the same symbols, such as x or y, (the numbers in front of

the x or y may change). Like terms can be combined.

Line
A one-dimensional element that only has length (i.e. no width or height).

Line graph
A graph that uses points connected by lines to represent a set of data.

Line of best fit
A line on a scatter diagram that shows the correlation or trend between variables.

Line of symmetry
A line that acts like a mirror, splitting a figure into two mirror-image parts.

Loan
An amount of money borrowed that has to be paid back (usually over a period of time).

Locus (plural: loci)
The path of a point, following certain conditions or rules.

Loss
Spending more money than has been earned creates a loss.

Major
The larger of the two or more objects referred to. It can be applied to arcs, segments, sectors, or ellipses.

Mean
The middle value of a set of data, found by adding up all the values, then dividing by the total number of values.

Measurement
A quantity, length, or size, found by measuring something.

Median
The number that lies in the middle of a set of data, after the data has been put into increasing order. The median is a type of average.

Mental arithmetic
Basic calculations done without writing anything down.

Minor
The smaller of the two or more objects it referred to. It can be applied to arcs, segments, sectors, or ellipses.

Minus
The sign for subtraction, represented as −.

Mixed operations
A combination of different actions used in a calculation, such as addition, subtraction, multiplication, and division.

Mode
The number that appears most often in a set of data. The mode is a type of average.

Mortgage
An agreement to borrow money to pay for a house. It is paid back with interest over a long period of time.

Multiply/multiplication
The process of adding a value to itself a set number of times. The symbol for multiplication is ×.

Mutually exclusive events
Two mutally exclusive events are events that cannot both be true at the same time.

Negative
Less than zero. Negative is the opposite of positive.

Net
A flat shape that can be folded to make a three-dimensional object.

Not equal to
Not of the same value. Not equal to is represented by the symbol ≠, e.g. $1 \neq 2$.

Numerator
The number at the top of a fraction, e.g. 2 is the numerator of $^2/_3$.

Obtuse angle
An angle measuring between 90° and 180°.

Octagon
A two-dimensional shape with 8 sides and 8 angles.

Odd number
A whole number that cannot be divided by 2, e.g. -7, 1, and 65.

Operation
An action done to a number, e.g. adding, subtracting, dividing, and multiplying.

Operator
A symbol that represents an operation, e.g. +, −, ×, and ÷.

Opposite
Angles or sides are opposite if they face each other.

Parallel
Two lines are parallel if they are always the same distance apart.

Parallelogram
A quadrilateral which has opposite sides that are equal and parallel to each other.

Pascal's triangle
A number pattern formed in a triangle. Each number is the sum of the two numbers directly above it. The number at the top is 1.

Pentagon
A two-dimensional shape that has 5 sides and 5 angles.

Percentage/per cent
A number of parts out of a hundred. Percentage is represented by the symbol %.

Perimeter
The boundary all the way around a shape. The perimeter also refers to the length of this boundary.

Perpendicular bisector
A line that cuts another line in half at right-angles to it.

Pi
A number that is approximately 3.142 and is represented by the Greek letter pi, π.

Plane
A completely flat surface that can be horizontal, vertical, or sloping.

Plus
The sign for addition, represented as +.

Point of contact
The place where two or more lines intersect or touch.

Polygon
A two-dimensional shape with 3 or more straight sides.

Polyhedron
A three-dimensional object with faces that are flat polygons.

Positive
More than zero. Positive is the opposite of negative.

Power
The number that indicates how many times a number is multiplied by itself. Powers are shown by a small number at the top-right hand corner of another number, e.g. 4 is the power in $2^4 = 2 \times 2 \times 2 \times 2$.

Prime number
A number which has exactly two factors: 1 and itself. The first 10 prime numbers are 2, 3, 5, 7, 11, 13, 17, 19, 23, and 29.

Prism
A three-dimensional object with ends that are identical polygons.

Probability
The likelihood that something will happen. This likelihood is given a value between 0 and 1. An impossible event has probability 0 and a certain event has probability 1.

Product
A number calculated when two or more numbers are multiplied together.

Profit
The amount of money left once costs have been paid.

Proper fraction
A fraction in which the numerator is less than the denominator, e.g. $^2/_5$ is a proper fraction.

Proportion/proportionality
Proportionality is when two or more quantities are related by a constant ratio, e.g. a recipe may contain three parts of one ingredient to two parts of another.

Protractor
A tool used to measure angles.

Pyramid
A three-dimensional object with a polygon as its base and triangular sides that meet in a point at the top.

Pythagorean theorem
A rule that states that the squared length of the hypotenuse of a right-angled triangle will equal the sum of the squares of the other two sides as represented by the equation $a^2 + b^2 = c^2$.

Quadrant
A quarter of a circle, or a quarter of a graph divided by the x- and y-axis.

Quadratic equation
Equations that include a squared variable, e.g. $x^2 + 3x + 2 = 0$.

Quadratic formula
A formula that allows any quadratic equation to be solved, by substituting values into it.

Quadrilateral
A two-dimensional shape that has 4 sides and 4 angles.

Quartiles
In statistics, quartiles are points that split an ordered set of data into 4 equal parts. The number that is a quarter of the way through is the lower quartile, halfway is the median, and three-quarters of the way through is the upper quartile.

Quotient
The whole number of times a number can be divided into another e.g. if $11 \div 2$ then the quotient is 5 (and the remainder is 1).

Radius (plural: radii)
The distance from the center of a circle to any point on its circumference.

Random
Something that has no special pattern in it, but has happened by chance.

Range
The span between the smallest and largest values in a set of data.

Ratio
A comparison of two numbers, written either side of the symbol : e.g. 2:3.

Rectangle
A quadrilateral with 2 pairs of opposite, parallel sides that are equal in length, and 4 right angles.

Rectangular prisms
A three-dimensional object made of 6 faces (2 squares at opposite ends with 4 rectangles between), 8 vertices, and 12 edges.

Recurring
Something that repeats over and over again, e.g. $^1/_9 = 0.11111...$ is a recurring decimal and is shown as $0.\dot{1}$.

Reflection
A type of transformation that produces a mirror-image of the original object.

Reflex angle
An angle between 180° and 360°.

Regular polygon
A two-dimensional shape with sides that are all the same length and angles that are all the same size.

Remainder
The number left over when a dividing a number into whole parts e.g. $11 \div 2 = 5$ with remainder 1.

Revolution
A complete turn of 360°.

Rhombus
A quadrilateral with 2 pairs of parallel sides and all 4 sides of the same length.

Right angle
An angle measuring exactly 90°.

Root
The number which, when multiplied by itself a number of times, results in the given value, e.g. 2 is the fourth root of 16 as $2 \times 2 \times 2 \times 2 = 16$.

Rotation
A type of transformation in which an object is turned around a point.

Rounding
The process of approximating a number by writing it to the nearest whole number or to a given number of decimal places.

Salary
An amount of money paid regularly for the work that someone has done.

Sample
A part of a whole group from which data is collected to give information about the whole group.

Savings
An amount of money kept aside or invested and not spent.

Scale/scale drawing
Scale is the amount by which an object is made larger or smaller. It is represented as a ratio. A scale drawing is a drawing that is in direct proportion to the object it represents.

Scalene triangle
A triangle where every side is a different length and every angle is a different size.

Scatter plot
A graph in which plotted points or dots are used to show the correlation or relationship between two sets of data.

Sector
Part of a circle, with edges that are two radii and an arc.

Segment
Part of a circle, whose edges are a chord and an arc.

Semi-circle
Half of a full circle, whose edges are the diameter and an arc.

Sequence
A list of numbers ordered according to a rule.

Similar
Shapes are similar if they have the same shape but not the same size.

Simplification
In algebra, writing something in its most basic or simple form, e.g. by cancelling terms.

Simultaneous equation
Two or more equations that must be solved at the same time.

Sine
In trigonometry, sine is the ratio of the side opposite to a given angle with the hypotenuse of a right triangle.

Solid
A three-dimensional shape that has length, width, and height.

Sphere
A three-dimensional, ball-shaped, perfectly round object, where each point on its surface is the same distance from its center.

Spread
The spread of a set of data is how the data is distributed over a range.

Square
A quadrilateral in which all the angles are the same (90°) and every side is the same length.

Square root
A number that, multiplied by itself, produces a given number, shown as $\sqrt{\ }$, e.g. $\sqrt{4} = 2$.

Squared number
The result of multiplying a number by itself, e.g. $4^2 = 4 \times 4 = 16$.

Standard deviation
A measure of spread that shows the amount of deviation from the mean. If the standard deviation is low the data is close to the mean, if it is high, it is widely spread.

Standard form
A number (usually very large or very small) written as a positive or negative number between 1 and 9 multiplied by a power of 10, e.g. 0.02 is 2×10^{-2}.

Statistics
The collection, presentation, and interpretation of data.

Stem-and-leaf diagram
A graph showing the shape of ordered data. Numbers are split in two digits and separated by a line. The first digits form the stem (written once) and the second digits form leaves (written many times in rows).

Substitution
Putting something in place of something else, e.g. using a constant number in place of a variable.

Subtraction/subtract
Taking a number away from another number. It is represented by the symbol −.

Sum
The total, or the number calculated when two numbers are added together.

Supplementary angle
Two angles that add up to 180°.

Symmetry/symmetrical
A shape or object is symmetrical if it looks the same after a reflection or a rotation.

Table
Information displayed in rows and columns.

Take-home pay
Take-home pay is the amount of earnings left after tax has been paid.

Tangent
1. A straight line that touches a curve at one point.
2. In trigonometry, tangent is the ratio of the side opposite to a given angle with the side adjacent to the given angle, in a right-angled triangle.

Tax
Money that is paid to the government, either as part of what a person buys, or as a part of their income.

Terms
Individual numbers in a sequence or series, or individual parts of an expression, e.g. in $7a^2 + 4xy - 5$ the terms are $7a^2$, $4xy$, and 5.

Tessellation
A pattern of shapes covering a surface without leaving any gaps.

Theoretical probability
The likelihood of an outcome based on mathematical ideas rather than experiments.

Three-dimensional
Objects that have length, width, and height. Three-dimensions is often written as 3D.

Transformation
A change of position, size, or orientation. Reflections, rotations, enlargements, and translations are all transformations.

Translation
Movement of an object without it being rotated.

Trapezoid
A quadrilateral with a pair of parallel sides that can be of different lengths.

Triangle
A two-dimensional shape with 3 sides and 3 angles.

Trigonometry
The study of triangles and the ratios of their sides and angles.

Two-dimensional
A flat figure that has length and width. Two-dimensions is often written as 2D.

Unit
1. The standard amount in measuring, e.g. cm, kg, and seconds.
2. Another name for one.

Unknown angle
An angle which is not specified, and for which the number of degrees need to be determined.

Variable
A quantity that can vary or change and is usually indicated by a letter.

Vector
A quantity that has both size and direction, e.g. velocity and force are vectors.

Velocity
The speed and direction in which something is moving, measured in metres per second m/s.

Vertex (plural: vertices)
The corner or point at which surfaces or lines meet.

Vertical
At right-angles to the horizon. A vertical line goes between up and down directions.

Volume
The amount of space within a three-dimensional object. Volume is measured in units cubed, e.g. cm^3.

Wage
The amount of money paid to a person in exchange for work.

Whole number
Counting numbers that do not have any fractional parts and are greater than or equal to 0, e.g. 1, 7, 46, 108.

Whole turn
A rotation of 360°, so that an object faces the same direction it started from.

Width
The sideways length, measuring between opposite sides. Width is the same as breadth.

X-axis
The horizontal axis of a graph, which determines the x-coordinate.

X-intercept
The value at which a line crosses the x-axis on a graph.

Y-axis
The vertical axis of a graph, which determines the y-coordinate.

Index

Acknowledgments

BARRY LEWIS would like to thank Toby, Lara, and Emily, for always asking why.

The publisher would like to thank David Summers, Cressida Tuson, and Ruth O'Rourke-Jones for additional editorial work; and Kenny Grant, Sunita Gahir, Peter Laws, Steve Woosnam-Savage, and Hugh Schermuly for additional design work. We would also like to thank Sarah Broadbent for her work on the glossary.

The publisher would like to thank the following for their kind permission to reproduce their photographs:

(Key: b-bottom; c-center; l-left; r-right; t-top)

Alamy Images: Bon Appetit 218bc (tub); K-PHOTOS 218bc (cone); **Corbis:** Doug Landreth/Science Faction 171cr; Charles O'Rear 205br; **Dorling Kindersley:** NASA 43tr, 93bl, 231br; Lindsey Stock 27br, 220cr; **Character from Halo 2 used with permission from Microsoft:** 118tr; **NASA:** JPL 43cr

All other images © Dorling Kindersley
For further information see: www.dkimages.com